The Changing Political Thought of
John Adams

Now I say, Virtue in a Society has a like Tendency to procure Superiority and additional Power. . . . And it has this Tendency, by rendering publick Good, an Object and End, to every Member of the Society; by putting every one upon Consideration and Diligence, Recollection and Self-government . . . by uniting a Society within itself, and so increasing its Strength; and, which is particularly to be mentioned, uniting it by Means of Veracity and Justice.

—JOSEPH BUTLER

The Analogy of Religion, 3rd ed. (1740)

The Changing
Political Thought of
John Adams

BY JOHN R. HOWE, JR.

PRINCETON, NEW JERSEY

PRINCETON UNIVERSITY PRESS

1966

Printed in the United States of America
by Princeton University Press, Princeton, New Jersey

To My Parents

Acknowledgments

I began the study of John Adams several years ago in a graduate seminar. Since then, as the manuscript expanded into a dissertation and then passed through successive drafts in revision, a number of people have provided valuable counsel. At Yale, Professors John Blum, Howard Lamar, and Leonard Labaree read the original thesis and offered helpful comment. Two fellow graduate students there, David Hall and John Murrin, listened to some of my ideas and showed where improvements might be made. More recently, Professors Shaw Livermore, John Shy, and Robert Faulkner have read the manuscript in various stages of revision and offered a number of suggestions which I have profitably exploited. Professor Frank Craven examined several chapters, and for his interest I also am grateful. Several other scholars kindly responded to inquiries concerning some of Adams' acquaintances; among them, Professors Harry Jackson and Lynn W. Turner. My several visits to the Massachusetts Historical Society were made both more pleasant and profitable through the helpfulness of Dr. Stephen T. Riley and his staff. Quotations from the Adams Papers are from the microfilm edition, by permission of the Massachusetts Historical Society. Officials at the New Hampshire State Library, the Boston Public Library, the New York State Library, the Connecticut Historical Society, the Buffalo and Erie County Historical Society, the Historical Society of Pennsylvania, and the Duke University Medical Center have likewise assisted by replying to my inquiries and granting permission to quote from certain of their materials. The Princeton University Research Fund provided funds for one summer's travel and research and for the final typing of the manuscript.

I should, in addition, like to thank two individuals

at Princeton University Press, Miss Miriam Brokaw and Mr. Roy Grisham, for their thoughtfulness and the care with which they considered the manuscript.

Finally, I wish to mention two persons in particular: Professor Edmund S. Morgan has read these pages several times and given constant advice and encouragement, often at the darkest moments. And my wife, Judith, has suffered the "traditional" inconveniences of academic wives with remarkable patience. For her continuing support I am especially grateful.

Whatever is of value in the pages following, I gladly share with all of the persons named above. The errors and omissions that remain are, of course, my own.

JOHN R. HOWE, JR.

Princeton, New Jersey
June 1965

Contents

Introduction

One theme more than any other occupied the attention of John Adams and informed both his thought and action; this was a concern with maintaining order and stability in American society. That he lived through a period of political revolution and attendant social dislocation is reason enough why the issue of social stability should have concerned him—especially when one remembers his training in the law and his dedication to orderly legal processes. Adams gave a great deal of consideration to this problem during the 1760's and 1770's while active in the colonial struggle against England. Though intent (at least after April of 1775) upon securing American independence, he was equally concerned with seeing that the American people regulated themselves effectively once independence had been achieved. During this earlier period, Adams' involvement with the problem of social regulation centered on the establishment of new state governments to replace the old colonial regimes.

By the 1790's, Adams' attention had shifted to the national scene, but his interest in the problem of social regulation continued and, in fact, became more intense. It inspired his political writings at the time: his *Defense of the Constitutions of Government of the United States of America* (1787-88), his "Discourses on Davila" (1790), and much of his correspondence. It explained his involvement in the controversy over the use of titles and ceremonials in the new national government and informed his most important action as President—deciding to avoid war with France in 1799.

Scholars have written frequently and at length about Adams' political thought. (Recent attempts to identify him as a spiritual forbear of twentieth century conservatism, or as an American Burke, have increased his popularity. For an interesting critique of this movement, see an unpublished senior honors essay in the Princeton University Library by John D. Hastie, entitled "Conservatism Revisited.") Much of their work, however, has been characterized by several related weaknesses.

For one thing, they have frequently defined Adams' thought too narrowly, emphasizing such themes as the separation and balance of powers or his insistence upon a strong, independent executive. Not enough care has been given to the social and moral assumptions which underlay his political and constitutional ideas. The quality of American character, the structure of American society, the meaning of America's historical experience—each of these had important implications for Adams' political thought.

Nor have students of Adams adequately understood how changes in his evaluation of the American character and the structure of American society between the 1770's and 1790's brought corresponding changes in his political thought. Too often the implications of Adams' later writings have been read back uncritically into his earlier years. The result has been to obscure our understanding of the ways in which his evaluation of American society and its political system altered. Citing Adams' "realistic" view of human nature, writers have gone on to emphasize his continuing fear of the passions, his concern to fragment and control political power, and his emphasis upon the separation and balance in government. The important thing about Adams' thought, scholars have declared, was its consistency.[1]

In certain important respects, Adams' political thought remained much the same from his early revolutionary years through the 1790's. In other equally important ways, however, the pattern of his thinking changed

[1] For example, Manning J. Dauer, *The Adams Federalists* (Baltimore, 1953), Chapter 3; and Correa M. Walsh, *The Political Science of John Adams* (New York, 1915), pp. 112-116.

dramatically. Most importantly, his assumptions about the moral condition of the American people and the make-up of American society altered quite significantly between the two periods—essentially from an emphasis upon moral virtue and social cohesion to notions of moral declension and social conflict. The interpretation that Adams gave to the political problem of maintaining social stability in America was a direct projection of his most basic assumptions about American origins and ambitions, character and values, failures and achievements, present condition and probable future circumstance. As his understanding of these matters altered, so did his evaluation of American society and the political problems facing it; that is, so did his political thought. These changes constitute a principal theme of the following pages.

More than this, scholars have made little effort to tie together Adams' political thought and his experiences as an active political leader. So far we have had two kinds of studies. One is a narrative account of Adams' life—setting forth his activities in the revolutionary crisis, in the establishment of new state governments, as American minister abroad during the 1780's, and as Vice-President and President in the decade following—but spends little time in systematic analysis of Adams' thought. Page Smith's recent biography stands out in this group, as do the studies by Stephen Kurtz and Catherine Drinker Bowen.[2]

The second type of study does undertake a detailed discussion of Adams' ideas but with little attention to their relationship with his experience. Of this group, Correa M. Walsh's cumbersome *Political Science of John Adams* is the archetype. Walsh's discussion focuses en-

[2] Page Smith, *John Adams*, 2 vols. (Garden City, New York, 1962); Stephen Kurtz, *The Presidency of John Adams: The Collapse of Federalism, 1795-1800* (Philadelphia, 1957); Catherine Drinker Bowen, *John Adams and the American Revolution* (Boston, 1950).

tirely on Adams' political ideology, busying itself with charting rigid periods in his thought and pointing up inconsistencies both within and between them, without any serious effort to consider the implications of Adams' political activities. Nowhere is there a book which brings both aspects of Adams' life, both thought and experience, into effective conjunction.[3]

Though Adams made some effort at the construction of a systematic body of thought—for example, in his "Thoughts on Government" (1776), *Defense of the Constitutions of Government of the United States* (1787-88), and "Davila" essays (1790)—he was never a social theorist in the manner of Marx or Rousseau, or even Calhoun. He wrestled with abstract problems of human nature and social organization, but this was not where his greatest interests or abilities lay. He was preeminently a man of action rather than of reflection. He was deeply involved with the specific problems confronting America during his lifetime, and his thinking about matters of politics and society derived essentially from this involvement. His interest in theory, moreover, grew out of its promise to assist in understanding the day-to-day issues with which he dealt. To understand Adams adequately, one must begin with these premises.

The relationship between experience and thought in Adams' life was twofold. As an active political leader, he was made constantly aware of the difficulties which America faced and of the efficiency with which they were or were not resolved. During the 1770's, he shared in the adventure of securing independence from England and establishing new American governments. The success with which the American people moved first to protect their liberties against outside attack and then to insure their survival against internal disorder impressed

[3] Dauer's *The Adams Federalists* comes closest to this, but his concern is solely with the 1790's; more particularly, with the Federalist split between Adamsites and Hamiltonians.

Adams greatly and went far to persuade him of America's capacity for self-government. Conversely, the social, economic, and political difficulties of the 1780's, of which, as we shall see, Adams was made painfully and personally aware, were instrumental in persuading him that a basic reconsideration of his earlier thinking was required.

There was, in addition, a second and more subjective relationship between Adams' experience and the development of his political thought. Put most baldly, a correspondence developed between the satisfactions of his own life—his early years as a confident political leader, successful in his ambitions and applauded by the people—and his outlook on American society. I have suggested that important to Adams' evaluation of American society was his understanding of its prevailing moral tone. One effective test he had for measuring this—other than simply observing the habits of the people—was his own condition. While supported by the people, he had no reason to doubt them. When later on they turned against him, however, he saw the fault as theirs. In his own mind, Adams had remained constant to his earlier principles, while the people had fallen away. There was an intimacy between his personal relationship with the American people and his conclusions about them that however subjective and imprecise was of real importance. His growing sense of estrangement, begun during the 1780's and continuing through 1800, both paralleled and informed his changing evaluation of American society.

In the following pages, then, I have attempted to view Adams' political thought not essentially as a product of his reading and reflection, but of the immediate experiences through which he passed—as an effort to come to grips with both the specific historical events in which he shared and the changing circumstances of his own life. Approached in these terms, the development of his political thinking should become considerably more clear.

The Changing Political Thought of

John Adams

Chapter I. "A Scaene of Much Confusion"

Few persons were more active on the American political scene during the years 1765 to 1800 than John Adams. First as constitutional adviser to the Massachusetts Patriots on matters of English liberty and empire organization, then as leader of the Whig cause in the Continental Congress, then as theoretician of the new state governments, next as American representative to the courts of western Europe, and finally as Vice-President and President under the national constitution, he served the American people faithfully and well. In each of these roles, Adams addressed himself to two basic problems.

The first arose as a consequence of Britain's efforts to strengthen her control over her North American colonies. For Adams, this created almost at once the issue of defining and then defending American liberties against encroachment by an "external" power. Ultimately this became a campaign to achieve and then to maintain full independence from the British Crown and Parliament. The second problem arose in conjunction with the first. It was to insure the continuing stability of American society once independence had been secured.

The two problems developed concurrently in Adams' mind. As long as he contemplated no final break with Britain, matters of social regulation posed no serious question. There were, of course, momentary disruptions of society during the earlier years of the Revolution. Before the decision for independence, however, such inconveniences, bothersome as they might be, seemed to him temporary and therefore tolerable. Once the crisis with Great Britain was resolved, the colonial adminis-

trations, purged and made consonant with the full enjoyment of Anglo-American liberties would resume their
operation. Society, at the same time, would return to its
accustomed regularity.

Adams continued in this attitude throughout the 1760's
and half of the 1770's, neither wishing for independence
nor thinking it inevitable. By mid-1774, he had moved
closer to a break, yet he still hesitated to go along with
the more radical Patriot leaders. He was ready to deny
Parliament all authority in the colonies other than that
mutually agreed upon for the regulation of empire
trade. In the fourth item of the Declaration of Rights,
written by Adams and adopted by the Continental Congress in October of 1774, he described his view of the
colonies' relationship with England. The American colonies, Adams explained, could not from their circumstances be represented in Parliament, and thus were "entitled to a free and exclusive power of legislation" in
their provincial legislatures "in all cases of taxation and
internal polity, subject only to the negative of their sovereign. . . ." From a regard for the mutual interest of
the colonies and mother country, however, they would
"cheerfully consent" to such acts of Parliament as were
"bona fide, restrained to the regulation of our external
commerce, for the purpose of securing the commercial
advantages of the whole empire. . . ."[1] In 1774, Adams
was, in essence, suggesting something closely resembling
the commonwealth theory of association.[2]

Even during the first months of 1775, he remained
committed to an accommodation of existing difficulties
with England consistent with American interests. In a
series of essays published from January to April of 1775

[1] W. C. Ford, ed., *Journals of the Continental Congress*, 34 vols.
(Washington, D.C., 1904-1937), I, 68-69. Also, C. F. Adams, ed.,
The Life and Works of John Adams, 10 vols. (Boston, 1856), II,
538-39. (Hereafter cited as *Works*.)
[2] R. G. Adams, *Political Ideas of the American Revolution* (New
York, 1958), pp. 107-27.

in the *Boston Gazette*, under the pseudonym "Novanglus," he expressed his hope for a resolution of the existing crisis in terms of America's continuing allegiance to
the Crown, even though he was becoming skeptical that
this was any longer possible. In the fourth essay, he openly denied the Tories' assertion that the Patriot leaders
were scheming for independence. Do they mean, he
asked, that we desire to be "independent of the Crown
of Great Britain" and to form "an independent republic
in America, or a confederation of independent republics?" Nothing could be "a greater slander."[3] To deny
that independence was the goal was the tactful course
for any Massachusetts politician anxious to retain the
support of the southern colonies in the struggle against
England—even if independence was in fact the end in
sight. There is no evidence in Adams' actions or writings, in his Diary or most personal correspondence
through the winter of 1775, however, that he sought independence or thought it more than a possible consequence of English acts.

In April of 1775, following the events at Lexington
and Concord, Adams' attitude toward independence
and consequently toward the problem of social regulation changed dramatically. The outbreak of fighting
convinced him finally that Britain was prepared to go
any length to subjugate the colonies, and that reconciliation was impossible. During the preceding year, he
had warned that an outbreak of fighting would end all
hope of accommodation. He had always thought that
hostilities "would terminate in incurable animosity between the two countries."[4] As the revolutionary crisis

[3] "Novanglus": *Works*, IV, 52 *passim*.
[4] Adams to Samuel Chase, July 1, 1776: Adams Papers Microfilm, Reel 89. (Hereafter cited as Adams Microfilm, Reel.) In
quoting material from the Adams microfilm, I have followed the
editorial method described by Messrs. Butterfield, et al., in the
most recent edition of John Adams' Diary and Autobiography. See
Lyman C. Butterfield, ed., *The Diary and Autobiography of John*

deepened, dangers of outright hostilities had increased, until by late 1774 only the greatest caution prevented an open clash. From Philadelphia, Adams had written home urging that the people of Massachusetts bend every effort to prevent a rupture. His reason had been that "the decisive sentiments" of the Congressional delegates were against any measures which might kindle war.[5] Again, Adams' comments gave no indication that he was personally anxious for the fighting to begin. If something like the arrangement he had described in his "Novanglus" essays could have been worked out to keep the colonies under the Crown, Adams would certainly have favored it even at this late date. After the fighting began, however, he concluded that a final separation was America's only safe course. Once persuaded, he never looked back.

A few days after the encounter, Adams rode out to the scene of the fighting, talking with the inhabitants as he went. His conversations convinced him that "the Die was cast," and that Americans must defend themselves.[6] From April of 1775 on, he believed the American states, by virtue of Britain's aggressive acts, were for all practical purposes independent. All of America's remaining ties with the King, he declared a year later in supporting the motion for a formal declaration of independence, had been dissolved by George III's levying war against the colonies. The King, by his actions, had declared the colonies out of his protection; and it being "a certain position in law" that allegiance and protection were re-

Adams, 4 vols. (Cambridge, Massachusetts, 1961), I, lv-lix. (Hereafter cited as _Diary and Autobiography_.)

[5] Adams to William Tudor, October 7, 1774: E. C. Burnett, ed., _Letters of Members of the Continental Congress_, 8 vols. (Washington, D.C., 1921-1934), I, 65.

[6] _Diary and Autobiography_, III, 314. Also, Adams to James Warren, July 6, 1775: "Warren-Adams Letters," Massachusetts Historical Society, _Collections_, Vols. LXXII, LXXIII (Boston, 1917-1925), LXXII, 74.

ciprocal, independence had at once become a legal fact.[7]
"Have We not been independent these twelve Months?"
he asked James Warren in April of 1776.[8] After Lexington and Concord, Adams worked diligently to secure
public acknowledgement of the legal fact. Convinced
now that all efforts at reconciliation were useless and in
fact only endangered American liberty, he labored both
in Congress and out to persuade the American people
that their only safety lay in a rapid and permanent separation. He urged that they seize all Crown officers as
hostages for the beleaguered city of Boston; that a continental army be formed and prepared for war; that
American ports be opened to foreign trade in defiance
of British orders; and that new state governments be
established free of all royal sanction—all of these in an
effort to move the American people rapidly toward formal independence.[9]

At the same time, Adams turned to the issue that logically next arose—making certain that the disruption of
established political authority did not invite social dis-
turbance. The problem confronting American society, as
Adams conceived it, was essentially political. Government was the ultimate guarantor of social order. Liberty,
he emphasized, could prevail only within the context of
stable political institutions. For liberty required order;
order, law; and law, government. Yet the regular opera-

[7] Adams to Horatio Gates, March 23, 1776: Burnett, ed., *Letters
of Congress*, I, 406.

[8] Adams to James Warren, April 16, 1776: "Warren-Adams
Letters," LXXII, 227. Also, Adams to Mercy Warren, May 12, 1776:
Massachusetts Historical Society, *Collections*, Series 5, IV (1878),
302.

[9] *Diary and Autobiography*, III, 315-16, 319, 327, 364. Also,
Adams to Abigail Adams, April 12 and 14, 1776: Lyman H. Butterfield, ed., *Adams Family Correspondence*, 2 vols. to date (Cambridge,
Massachusetts, 1963-   ), I, 376-77, 381-82. In the summer of
1775, Adams toyed briefly with the idea of a temporary declaration
of independence, wondering whether this would not be enough to
shake England back to sense. However, he quickly dropped the
idea. *Diary and Autobiography*, III, 315.

tion of America's political institutions had been in significant measure destroyed.

While at Congress in May of 1776, he heard from his wife Abigail of the problems caused by inadequate political regulation. "A Government of more Stability," she warned, "is much wanted in this colony. . . ."[10] James Warren wrote similarly of the "extreme want of the Exercise of a fixt Government" under which Massachusetts suffered.[11] Their anxieties but confirmed Adams' own. Provision had to be made for the immediate restoration of regular political processes, for the orderly transfer of authority from colonial to independent regimes capable of ordering American society permanently and effectively. He had thought it "the most difficult and dangerous Part of the Business Americans have to do in this mighty Contest . . . to contrive some Method for the Colonies to glide insensibly, from under the old Government, into a peaceable and contented submission to new ones." From April of 1775 on, his "constant Endeavor" was "to convince Gentlemen of the Necessity of turning their Thoughts to these subjects."[12] This, more than anything else, became the theme of his thought and action.

Adams applauded from the first the efforts of the several colonies to provide themselves with temporary agencies of government. Town committees and provincial conventions, he noted approvingly, were devised to take up the slack. Since the people were familiar with the processes of self-government, they quickly devised effective expedients of their own.[13] "Nature and experience" pointed out a solution to their dilemma in the

[10] Abigail Adams to Adams, May 7, 1776: Butterfield, ed., *Adams Family Correspondence*, I, 402.

[11] James Warren to Adams, May 7, 1775: "Warren-Adams Letters," LXXII, 48.

[12] Adams to Mercy Warren, April 16, 1776: *Ibid.*, p. 222.

[13] "Novanglus": *Works*, IV, 31.

choice of conventions and committees of public safety.[14]

But he warned that such temporary agencies of government could not long be adequate. There were limits to such improvisation beyond which the American people could not safely go. At times, it seemed that these limits were in danger of being reached. In several of the colonies, government by late 1774 was at a standstill. Courts were not meeting, trade was almost wholly stopped, men were unable to pay their debts. The consequences were serious. "We are trying by a Thousand Experiments, the Ingenuity as well as the Virtue of our People," Adams warned one correspondent. "The Effects are such as would divert you. Imagine 400,000 People without Government or Law, forming themselves in companies for various Purposes of Justice, Policy, and War. You must allow for a great deal of the ridiculous, much of the melancholly, and some of the Marvellous."[15] It was necessary, he wrote in the preamble to a Congressional resolution of May 1776, that "all the Powers of Government under the Authority of the People of the Colonies [be] exerted for the Preservation of internal Peace, Virtue and good order, as well as to defend our Lives, Liberties, and Properties, from the hostile Invasions . . . of our Enemies. . . ."[16] The full power of government could not be exercised except by regularly functioning, permanently established government.

The problem of guaranteeing adequate social regulation appeared more urgent as it became evident that the military struggle with Britain would be protracted. Adams had first expected that the contest would be brief. To General Nathanael Greene, he admitted in March

[14] Adams to R. H. Lee, November 15, 1775: *Ibid.*, p. 185.

[15] Adams to Edward Biddle, December 12, 1774: Adams Microfilm, Reel 344.

[16] Adams to James Warren, May 15, 1776: "Warren-Adams Letters," LXXII, 246.

of 1777 that he had hoped "two or three such Actions" as Bunker Hill would be sufficient to convince the British of American firmness and force them into an acceptable peace.[17] The prospect of a long contest with the instruments of civil control so lax, Adams feared from the first. There was reason to apprehend that the people would panic at the news of American reversals, "that in the fright and confusion" whole states would fall into disorder and seek a peace of their own.[18]

The long-term effect of living without permanent government, Adams warned, might well prove destructive of the "internal Peace, Virtue and good order" of the people. There seemed danger that if continued in this condition for long, Americans would lose their habitual respect for authority and be unwilling to submit to proper discipline again. The continuation of power in the hands of temporary bodies, Adams later recalled, "composed a Scaene [sic] of much Confusion and Injustice the Continuance of which was much dreaded by me, as tending to injure the Morals of the People and destroy the habits of order, and attachment to regular Government."[19] Revolution tended to foster disrespect for law and authority anyway. Americans were being called upon in the name of personal liberty to challenge the actions of their governors, to deny the jurisdiction of Royal courts, to disobey tax laws and other legislative acts; in short, to question and ultimately resist established government. The experience encouraged tendencies which, if left unchecked, could prove fatal to all orderly processes of social regulation. Too many persons, Adams worried, seemed to love liberty better than they understood it, and to be unwilling to acknowledge their ignorance.[20]

---

[17] Adams to Nathanael Greene, March 9, 1777: Adams Microfilm, Reel 91.
[18] *Ibid.*   [19] *Diary and Autobiography*, III, 370.
[20] Adams to James Warren, February 3, 1777: *Works*, IX, 451.

In the fall of 1775, Adams had an experience that brought the point home forcefully to him. While riding near Braintree one afternoon, he was approached by another rider—"a common Horse Jockey," Adams later remembered, who had frequently been in trouble with the law and just as frequently come to Adams for counsel. "Oh! Mr. Adams," exclaimed the other man excitedly, "what great Things have you and your Colleagues done for Us! We can never be grateful enough to you. There are no Courts of Justice now in this Province, and I hope there never will be another!" Adams recalled sourly that he had ridden ahead without an answer.[21] The experience impressed him. Was this, he wondered, the attitude generally of the people? If power should get into the hands of such individuals, the fate of Americans under their own control would be darker than under Parliament's domination. Surely to substitute anarchy for oppression was no gain. "We must guard against this Spirit and these Principles," he concluded, "or We shall repent of all our Conduct."[22]

There were other indications of restlessness among the people that gave Adams pause—particularly the outbursts of mob violence that periodically disturbed the colonies, even reaching into New England. Adams made efforts to keep the instances of mob action in perspective, especially those involving Whig activity against Royal officials and Tory sympathizers. About these, he never demonstrated undue alarm. Given the great provocations of the American people, he observed, the incidence of mob action had been remarkably low. The noteworthy thing had been the orderly manner in which the people carried on their protest. In any time of high emotion, there would inevitably be a certain amount of extra-legal activity; there was "no avoiding all inconveniences in human affairs," he explained.[23] When peti-

[21] Diary and Autobiography, III, 326.   [22] Ibid.
[23] "Novanglus": Works, IV, 116.

tions were scorned and resolutions ignored, force became the only way of making one's protests felt. Americans should remember, Adams counselled, repeating the
admonition of Grotius, that there were "tumults, seditions, popular commotions, insurrections, and civil wars,
upon just occasions as well as unjust"; that it was "not
repugnant to the law of nature, for any one to repel
injuries by force."[24] Such violence as had occurred,
Adams inclined to say, was the responsibility of the
British and their American agents. "Hutchinson [Gov-
ernor of Massachusetts], Oliver [Peter Oliver, Chief
Justice of the Superior Court of Massachusetts], and
others of their circle" who for their own ends of ambition had encouraged Parliament's taxation of America,
had been "the real tempters of their countrymen . . .
into all the . . . crimes, and follies" which British measures had occasioned.[25]

Though Adams seems never to have joined any Patriot mobs, he was not quick to condemn them. When
directed toward necessary public ends, mob pressure
might well be justified. The sacking of the stamp office,
for example, he defended as a militant demonstration
of public will. The stamp affair in Boston was "an hon-
ourable and glorious action, not a riot."[26] Enthralled by
the "patriotism" of the people, Adams went so far as
to recount with obvious relish how every man who dared
speak in favor of the stamps, "how great soever his Abilities and Virtues had been esteemed before, or whatever
his fortune . . . and Influence had been," had been seen
to sink into "universal Contempt and Ignominy." Crown
officers had "every where trembled, and all their little
Tools and Creatures, been afraid to Speak and ashamed

[24] *Ibid.*, p. 79.
[25] Adams to Abigail Adams, July 6, 1774: Butterfield, ed., *Adams Family Correspondence*, I, 126-27.
[26] "Novanglus": *Works*, IV, 74-75. Also, *Diary and Autobiography*, I, 259-61.

to be seen."[27] Adams was not typically so cavalier about
violence, but in the enthusiasm of the moment he could
accept and even applaud certain kinds of it. The destruction of the tea, he thought "the grandest event" which
had happened since the controversy with England had
opened.[28] If any fault was to be claimed, it lay with
Hutchinson for not allowing the tea to be sent back.

Adams' apologies, however, betrayed a nervousness
at the use of force at any time, under any circumstances.
One can sense this in his exaggerated insistence that in
disposing of the tea the people acted "with great order,
decency, and *perfect submission to government*."[29] Moreover, he labored to distinguish between "public mobs"
aimed at the defense of essential public liberties (which
he condoned) and "private mobs" cloaked often in pa-
triotic garb but prompted by personal vendetta (which
he condemned). Even "legitimate" public violence, he
acknowledged, encouraged the "excesses of a few, who
. . . took advantage of the general enthusiasm, to per-
petuate their ill designs."[30]

Upon several occasions, Adams saw for himself the
consequences of such personal violence. In July of 1774
while riding circuit, he was engaged in a case arising
from private mob action against John King of Scarbor-
ough. In a letter to Abigail he recounted his reaction
to the terror and distress which had resulted. "A Mind
susceptible of the Feelings of Humanity," he exclaimed,
"an Heart which can be touch'd with Sensibi[li]ty for
human Misery and Wretchedness must reluct [*sic*], must
burn with Resentment and Indignation, at such out-
rageous Injuries. These private Mobs, I do and will de-
test." If popular commotions could be justified in oppo-

---

[27] Diary, December 18, 1765: *Diary and Autobiography*, I, 263.
[28] Adams to James Warren, December 17, 1773: *Works*, IX, 333.
[29] *Ibid.*, p. 334.
[30] "Clarendon" (Adams' pseudonym): *Boston Gazette*, January
27, 1776.

sition to attacks upon the constitution—and Adams wondered if this could safely be admitted—it was only when fundamental liberties were invaded; nor then, unless as an absolute necessity and with great caution. Certainly "these Tarrings and Featherings, these breaking open Houses by rude and insolent Rabbles, in Resentment for private Wrongs" had to be discountenanced.[31]

Adams, in fact, never felt easy defending the most obvious of "public mobs." Argue as he might that Americans resorted to force only in defense of their basic rights, he always wished such acts could be entirely avoided, for they ran counter to his whole emphasis upon social order and stability. At best, he regarded them as temporary expedients, necessitated by the exceptional conditions of the times. He could never escape the thought that the use of force, even for public ends, might too easily become habitual. It was, he reflected, a situation "of dangerous Tendency and Consequence," and could be controlled only by the rapid implementation of established authority.[32]

Adams' concern about the potentially unsettling effects of the Revolution was based upon certain assumptions he held concerning human nature. As important in considering the problem of social order as the historical circumstances in which individuals lived, he believed, was the moral character of the individuals themselves—their capacity for reasoned and sociable behavior, or their inclination to be governed by selfish emotion.

No area of human knowledge, with the possible exception of physics, received more attention among eighteenth-century men than moral philosophy. In America as in Europe, books treating the conflict between reason and the passions, or the importance of conscience and

[31] Adams to Abigail Adams, July 7, 1774: Butterfield, ed., *Adams Family Correspondence*, I, 131.
[32] Diary, August 15, 1765: *Diary and Autobiography*, I, 260.

the moral sense for human behavior, appeared in a steady stream. Whatever the subject men considered—whether politics, religion, or economics—underlying the discussion were certain presuppositions about human nature. It was, in fact, during the eighteenth century that the term "human nature" came into general use. "The Proper Study of Mankind is Man," wrote Pope, thus capturing in an aphorism the theme of an entire age.

Adams fully shared in this fascination with moral thought. During the course of his life, he read nearly every significant moralist of the day. Locke he knew by heart. Hutcheson, Adam Smith, Shaftesbury, Condorcet, Rousseau, Mandeville, Butler: these he mastered as well. With all of them he agreed on one thing: that the effort to understand society, to speculate about constitutions and systems of government must begin from a clear understanding of human nature. One could not employ with full advantage the force of one's mind "in study, in council, or in argument," Adams wrote,

> . . . without examining with great attention and exactness, all our mental faculties, in all their operations, as explained by writers on the human understanding, and exerted by geometricians.
>
> 'Tis impossible to judge with much precision, of the true motives and qualities of human actions, or of the propriety of rules contrived to govern them, without considering with like attention, all the passions, appetites, affections in nature, from which they flow. An intimate knowledge therefore of the intellectual and moral world is the sole foundation on which a stable structure of knowledge can be erected.[33]

It was futile, he explained, "to study all arts but that of living in the world, and all sciences but that of man-

[33] Adams to Jonathan Sewall, October 1759: *Works*, II, 79.

kind."[34] In accordance with this precept, Adams set himself early in life to a careful and continuing examination of human psychology and moral behavior.

His approach professed to be scientific; his method, the examination of his own heart (this he developed into a fine skill) and the careful observation of others. The principles of human conduct were not to be produced deductively, either by religious inspiration or pure cerebration. Rather, they should be determined by observation and analysis, by a cross-examination of theory and circumstance until certain patterns, certain laws of human behavior could be empirically defined. In the everyday actions of individuals lay the only sure revelation of human nature. Wherever he went, Adams missed no opportunity to search out the springs of human conduct. "Let me search for the Clue, which Led great Shakespeare into the Labyrinth of mental Nature," he admonished himself.[35] In his own experience and in his reading of history, he searched for the clue endlessly.

As with most men of his day, Adams framed his discussion in terms of an inner tension between man's reason and his passions. The explanation of human conduct, of human failings as well as accomplishments, could be found in the continuing interplay between these two forces. By reason, Adams meant several things. With John Locke, he meant the capacity for marshalling ideas gained through sense impressions.[36] He signified by it as well an instrument for perceiving the order and finding out the meaning of nature. The Creator, Adams wrote, had given men reason "to find out the Truth" and the design of their existence.[37] Reason was also an in-

---

[34] Diary, 1759: *Diary and Autobiography*, I, 106.

[35] Diary, December 5 (?), 1758: *Ibid.*, p. 61.

[36] Reason's function, Adams explained on one occasion, was in "retaining, compounding, and arranging the vigorous impressions which we receive . . . into all the varieties of Picture and Figure." Adams to ?, August 29, 1756: Adams Microfilm, Reel 114.

[37] Adams to Richard Cranch, August 29, 1765: *Ibid.*

strument of creation by which men shaped their environment to their own needs. The capacities of the human mind for such constructive endeavor Adams believed to be great. Through reason men invented "Engines and Instruments, to take advantage of the Powers in Nature," and accomplished "the most astonishing Designs": levelling mountains, raising cities, communicating from remote areas, peering into the farthest heavens.[38] Reason, Locke had declared, "sets man above the rest of sensible beings, and gives him all the advantages and Dominion he has over them."[39] Adams echoed his own assent.

More significantly, however, reason signified for Adams certain characteristics of mood and temperament: calmness and reflection, a willingness to weigh action carefully and consider the social as well as the personal consequences—qualities the opposite of those demonstrated by the passions. Reason's function was to overrule the passions and keep them within strict bounds of order and moderation. Men should endeavor at a balance of affections and appetites under the monarchy of reason. Every man was unfit to fill any important station in society who "left one Passion in his Soul unsubdued." The affections should "be bound fast and brought under the Yoke."[40]

Though men frequently acted according to the dictates of reason, Adams was particularly impressed with the way in which emotion often gained the upper hand. The tension between reason and affection was a delicate one. Men were curiously possessed of both influences. The number of "pure Characters" among mankind was few. Virtues and vices, wisdom and folly were blended in

[38] Diary, May 17, 1756: *Diary and Autobiography*, I, 27.

[39] Quoted in Russell Nye, *The Cultural Life of the New Nation* (New York, 1961), p. 20.

[40] Diary, June 14, 1756: *Diary and Autobiography*, I, 33.

all men. Too often, however, the emotions won out and men lapsed into selfishness, forgetting sociability.

The passions, Adam made clear, were a fixed part of human nature, wrought into the very texture of the soul. Indeed, they were necessary for survival. They stirred the soul, awakened the understanding, informed the will, and made the whole man vigorous and attentive. "I find that the Mind must be agitated with some Passion, either Love, fear, Hope &.," Adams commented, "before she will do her best."[41] Frequently enough, the affections served a constructive purpose by impelling men to actions both personally and socially advantageous. Ambition, for example, was responsible for many of mankind's most wonderful achievements. It prompted men to write books, form governments, develop commerce, and even compose sermons.[42] There were, as well, certain "social affections."

Most often, however, the passions exerted an influence disadvantageous to both the individual and society. Their inspiration was typically selfish; their effect destructive. Even the affections which in moderate form served desirable ends easily became inflamed and took on a quite different aspect. The same ambition, for example, which could impel men to pursue a useful profession, inclined to slip into a cruel grasping for power. In every person's life, the selfish affections constantly threatened to take control—and too frequently did.

Adams' doubts about the adequacy of reason when confronted by aroused passions increased considerably with the passing of years. (By 1790, as we shall see, he had become extremely pessimistic about human nature.) Yet he believed from the first that in the majority of men, prejudice, fancy, and self-interest often proved too great. "We see every Day," he wrote, "that our Imaginations are so strong and our Reason so weak, the Charms of

[41] Diary, June 10, 1760: *Ibid.*, p. 133.
[42] "Literary Commonplace Book": Adams Microfilm, Reel 187.

Wealth and Power are so enchanting, and the Belief of future Punishments so faint, that Men find Ways to persuade themselves, to believe any Absurdity, to submit to any Prostitution, rather than forego their Wishes and Desires. Their Reason becomes at last an eloquent Advocate on the Side of their Passions, and [they] bring themselves to believe that black is white, that Vice is Virtue, that Folly is Wisdom and Eternity a Moment."[43]

Once the precarious balance was broken and reason's tenuous control upset, nothing remained but for the evil to work itself out. The passions were insatiable. They increased, "by exercise, like the body," gathering strength when indulged until they overbore whatever stood in their way. Each passion was "a usurping, cruel, domineering tyrant," seeking to extend its sway as far as it could.[44]

Men had a difficult enough time keeping their passions under account in their own private lives. Again and again, the entries in Adams' diary attested to this. The problem was infinitely compounded when individuals confronted each other in society. In the abrasive effect of social contact, Adams found the main irritant of human emotions. Man, Adams emphasized again and again, was essentially a social creature. Never had men existed in isolation. The "Instinct of Nature" was against it.[45] In the most primitive conditions, they had been "undoubtedly gregarious." Not even during the Revolution did Adams argue in terms of a state of nature. To Rousseau's description of it, he took firm exception. Adams first read the *Social Contract* in 1762, then again about 15 years later, and once more in 1794, speckling the margins of his copy each time with argumentative comments. "Nature never intended any society," he scoffed in disbelief. "All society is art. Nothing will do but a

---

[43] Diary, February 9, 1772: *Diary and Autobiography*, II, 54.
[44] "Literary Notes and Drafts": Adams Microfilm, Reel 118.
[45] Diary, February 10, 1772: *Diary and Autobiography*, II, 57.

paradox."[46] The first two men or women who met, Adams countered, setting the Frenchman straight, felt an affection for each other. At that moment "society" was established.[47] Only in terms of the individual's relations with his fellow man, then, could one meaningfully discuss human nature.

The effects of social intercourse upon the individual, Adams emphasized, were commonly disquieting. "Such is the social Constitution of our Nature," he wrote as early as 1759, "that Conversation arouses Passions in our Breasts, which give a new Vigour and Freedom to our Thoughts, raises Hints and arguments which we should never find in solitude, and is at least the best scene to gather Ideas, if not to compare and separate them. . . ."[48] Contact with one's fellows typically served to excite the affections, stimulate the passions and disrupt all rational capacity. If, as Adams suggested, conversation alone could do so much, what awful effect would the open clash of ambitions have?

Adams observed every day in his legal practice the hurtful effects of personal controversy: the inflammation of passions until "Malice, Hatred, Envy, Pride, fear, Rage, Despair," all took their turn and set neighbor against neighbor, family against family.[49] In August of 1765, Adams traveled to Martha's Vineyard for the trial of a cause between Jerusha Mayhew and her relations. The experience made a lasting impression upon him. "The keen Understanding of this Woman, and the uncontroulable Violence of her irascible Passions," Adams recalled some years later, had excited within the family a quarrel of "the most invidious, inveterate and irreconcileable nature. . . ." Never before had "the Rancour of

[46] Zoltan Haraszti, *John Adams and the Prophets of Progress* (Cambridge, Massachusetts, 1952), p. 85.

[47] *Ibid.*, pp. 89, 92.

[48] Adams to R. T. Paine, December 6, 1759: Paine Papers, Massachusetts Historical Society.

[49] Diary, May 16, 1767: *Diary and Autobiography*, I, 335.

that fiend the Spirit of Party" appeared to him so malig-
nant. It seemed to have wrought "an entire metamor-
phosis of the human Character"; to have destroyed "all
sense and Understanding, all Equity and Humanity, all
Memory and regard to Truth, all Virtue, Honor, Decorum and Veracity."[50] So it was when men became inflamed against each other. Adams made similar observations elsewhere: the clash of ambition among young law-
yers in Boston, the enmities developed between members
of the Continental Congress in Philadelphia. They all
pointed the same moral: in society, men tended naturally
toward conflict.

Beyond such observations, however, Adams' most effective teacher was his own personal experience. "Experience," he copied into his literary notebook, "[is]
the only Source of human Knowledge. It is the crutch
men hobble on in the course of reasoning."[51] For Adams,
this was more than aphorism. It described the intimate
relationship between thought and event in his own life.
The most vivid and compelling information always came
to him from his personal contacts with the society about
him. His insights were essentially emotional rather than
cerebral. "There must be action, passion, sentiment, and
moral," he observed, "to gain my attention very much."[52]
For nothing was this of more importance than his conclusions about human nature.

Adams' relationships with other individuals were typically difficult and unsettling. He was never comfortable,
he complained, in the "large and promiscuous com-

[50] Autobiography: *Ibid.*, III, 284-85.

[51] "Literary Commonplace Book": Adams Microfilm, Reel 188.
Also, Diary, Spring 1759: *Diary and Autobiography*, I, 98.

[52] Diary, July 1766: *Ibid.*, p. 318. Professor Bernard Bailyn
touches upon the same point in his discussion of Adams' "sensuous"
response to the world about him. Events, Professor Bailyn asserts,
never appeared as abstractions to Adams; "they were human en-
counters, exchanges between sentient, visible and audible people."
Bernard Bailyn, "Butterfield's Adams: Notes for a Sketch": *William
and Mary Quarterly*, Series 3, XIX (1962), 247.

panies" that his duties constantly forced upon him. "Business alone, with the intimate, unreserved conversation of a very few friends, books, and familiar correspondence" gratified him. He found "no pleasure, no ease, in any other way."[53] Though he took pride in his many accomplishments and relished the fame he achieved, his public career weighed heavily upon him, draining him of energy both mental and physical not simply because of the responsibilities undertaken, for he did not lack confidence in his own abilities, but because these responsibilities so often involved him in difficult situations with other people. "The Reflections that are made in a Grove," he observed in an important bit of self-revelation, "are forgotten in the Town, and the Man who resembles a saint in his Thoughts in the first, shall resemble [a] Devil in his Actions in the last." That Adams had himself in mind became clear in the next sentence: "In such silent scenes, as riding or walking thro the Woods or sitting alone in my Chamber, or lying awake in my Bed my Thoughts commonly run upon Knowledge, Virtue, Books, etc. tho I am apt to forget these, in the distracting Bustle of the Town, and ceremonious Converse with Mankind."[54] This was the effect that living in the world had upon him.

His typical reaction to strangers was caution and distrust until they had proven themselves reliable—and the proving was not easy. Contemporaries frequently remarked upon the difficulties of associating with him. There was in his behavior, noted one, "a natural restraint" that prevented free communication.[55] Another complained that though Adams seemed friendly enough to some, he was "rather implacable" to those he thought

[53] Adams to Mercy Warren, November 25, 1775: *Works*, IX, 368.
[54] Diary, Spring 1759: *Diary and Autobiography*, I, 85.
[55] D. M. Erskine to his father, January 1, 1799: *William and Mary Quarterly*, Series 3, VI (1949), 281.

his enemies.[56] This observation struck close to the point, for it suggested perhaps the most important reason for the tension that seemed constantly to grip Adams' life. More than anything else, he yearned for solid and lasting fame; not simply the applause that would gratify shallow ambition, but the considered approbation of his society for valuable services rendered.[57] All his life he struggled for greatness—and feared he would miss it. "Reputation," he advised, "ought to be the perpetual subject of my Thoughts, and Aim of my Behavior. How shall I gain a Reputation! How shall I Spread an Opinion of myself as a Lawyer of distinguished Genius, Learning and Virtue.]"[58] However substantial his achievements, he could never rest easily with them. He could never shake the lingering fear that in the end he would turn out to have been quite ordinary after all. "The man to whom Nature has given a great and Surprizing Genius," he worried in his diary, "will perform Great and Surprizing Atchievements [sic], but a Soul originally narrow and confined, will never be enlarged to a distinguishing Capacity." Such a person would have to be content "to grovel amidst pebles [sic]" through the whole of his life. By diligence he might possibly secure the character of "a Man of Sence [sic]," but never that of a great Man."[59] All his life he examined his situation to determine whether greatness would in fact be his.

Much of Adams' difficulty with others derived from this compulsion to succeed. Anyone who seemed to challenge him for preferment (and in one way or another nearly everyone did) or even to question his position was immediately marked out for opposition. (It was this ex-

[56] Quoted in Adams' *Works*, I, 57n.

[57] Professor Edmund S. Morgan has examined Adams' motives, compounded equally of ambition and a sense of public duty, in a model review essay, "John Adams and the Puritan Tradition": *New England Quarterly*, XXXIV (1961), 518-29.

[58] Diary, March 14, 1759: *Diary and Autobiography*, I, 78.

[59] Diary, April 10, 1756: *Ibid.*, p. 20.

cessive sensitivity to criticism that Mercy Warren later described as "a natural irratibility [*sic*] of temper.")[60] So it was with Robert Treat Paine, another bright young lawyer sworn at the same time as Adams before the Boston bar. Adams disliked Paine intensely because of his obvious ability and sharp wit, which Adams frequently found turned against himself. "Bob Paine is conceited and pretends to more Knowledge and Genius than he has," Adams complained after one unfortunate encounter. Paine had declared that Adams could not understand Vinnius; yet, Adams fumed, "he has no Right to say that I dont understand every Word" of it. Moreover, at a dinner of the Superior Court judges in Worcester, Adams continued grumpily, Paine had engrossed the whole conversation, when "a modest attentive Behaviour" would have been proper. Such impudence might "sett the Million a Gape [*sic*]," noted Adams, but would "make all Persons of Sense despize him. . . ." For the future, Adams would "act the Part of a critical spy" upon Paine, "not that of an open unsuspicious friend."[61]

Similarly with Franklin when both he and Adams were abroad during the 1780's. There were matters of temperament that set Adams and the Doctor apart. Never could Adams feel at ease with Franklin's urbane manner, so much the opposite of his own. In addition, they disagreed over the definition of their function as American representatives. Franklin, assuming that the important thing was to keep the French as friends, entered easily into the social life of Paris and the Court. Adams, more suspicious of both French morals and intentions, chose to remain aloof, directing his energies to the details of the mission and berating Franklin for ignoring them. More than this, however, Adams was dis-

[60] Mercy Warren to Adams, July 16, 1807: Massachusetts Historical Society, *Collections*, Series 5, IV (1878), 330.

[61] Diary, December 5, 1758: *Diary and Autobiography*, I, 59-60.

gruntled at being overshadowed by Franklin both in France and back in Congress. Franklin's casual attitude of superiority and his effectiveness at contesting for pre-eminence was more than Adams could easily endure.

There were other factors as well that added to Adams' difficulties—what Professor Bailyn, for example, has described as a "feeling of gracelessness and social clumsiness."[62] Adams had constantly to be on guard against his own impulsiveness. Too often he failed. Perhaps his most distinguishing characteristic was his tactlessness. He was distressingly blunt and outspoken. "Mr Adams," declared Lord Howe in British understatement, "is a decided Character."[63] A century later, Theodore Parker said the same thing less cautiously. Adams, he observed, was "terribly open, earnest, and direct, and could not keep his mouth shut."[64] Adams had sharp opinions about men and events, and spoke them with a ferocity that brooked no opposition. Repeatedly, he spoke out before thinking, realizing the consequences only too late. No one knew it better than he. "Zeal, and fire, and activity, and enterprise," he admitted ruefully, "strike my imagination too much. I am obliged to be constantly on my guard; yet the heat within will burst forth at times."[65] There were numerous occasions, he acknowledged, when he was so agitated that he had no consideration of the way his words would be regarded by others.[66] His impulsiveness left him exposed to the criticism and mockery of calmer men. "How great," he reflected, "is the Dread of Satyr and Ridicule in human Nature."[67] From his own experience, he knew.

His physical stature, moreover, caused him discom-

[62] Bailyn, "Butterfield's Adams": *William and Mary Quarterly*, Series 3, XIX (1962), 245.

[63] Autobiography: *Diary and Autobiography*, III, 423.

[64] Theodore Parker, *Historic Americans* (Boston, 1907), p. 210.

[65] Adams to Mercy Warren, November 25, 1775: *Works*, IX, 369.

[66] Diary, December 31, 1772: *Diary and Autobiography*, II, 76.

[67] Diary, April 1759: *Ibid.*, I, 83.

fort. His appearance gave the lie outright to the mood of high seriousness which he constantly struck. He wanted above all to be impressive; yet physically he was not, and he felt the fact keenly. He was short and plump —increasingly so. His arms and legs were too spindly for the rest of him and moved awkwardly when he became excited. His rounded head, balding on top and encircled by an unruly fringe of hair, sat immediately upon his shoulders. He had a rather small face, with eyes reddened and heavy-lidded from constant use set close on either side of a thin nose. Almost lost among his full jowls rested his mouth: small and prim, distinctly feminine.

Neither in its parts nor as a whole was it a physique to command respect. From Ralph Izard, it inspired the derisive title, His Rotundity. At times, Adams could be mildly amused at the figure he struck. To one friend, he remarked late in life that he looked most of all like "a short, thick Archbishop of Canterbury. . . ."[68] Normally, however, he was not so detached. "By my Physical Constitution," he lamented in 1779, "I am but an ordinary Man." When he looked in the glass, his eye, his forehead, his lips all betrayed relaxation. Some great events, some "cutting Expressions, some mean Hypocrisies," he hoped, might throw "this Assemblage of Sloth, Sleep, and littleness into Rage a little like a Lion." Yet he was not like a lion, he concluded glumly. There was "Extravagance and Distraction" in his manner that betrayed weakness.[69]

Adams, then, mixed uneasily with the society about him. He developed, of course, a number of warm and lasting relationships which he valued highly. Yet, characteristically, his contacts with other people impressed

[68] Adams to Benjamin Waterhouse, March 25, 1817: W. C. Ford, ed., *Statesman and Friend, Correspondence of John Adams with Benjamin Waterhouse, 1784-1822* (Boston, 1927), p. 131.
[69] Diary, April 26, 1779: *Diary and Autobiography*, II, 362-63.

him more as challenges than opportunities, more to be approached warily than rushed into with open arms. In one of his countless letters to Abigail, he made some of his difficulties clear. "There are very few People in this World, with whom I can bear to converse," he lamented. "I can treat all with Decency and Civility, and converse with them, when it is necessary, on Points of Business. But I am never happy in their Company. This has made me a Recluse," he lamented, "and will one day make me an Hermit."[70]

The lesson of his experience was not lost upon him. It provided further confirmation of what reading and observation had declared as well: that men were naturally contentious and got along together only with difficulty. This was the basic assumption about human nature that Adams carried with him as he turned after April of 1775 to the task of regulating American society; a task of crucial importance and awesome dimension.

[70] Adams to Abigail Adams, August 18, 1776: Butterfield, ed., *Adams Family Correspondence*, II, 100.

Chapter II. A Virtuous People

I f Adams worried about American society and warned of the difficulties into which it could fall, however, he remained ultimately confident throughout the Revolution that these difficulties could be overcome. Though he lamented the excesses into which public behavior occasionally ran, he was most impressed by the moderation with which Americans usually conducted themselves. In spite of disturbed conditions and roused emotions, they demonstrated admirable prudence and caution. In the face of the most desperate challenges, they steadfastly maintained their composure.

The people of Massachusetts especially received his commendation. "Such an example of patience and order" this people exhibited under the most "cruel insults, distresses, and provocations," he applauded, "as the history of mankind cannot parallel."[1] Some elements in the population, of course, took advantage of the prevailing confusion to attack their personal enemies. And public disfavor fell rather heavily upon merchants and others whose patriotism the Revolutionary leaders deemed insufficient. Tories had to flee for their lives to Canada or England, almost always at the expense of their property. Never was Adams unduly disturbed by these activities, however. Uncompromising hostility toward Tories and their sympathizers he believed warranted by America's desperate situation. The notable thing to him was that more violence had not occurred.

Adams turned aside Joseph Galloway's dark warning that if the authority of the parent state was weakened, "unsettled disputes" would involve the people in "all

[1] "Novanglus": *Works*, IV, 31.

the horrors of civil war."[2] Adams denied that the Patriots constituted the lower elements of society as Galloway implied, or that they were bent upon remaking America. The notion too much prevails, he protested, that the "politest and genteelist" were all on the side of the administration; "that the better Sort, the Wiser Few" were on one side, and "the Multitude, the Vulgar, the Herd, the Rabble, the Mob only" on the other. So difficult it was, he concluded, "for the frail, feeble Mind of Man to shake itself loose from all Prejudices and Habits."[3] The Americans, he insisted, were a sober and responsible people, fixed in their dedication to a free, yet orderly society—a society given stability by its own regularly functioning political institutions.

The key to Adams' optimism was his abiding belief in American virtue. Though he became disenchanted at times during the 1770's with the behavior of particular Americans, he remained utterly convinced of the predominant virtue of American society as a whole. In this he found an influence capable of overruling the foolishness of individuals. He relied on "the honesty and sobriety as well as good sense of the people," he acknowledged to Abigail. "These qualities will overawe the passions of individuals and preserve a steady administration of the laws."[4] This was the single most important assumption of his early political thought.

Adams' belief in American virtue was supported by the historical context in which he placed the revolutionary experience. Americans, of course, shared a common humanity with other men, and consequently demonstrated the weaknesses to which individuals were subject everywhere. Yet during the 1770's, Adams did not

[2] Joseph Galloway, *Historical and Political Reflections* (London, 1770), p. 77.

[3] Adams to Abigail Adams, July 7, 1774: Butterfield, ed., *Adams Family Correspondence*, I, 130.

[4] Adams to Abigail Adams, September 17, 1782: C. F. Adams, ed., *Familiar Letters of John Adams and his Wife* (Boston, 1875), p. 405.

think of the American people only, or even primarily, in such universal terms. The point of greatest significance to him was America's uniqueness—the "differentness" of America's historical circumstance and thus, most importantly, of her people's moral character. From his own experience and observations of the conduct of other men, he did, as we have seen, fashion certain principles of human behavior valid for all men everywhere. But during the revolutionary years, he subordinated these considerations to a stronger belief in American particularity; a belief fashioned by his understanding of America's historical situation.

For every age, one can discover a few key words which illuminate prevailing patterns of thought. "Virtue," like "Reason" and "Nature," was one such word for the eighteenth century. Its meanings were many. For Adams it signified on the one hand the qualities of industry, frugality, and prudence which classical philosophy and political theory declared to be good.[5] In Adams' mind, of course, these were more immediately the virtues of the Puritan ethic, cleansed somewhat of their theological trappings.

Virtue most often, however, meant something more than this to Adams. It meant, above all, a concern for the welfare of society as a whole as opposed to one's own purely selfish interests. Though manifested by individuals, virtue, as Adams most often used the term, did not have individuals as its primary object; humanitarianism was not its theme. (In this, Adams differed

[5] Adams read widely and carefully in the classics and admired particularly the wisdom of the Stoics. The classics represented in his library about one hundred volumes in the original, besides translations of a number of authors into French and English. Typically, his interests ran strongly to history and philosophy, rather than poetry. See D. M. Robatham, "John Adams and the Classics": *New England Quarterly*, XIX (1946), 91-98. Also, *Catalogue of the John Adams Library in the Public Library of the City of Boston* (Boston, 1917). Relevant material can also be found in Alfred Iacuzzi, *John Adams, Scholar* (New York, 1952).

from Jefferson who described virtue as "a love of others, a sense of duty to them, a moral instinct, in short, which prompts us irresistibly to feel and to succor their distresses. . . .")[6] For Adams, the proper object of virtue was society as a whole. In the virtuous man, social affections predominated over selfish and first priority was given to social responsibilities.

In 1765, Adams read Joseph Butler's *Analogy of Religion* (1740). In it, he found a definition of virtue that he made his own. Adams transcribed the passage carefully in his notebook. "Now I say," Adams copied,

> . . . Virtue in a society has a . . . tendency to procure superiority and additional power . . . by rendering public good, an object and end, to every member of the society by putting every one upon consideration and diligence, resollution and self-government, both in order to see what is the most effectual method, and also in order to perform their proposed part, for obtaining and preserving it; by uniting a society within itself, and so increasing its strength; and, which is particularly to be mentioned, uniting it by means of veracity and justice. For as these last are principle bonds of union, so benevolence or public spirit, undirected, unrestrained by them, is, nobody knows what.[7]

A decade later, in a letter to Mercy Warren, Adams explained the matter in his own words. Public virtue, he asserted, was the necessary foundation of America's new governments. That is, there had to be "a positive Passion for the public good, the public Interest, Honour, Power and Glory, established in the Minds of the People," and this public passion had to "be Superiour to all pri-

[6] Thomas Jefferson to Thomas Law, June 13, 1814: Adrienne Koch and William Peden, eds., *The Life and Selected Writings of Thomas Jefferson* (New York, 1944), p. 638.
[7] "Literary Commonplace Book": Adams Microfilm, Reel 187.

vate Passions." Men had to pride themselves on sacrificing their private pleasures, interests, and connections when these stood in competition with the good of society. "The only reputable Principle and Doctrine," he concluded, was that "all Things must give Way to the public."[8]

Not all socially beneficial attitudes would Adams classify as virtuous. An individual's conscience which stood in the way of his gratification of some selfish desire could not strictly be identified as virtue. And oftentimes self-interest and social advantage coincided. By their desire for social approbation, for example, men even of little virtue could be persuaded to serve their fellow creatures. Acts taken upon the calculation of self-interest, however, were not virtuous whatever their results might be. Virtue, by definition, involved the willful discipline of one's own selfish passions, and the conscious choosing of social good over immediate personal advantage.

Adams explained the peculiar virtuousness of the American people as a function of America's historical circumstance. Experience manifested American virtue to Adams; the experience of the Revolution, which called American virtue so forcefully to his attention, and the broader historical experience of past generations in which the singular character of the American people had been fashioned.

Adams' understanding of the American condition was ordered around a cyclical theory of historical development. History, he affirmed, consisted of the gradual rise and fall of successive empires, each for a period dominating the world and then giving way to another. Over the centuries, there had taken place a constant ebb and flow of ascendant nations. Various empires had risen to preeminence; but after a period of supremacy, each had entered upon a period of decline, ultimately giving way to another.[9] Initially, the Assyrian and Egyptian empires had flourished. They then succumbed to Greek and Roman supremacy. Eventually, these too encountered a time of dissolution. The seat of empire had next moved to France, and finally to England.

To the rise and fall of empires, Adams gave an almost biological description. Lord Bolingbroke, the English statesman and historian, in his *Patriot King* (1738)—a book Adams read carefully—pointed up the close analogy between the life cycles of nations and organisms. Political societies, like animal bodies, noted Bolingbroke, had a natural cycle of infancy, youth, maturity, old age, and death. Every nation unavoidably had to pass through the full revolution.[10] Governor James Bowdoin of Massachusetts, in an address of 1780 inaugurating the American Academy of Arts and Sciences, described with particular clarity the law of cyclical development to which Adams adhered. "It is very pleasing and instructive," Bowdoin declared,

> ... to recur back to the early ages of mankind, and trace the progressive state of nations and empires, from infancy to maturity, to old age and dissolution:—to observe their origin, their growth and improvement ... to observe the progress of the arts among them ... to observe the rise and gradual advancement of civilization, of science, of wealth, elegance, and politeness, until they had obtained the

[9] On the subject of American historical theory during the eighteenth century, Stow Persons' *American Minds* (New York, 1958) has been particularly helpful, especially pages 122ff. The whole matter of historical writing during the late colonial and early national periods needs more careful work than it has yet received. For useful discussions of European historical writing during this period, see Carl Becker's *The Heavenly City of the Eighteenth Century Philosophers* (New Haven, 1932), Chapters 3 and 4, and J. B. Bury's *The Idea of Progress* (London, 1921). Bury recalls the classical origins of the cyclical theory of history.

[10] Cited in Persons, *American Minds*, p. 122.

> summit of their greatness:—to observe at this pe-
> riod the principle of mortality, produced by afflu-
> ence and luxury, beginning to operate in them . . .
> and finally terminating in their dissolution. . . . In
> fine—to observe, after this catastrophe, a new face
> of things; new kingdoms and empires rising upon
> the ruins of the old; all of them to undergo like
> changes, and to suffer a similar dissolution.[11]

Not only did empires wax and wane, but as Governor Bowdoin suggested, the life cycle of each empire was reflected in the character of its people. Every phase in the process of growth, maturity, decline, and decay manifested different qualities of individual and social life. David Tappan, Hollis Professor of Divinity at Harvard, explained how this was true. In the early stages of development, he observed, nations were inhabited by men "industrious and frugal, simple in their manners, just and kind in their intercourse, active and hardy, united and brave." Gradually the practice of such virtues brought the people to a state of manly vigor. They matured and became flourishing in wealth and population, in arts and arms. Once they reached a certain point, however, their manners began to change. Prosperity infected their morals, leading them into "pride and avarice, luxury and dissipation, idleness and sensuality, and too often into . . . impiety." These and kindred vices hastened their downfall and ruin.[12] Between national character and the stages of empire, then, there was a direct correlation. The cycle of development of any nation could be traced in the customs and manners of the people.

The cyclical theory of history provided the rationale Adams needed to put the events of the Revolution and the behavior of the American people in perspective. It explained in clearest terms the actions of both England and America. England's attack upon American liberties

[11] *Ibid.*, p. 123.   [12] *Ibid.*, p. 125.

revealed a quite drastic declension in her national character. Adams' conclusion was that England had passed the high point and entered the downward swing of her development. Only this could explain her immoral actions. The change, Adams believed, had come with disarming speed. In 1763 with her final triumph over France, England had reached the peak of her strength. One might have expected a bit of time to elapse before decline set in. Yet such had not been the case. For Adams the lesson of events was clear: when nations reached the summit of their careers, any slight influence, any "minute and unsuspected cause" could start the irretrievable slide downhill.

The attack upon American liberties brought to Adams' attention the first certain signs of England's moral decay: selfishness among her people, ostentation, political corruption, the inclination to tyrannize over others. For a while, it seemed to him that the disease had spread no farther than Parliament and the royal officials. "We distinguish," he remarked as late as 1775, "between the ministry, the house of commons, the officers of the army, navy, excise, customs, &., who are dependent on the ministry, and tempted, if not obliged, to echo their voices, and the body of the people." It seemed certain to him that the people still were "friends to America" and wished her success in the struggle against Parliament and the administration.[18]

Ultimately, however, Adams was forced to admit that the debilitating influence of the Court had corrupted the whole English people. "Luxury, effeminacy, and venality," he wrote, "are arrived at such a shocking pitch in

---

[18] "Novanglus": *Works*, IV, 36-37. The representatives of royal authority in the colonies Adams described as the most degenerate of all. The "Junto" in Massachusetts, comprised of Governors Bernard and Hutchinson, Peter and Andrew Oliver, and their cohorts, Adams warned, were engaged in a plot to subvert the constitution of Massachusetts, the rights of all Americans, and English liberties to boot just for their own advantage. *Works*, IV, 19ff.

England" that "both electors and elected are become one mass of corruption. . . ." When Americans were told that the people of England were depraved, the Parliament venal, and the ministry corrupt, he asked, were they not told melancholy truths? Every man who came from there, whether Whig or Tory, told the same thing: that corruption was "so established . . . as to be incurable, and a necessary instrument of government." England, he concluded, had arrived nearly to the point of the Roman Empire when Jurgutha pronounced it "a venal city, ripe for destruction. . . ."[14] So far had England already fallen from her once proud pinnacle that there was no virtue left in her.

This theory of empire, which explained to Adams the cause of England's decline, had even more momentous implications for America. For if England was on the wane, a new empire must be rising to take her place, and America was the obvious successor. By all observable indices, England had entered her period of decay; by an obverse set of criteria, America was just beginning her rise.

In point of years, Adams declared, America was young —an "Infant Country."[15] In contrast to the tired societies of Europe, she was just now entering upon her full rate of growth. Americans of the mid-eighteenth century were fascinated with the development of their land. Their struggle and ultimate victory over England gave a great fillip to their notions of future empire. Franklin, among others, speculated upon the growth of the American population, predicting freely that it would outnumber England's by 1800. Declared Reverend Ebenezer Baldwin: the American colonies were certain to become the "Foundation of a great and mighty Empire; the Largest the World ever saw, to be founded on such

[14] "Novanglus": *Works*, IV, 28, 54-55. Also, Adams to R. H. Lee, December 24, 1785: Adams Microfilm, Reel 112.
[15] *Boston Gazette*, January 20, 1776.

Principles of Liberty and Freedom, both civil and religious, as never before took place in the World. . . ."[16]
Samuel Adams believed much the same thing. It required but a little discernment, he observed, to see that
there would be erected a mighty empire in America while
England sank into obscurity.[17]

No one wrote more enthusiastically of America's rising
fortunes than John Adams. His earliest view of America's future place in the continuing succession of nations,
he spelled out in a letter of October 1755 to his cousin,
Nathan Webb. "All that part of creation which lies within our observation," Adams wrote, "is liable to change.
Even mighty states and Kingdoms are not exempted."
Then he continued:

> If we look into history, we shall find some nations
> rising from contemptible beginnings, and spreading
> their influence till the whole globe is subjected to
> their sway. When they have reached the summit of
> grandeur, some minute and unsuspected cause com-
> monly effects their ruin, and the empire of the world
> is transferred to some other place. Immortal Rome
> . . . by degrees . . . rose to a stupendous height,
> and excelled, in arts and arms, all the nations that
> preceded it. But . . . [it sank] into a debauchery,
> and . . . [became] at length an easy prey to bar-
> barians.

Following Rome's decline, England began to increase in
power and wealth, and became the greatest nation upon
earth. Soon after the Reformation, however, a few people
had come over to the New World for conscience's sake.
"Perhaps this apparently trivial incident," Adams speculated, "may transfer the great seat of empire into America. It looks likely to me. . . ." If Americans could re-

---

[16] Quoted in Persons, *American Minds*, p. 126.
[17] William V. Wells, *The Life and Public Services of Samuel Adams*, 3 vols. (Boston, 1865), II, 149-50.

move "the turbulent Gallicks," her people "according to the exactest computations" would in the next century become more numerous than England's. Then, he concluded, "the united force of all Europe will not be able to subdue us."[18] As the Revolution progressed, Adams became convinced that America was growing even more rapidly than he had anticipated.

Adams was impressed with America's growing physical and economic strength; yet it was not this that most interested him.[19] Never did he share much of Hamilton's, or Robert Morris's, or Tench Coxe's vision of future material greatness. America's strength, Adams thought, would lie in the peculiar virtuousness of her people. On this would her influence in the world depend.

The logic of Adams' historical thought gave good reason for expecting that Americans would be particularly virtuous. One would expect the inhabitants of an "Infant Country" to be industrious and frugal, simple and unspoiled. American principles, Adams explained, were similar to "the high sentiments of Romans in the most prosperous and virtuous Times of that Commonwealth."[20] American society was sparse and vigorous, free from the great cities and attendant corruptions characteristic of Europe.

Adams did not, of course, depend alone for his conviction of American virtue upon the logic of historical theory. As always, he found in experience—the historical experience of his ancestors and the events of his own generation—the convincing truth which theory postulated.

Virtue, as we have seen, signified for Adams a pri-

[18] Adams to Nathan Webb, October 12, 1755: *Works*, I, 23. Also, *Diary and Autobiography*, I, 34.
[19] See especially Adams' early Diary entries—for example, May 17, 1756: *Diary and Autobiography*, I, 27.
[20] "Clarendon": *Ibid.*, p. 272.

mary concern for society. In the context of the Revolution, it meant something a good deal more specific: dedication to liberty, particularly American liberty, and a willingness to defend it at whatever cost. Adams was saying this when he linked together as attributes of the American people the "most habitual, radical sense of Liberty, and the highest Reverence for Virtue."[21] Or when in his "Novanglus" essays of 1775 he wrote of "the republican spirit, which is a spirit of true virtue and honest independence. . . ."[22] The virtuous man was he who dedicated himself to the preservation and extension of human liberty. Virtue, in this sense of the word, became for Adams the key to an understanding of the whole American experience, up to and including the Revolution.

Though Adams interpreted history in terms of the rise and fall of successive empires, he combined it with the notion of gradual progress. The cycles of empire did not oscillate along the horizontal, but rather along an inclined axis so that each empire succeeded the one preceding at a higher level of development. As Adam Ferguson, Scottish Common Sense philosopher widely read in America and well known to Adams, wrote: "When nations succeed one another . . . the last is always the most knowing."[23] Adams began from the assumption that history was the story of human progress. His belief in this was never as expansive as Turgot's or Condorcet's; never did he talk in terms of human perfectibility. And, as is well known, he became more skeptical about human progress after the French Revolution. In an observation made to Jefferson late in life, long after both had retired from public affairs, Adams expressed his considered views on the matter. "I am a Believer, in the probable improvability and Improvement, the Ameliora-

[21] *Ibid.*
[22] "Novanglus": *Works*, IV, p. 68.
[23] Diary, July 16, 1786: *Diary and Autobiography*, III, 194.

bi[li]ty and Amelioration in human Affairs: though I never could understand the Doctrine of the Perfectability [*sic*] of the human Mind."[24] During the 1770's, his view was somewhat more hopeful, but still not so different. Over the years, men had obviously improved their lot and would continue to do so.

The reality of progress Adams identified not primarily in economic or material terms, but by the advance of human liberty and the decline of tyranny. The theme of liberty Adams declared to be the gradual emancipation of men from religious, political, and intellectual oppression; the steady succession of reason over superstition, freedom over coercion, knowledge over ignorance. In these terms did he explain the American experience. They made the reality of American virtue evident to him.

Adams set down his fullest discussion of America's role in the progressive unfolding of human liberty in his "Dissertation on the Canon and Feudal Law," written and published in 1765. The modern struggle between liberty and tyranny, Adams observed, had begun with the Reformation. During the Middle Ages, priests and monarchs, "the artificers of the canon and feudal law," had joined in a "wicked confederacy" to keep the people "ignorant of everything but the tools of agriculture and of war." Under this unholy alliance, men had sunk into a condition of "sordid ignorance and staring timidity."[25] With ecclesiastical reform, the dissolution of both the religious and civil tyranny that had for centuries held men in submission began. Since the days of the church reformers, history had become the story of

[24] Adams to Thomas Jefferson, July 16, 1814: Lester Cappon, ed., *The Adams-Jefferson Letters*, 2 vols. (Chapel Hill, 1959), II, 435.

[25] "Dissertation on the Canon and Feudal Law": *Works*, III, 450-51.

the spread of knowledge and liberty. In direct proportion to their advance, oppression had fallen away.[26]

Enlightenment first appeared in Europe, yet found its greatest success in England. There the Roman church lost its authority. There, also, men developed a tradition of political liberty, unrivalled in any other nation. On two occasions during the seventeenth century, they demonstrated how deeply rooted in their lives this tradition was, by casting down "the execrable race of the Stuarts."[27]

The struggle against the tyranny of priest and king, however, had not been confined to the Old World, for out of it had come the settlement of North America. The English colonies, Adams asserted, had been settled by persons unwilling to live with even the remnants of the old canon and feudal systems. In America, they found a place where liberty could flourish unmolested.

Adams insisted that the earliest English settlers had come for more than narrowly religious motives. (Rather apologetically, he acknowledged that many of them had been religious to the point of enthusiasm.) The original settlers had left their ancient homes to face the rigors of a hostile land, he asserted, out of "a love of universal liberty, and a hatred, a dread, a horror, of the infernal confederacy [of civil and ecclesiastical powers]. . . ."[28] Vexed by church and state, they had fled into the wilderness for refuge from "the temporal and spiritual principalities" of their native country.[29]

In America, the settlers took great pains to protect the liberties they had come to enjoy. They formed policies of self-government, founded in the most "wise, humane, and benevolent principles."[30] They were convinced that the only foundation upon which freedom could be safely built was knowledge diffused broadly among the people. Accordingly, these "men of sense and learning"—Adams

26 *Ibid.*, p. 448.   27 *Ibid.*, p. 451.   28 *Ibid.*
29 *Ibid.*   30 *Ibid.*, p. 452.

was as much taken with their intellect as with their piety —set about to establish schools and universities. In their libraries they possessed "the wisdom of the most enlightened ages and nations," to be passed along to future generations.[31] Declaring that the people "have a right, from the frame of their nature" to knowledge, the founders had provided by law that every town should erect and support a school.

From both civil and ecclesiastical government, taking as their model not only scripture but "the best and wisest legislation of humanity" as well, they removed as many feudal inequalities as possible. Holding in "utter contempt . . . all that dark ribaldry of hereditary, indefeasible right . . . and the divine, miraculous original of all government," they established the popular will as a firm balance to the remaining powers of the monarch.[32] The whole system of ecclesiastical control, they utterly demolished. As the years passed, noted Adams, the settlers and their descendants continued to nurture the love of liberty and knowledge that had been their original inspiration.

As an essay in seventeenth-century history, Adams' analysis leaves something to be desired. Its importance, of course, lies in its reflection of his own preoccupations. The significance of the story he told was its timelessness. It offered to Americans of the eighteenth century at once an explanation of their heritage and instructions for their own conduct. The experience of the founders was intended as prologue to the experience of Adams' own generation.

The troubles that Americans encountered after 1765, Adams explained, were a continuation of the struggles their ancestors had begun. Once again, liberty was under attack; and now more than ever before the New World was being called upon to rally to its defense. The setting had shifted decisively to America, but the contest remained essentially the same. The colonies, Adams observed, were acting in defense of the liberties their forefathers had established at such great risk. "We are not exciting a rebellion," he wrote in 1775; Americans were but resisting "usurpation" and "lawless violence" against their liberty.[33] Throughout his life, Adams repeated his theme. America fought only to protect its traditional liberties against the "innovations and . . . unlimited claims of Parliament. . . ."[34]

As early as 1765, Adams had detected the scent of tyranny upon the breeze. Many of the measures of Parliament, he warned, had a tendency "to divest us of our most essential rights and liberties."[35] Before a decade was out, Adams was certain that a conscious attack upon American freedom was under way. England, he asserted in his "Novanglus" essays, was engaged in "a settled plan to deprive the people of all the benefits, blessings, and ends of the contract [between king and people], to subvert the fundamentals of the constitution, to deprive them of all share in making and executing laws. . . ."[36] He offered as evidence the extension of the courts of admiralty, the effort to begin royal payment of judicial salaries, and in 1774 the abrogation of the Massachusetts charter.[37] Repeated oppressions had "placed it beyond doubt" that there was a design to deprive the American people of their basic liberties.[38]

Throughout the Revolution, Adams emphasized that Americans were continuing the struggle for freedom begun by their fathers. "The principles and feelings which

[33] *Ibid.*, p. 57.
[34] Adams to Mercy Warren, July 20, 1807: Massachusetts Historical Society, *Collections*, Series 5, IV (1878), 352.
[35] "Instructions of the Town of Braintree, 1765": *Works*, III, 465. See also an early draft of one of Adams' "Clarendon" essays in his Diary for January 18, 1766: *Diary and Autobiography*, I, 297-98.
[36] "Novanglus": *Works*, IV, 16. Also, *ibid.*, p. 33.
[37] "Instructions of the Town of Braintree, 1765": *Ibid.*, III, pp. 466-67. Also, *Diary and Autobiography*, I, 297.
[38] "Novanglus": *Works*, IV, 17. Also, *ibid.*, p. 14.

contributed to produce the revolution," he explained many years later, "ought to be traced back for two hundred years, and sought in the history of the country from the first plantation in America."[39] Americans should set before themselves the conduct of their ancestors, who "defended for us the inherent rights of mankind against foreign and domestic . . . usurpers . . . arbitrary kings and cruel priests. . . ." He called upon his contemporaries to examine the nature of the oppressions that had driven the exiles from their homes; to "read and recollect and impress upon" their souls the purposes of the founders. Above all, Americans needed to set before themselves "the civil and religious principles . . . which constantly supported" the founders through all their hardships.[40]

America had now become the keeper of the heritage England had cast aside. The importance of America's mission Adams made abundantly clear. "I always considered the Settlement of America with Reverence and Wonder," he wrote solemnly in 1765, "as the opening of a grand Scene and Design of Providence, for the Illumination of the Slavish Part of Mankind all over the Earth."[41] The American people, he repeated, thought that "the Liberties of Mankind and the Glory of human Nature" were in their keeping. They knew that liberty had been hunted and persecuted in all countries. But they flattered themselves that America "was designed by Providence for the Theatre, on which Man was to make his true figure, on which science, Virtue, Liberty, Happiness and Glory were to exist in Peace."[42]

Adams identified the Revolution as a major step toward the realization of this goal. In their struggle against England, Americans were establishing liberty for

[39] Adams to Hezekiah Niles, February 13, 1818: *Ibid.*, X, 284.

[40] "Canon and Feudal Law": *Ibid.*, III, 462.

[41] Early draft of "Canon and Feudal Law": Adams Microfilm, Reel 1.

[42] "Clarendon": *Diary and Autobiography*, I, 282.

themselves and their posterity, for "future Millions, and Millions of Millions. . . ."[43] The progress of society, Adams asserted in one of his more expansive moments, "will be accelerated by centuries by this Revolution." Because of America's efforts, religious toleration and political liberty would prevail not only in America, but in Europe as well. "Light spreads from the dayspring in the west," he exulted, "and may it shine more and more until the perfect day!"[44]

Virtue, then, while signifying an overruling concern for the welfare of society, became transmuted in the context of the Revolutionary experience into patriotism, or a defense of American liberty against British attack. Merchants were asked to forego their trade, and housewives certain of their comforts. Husbands were required to offer military service, and some of them their lives. The whole Revolution was one grand exercise in virtuous conduct.

During the Revolution, Adams painstakingly examined the ways in which Americans reacted to the decisions thrust upon them—whether they were willing to make the sacrifices necessary to defend their freedom, or would compromise to accept a settlement less satisfactory. In 1776, Congress solicited designs for an American seal. The suggestion offered by Adams defined succinctly the choice he believed the American people faced. Emblazoned on the seal he would have had the figure of Hercules, representing the young republic, leaning on his club contemplating his future course. To one side would stand Virtue, pointing to her rugged mountain and urging him to ascend. To the other, Sloth "wantonly reclining on the ground, displaying the charms both of her eloquence and person," and beckoning toward "her flowery paths

[43] Adams to Abigail Adams, February 11, 1776: Butterfield, ed., *Adams Family Correspondence*, I, 346.
[44] Adams to Abigail Adams, December 18, 1781: C. F. Adams, ed., *Familiar Letters*, p. 133.

of pleasure."[45] Perhaps understandably, Adams' recommendation was not adopted. (He himself thought it "too complicated a group" and not original enough.) Yet it represented graphically for him the situation America was in. The Revolution was the supreme testing of the American character. By their adherence to principles of virtue, by their effective prosecution of the struggle, Americans would prove themselves the virtuous people history demanded them to be.

The fact that the Revolution was a period of trial fit for testing and tempering American character, Adams was convinced, was not an accident of history, but part of a grand design intended to mold the American people for the job history had assigned them. History was not governed by "Blind and Unintelligent Necessity." It was rather the visible working out of Providential will. In completely unexceptional eighteenth-century terms, Adams spelled out his belief in design and in the continuing influence of God on human affairs.[46] Adams' ideas were in keeping with the rationalist tradition of Samuel Clarke, Richard Bentley, and others. The "varieties of Harmonized Concord" in every area of creation revealed a Supreme Intelligence. And the regular ordering of nature's "prodigious Variety of Species's" demonstrated "the continual and vigilant Providence of God."[47] No longer did God determine the course of events

[45] Adams to Abigail Adams, August 14, 1776: Butterfield, ed., *Adams Family Correspondence*, II, 96-97.

[46] For a discussion of this concept in early New England Puritanism, see Perry Miller, *The New England Mind: The Seventeenth Century* (Boston, 1934), pp. 228-35. For an excellent treatment of eighteenth-century extensions of this doctrine, see Conrad Wright, *The Beginnings of Unitarianism in America* (Boston, 1955), pp. 161-84. See also, Joseph Haroutunian, *Piety Versus Moralism* (New York, 1932).

[47] Diary, July 31, 1756: *Diary and Autobiography*, I, 39. Also, *ibid.*, p. 38. See further jottings of "Instances of wise and good Designs in the Constitution and course of Nature," in Adams' "Literary Commonplace Book": Adams Microfilm, Reel 187.

through miraculous dispensations. Rather, he governed indirectly, through means both general and special.

The breakdown of civil and religious tyranny, which Adams described as the great theme of history, he identified confidently as a reflection of God's will. America's struggle was God's. The American people were His present agents for effecting His design. Our trial, Adams wrote to Josiah Quincy in 1775, "seems to be in the designs of providence. . . ."[48] America's fight against British tyranny was clearly "the work of the Lord. . . ."[49]

Even as God was using Americans to accomplish His purposes, however, He was in the process of making them more effectual agents. He was making them capable of serving His ends by setting them to the task of it—specifically, by placing the trials of the Revolution upon them. God, Adams believed, had not brought the Revolution upon America out of anger or in punishment. The old Jeremiad rationale which for generations had explained to Americans their troubles in terms of divine wrath, Adams found of only partial help in explaining the Revolution.[50] Only occasionally did he lapse into the familiar pattern, attributing America's suffering to her decline in piety and calling for public penitence to regain divine favor.[51] The initiating causes of the Revolution were not, after all, to be found in failures of the American character, but in the tyrannical actions of the British.

[48] Adams to Josiah Quincy, July 29, 1775: Works, IX, 361.

[49] Adams to Samuel Chase, June 24, 1776: Ibid., p. 413.

[50] For the fullest discussion of the Jeremiad rationale and its earlier development, see Perry Miller, The New England Mind: From Colony to Province (Cambridge, Massachusetts, 1953). Adams gave earlier evidence of finding the Jeremiad repugnant to his Arminian faith. See, for example, his reaction to the controversy that surrounded the earthquake of 1755, Diary and Autobiography, I, 61-62. See also his marginalia in his copy of Professor John Winthrop's Lecture on Earthquakes (1755) in the Adams' collection, Boston Public Library.

[51] Adams to Abigail Adams, July 6, 1774 and February 11, 1776: Butterfield, ed., Adams Family Correspondence, I, 126-27, 345-46.

The place where blame should be placed was clear: "on the ministry, and their instruments."[52]

God was using the trials of the Revolution not to punish Americans, but to cleanse them further for the tasks He had appointed them; to purify them, as Adams frequently suggested, in "the furnace of affliction." Out of America's struggle, he wrote confidently to William Gordon, the people's "Vigour, Fortitude and Perseverance" would be increased.[53] America would come out of the test "doubly refined."[54] As was so often true, Adams expressed his thoughts most fully in a letter to his wife. "It may be the Will of Heaven," he wrote to Abigail on the evening before independence was formally declared,

> that America shall suffer Calamities still more wasting and Distresses yet more dreadfull [than any so far experienced]. If this is to be the Case, it will have this good Effect, at least: it will inspire us with many Virtues, which We have not, and correct many Errors, Follies, and Vices, which threaten to disturb, dishonour, and destroy us. The furnace of Affliction produces Refinement, in States as well as Individuals. And the new Governments we are assuming, in every Part, will require a Purification from our Vices, and an Augmentation of our Virtues or they will be no Blessings.[55]

The great difficulties which America faced, would "lay

[52] "Novanglus": *Works*, IV, 71. Concerning the Jeremiad's application to the Revolution, see an article by Perry Miller entitled "From Covenant to Revival," in *The Shaping of American Religion*, James W. Smith and Leland Jameson, eds., 3 vols. (Princeton, 1961), I, 322-63.

[53] Adams to William Gordon, June 23, 1776: Adams Microfilm, Reel 89.

[54] Adams to Colonel Reed, July 7, 1776: *Ibid.*

[55] Adams to Abigail Adams, July 3, 1776: Butterfield, ed., *Adams Family Correspondence*, II, 28.

the Foundations of a full and flourishing People, deep
and strong in great Virtues and abilities."[56] The Revolution, then, was not intended as punishment for past failings, but as a means of strengthening America so that
she might be adequate to future demands. By requiring
Americans to choose virtue, God was making them into
a people more virtuous than ever before. By meeting and
overcoming adversity, they would emerge strengthened
and renewed. In this struggle, God would support them.
The God for whom they did battle would not allow
them to fall. And He would reward their obedience.
"The Arbiter of Events, the Sovereign of the World
only knows, which Way the Torrent will be turned," he
reflected to Abigail during the trying days of early 1776.
"Judging by Experience, by Probabilities, and by all
Appearances, I conclude, it will roll on to Dominion and
Glory, tho the Circumstances . . . may be bloody."[57]
It made a difference that the American people had divine
resources at their disposal.

Adams' reflections upon the Providential guarantee of
American success, were an extension, a socialization of
classical Puritan covenant theology. In it, salvation was
not to be won by individuals on their own merit alone.
If, however, they devoted themselves to praising God
and attempted to live a holy life, He would contract
with them to prosper the effort and bring them to glory.
So with the Revolution. If the American people would
strive to be virtuous, to surmount the challenges placed
before them, in a word to promote their Revoluton, He
would make them adequate to the task and bring them
through, tempered and stronger than ever before.

The reality, both of God's favor and of American
virtue, then, would be manifest in the unfolding of

---

[56] Adams to Samuel Adams, November 27, 1778: Adams Microfilm, Reel 93.
[57] Adams to Abigail Adams, February 11, 1776: Butterfield, ed.,
Adams Family Correspondence, I, 346.

Revolutionary events. The prevalence of "the republican spirit," the "spirit of true virtue," could be empirically determined. "There are certain marks," Adams observed, "by which the opinions, principles, inclinations, and wishes of a people may be discovered with infallible certainty, without recurring to . . . far-fetched arguments."[58] The success with which the American people met the Revolutionary challenge provided Adams with the ultimate proof of how virtuous American opinions and principles, inclinations and wishes in fact were.

From the first, Adams had few doubts about the character of New Englanders. He was fully persuaded of their devotion to liberty and their willingness to sacrifice for its preservation. The firm opposition of the northern colonies to both Stamp Act and Townshend duties demonstrated stoutness of heart. The embargoes had required homespun and hardship, but the people willingly made the sacrifice. Later yet, in 1774, they gave solid support to the beleaguered city of Boston.[59]

Of the colonies to the south, however, Adams was considerably less confident. There were encouraging signs from 1765 on, that their principles were acceptable. Yet Adams was unsure how far the southern and middle colonies would be willing to go in opposing England, especially if their own interests were not immediately threatened. Adams had the opportunity to find out in 1774, when Massachusetts fell victim to the Coercive Acts. Would the other colonies come to her aid? Their willingness to join their destinies with the Bay Colony would be the test of their virtue.

In resolving his doubts about the colonies to the south,

[58] Adams to Congress, June 2, 1780: Francis Wharton, ed., *The Revolutionary Diplomatic Correspondence of the United States*, 6 vols. (Washington, D.C., 1889), III, 754.
[59] Peter Force, *American Archives*, Series 4, I, 423. John C. Miller, *Origins of the American Revolution* (Boston, 1943), 362ff. Robert J. Taylor, *Western Massachusetts in the Revolution* (Providence, 1954).

Adams' seven weeks' stay at the first Continental Congress was decisive. Before his trip to Philadelphia with the other Massachusetts delegates in August of 1774, he had never been outside New England.[60] Though aware of the interdependence of the thirteen colonies, he had little knowledge or understanding of the large area south of Connecticut. "I feel myself unequal to this Business," he confided to his Diary just three days after his election as a delegate. "A more extensive Knowledge of the Realm, the Colonies, and of Commerce, as well as of Law and Policy, is necessary, than I am Master of."[61] At Philadelphia, he met for the first time with leaders from Virginia, Pennsylvania, and elsewhere and learned for himself what their sentiments were. The experience was an enlightening one for him.

Adams approached the first Congress with considerable trepidation. Its outcome seemed terribly uncertain. He feared, above all, that nothing substantial would be accomplished; that adequate support would not be given Massachusetts. The essential task of Congress, he believed, was to establish a firm basis for cooperative action. "Deliberations alone," would not do.[62] The prospects, however, seemed dim.

The trip southward provided an auspicious beginning to his venture. He expected that the Massachusetts delegation would be well received in Connecticut, but they were greeted as enthusiastically in New York, New Jersey, and Pennsylvania.[63] During the stopover at Princeton, Adams wrote to Abigail about the trip so far. "The

[60] The other delegates were Samuel Adams, R. T. Paine, and Thomas Cushing.

[61] Diary, June 20, 1774: *Diary and Autobiography*, II, 96. Adams feared that neither he nor his New England colleagues would compare favorably with the polished gentlemen from Virginia. At Philadelphia, as in France ten years later, refinement and polish in others which he did not himself possess made him uneasy.

[62] Diary, June 20, 1774: *Ibid.*, p. 96.

[63] Diary, August 1774: *Ibid.*, p. 97ff.

Spirit of the People wherever we have been," he informed her, "seems to be very favourable. They universally consider our Cause as their own, and express the firmest Resolution, to abide the Determination of the Congress."[64] Had Camden, Chatham, Richmond, and St. Asaph travelled through the country, he remarked, they would have enjoyed no greater demonstrations of respect than Cushing, Paine, and "the brace of Adamses."[65]

Adams began the task of sounding out the other delegates and testing their sentiments even before he reached Philadelphia. A number of gentlemen, Benjamin Rush among them, rode out from the city to meet the Massachusetts delegation. Rush rode back into town in Adams' carriage, Adams setting about at once, Rush later recalled, to quiz him. He "asked me many questions," remembered Rush, "relative to the state of public opinion upon politicks and the characters of the most active citizens on both sides of the controversy."[66]

Throughout the first weeks of his stay, Adams continued his examination. On every occasion—in Congress, during dinner at the boarding houses, or over ale and wine at the City Tavern—he listened to the views of the other delegates, searching for some clue to their sentiments, and jotting his findings down each evening in his notebook. One by one, he evaluated the representatives, noting his findings for future reference. There was James Duane of New York with his "sly surveying Eye" and "artfull" countenance—clearly not a man to be trusted; and John Rutledge of South Carolina, with "no Keenness in his Eye. No Depth in his Countenance. Nothing of the profound, sagacious, brilliant, or sparkling in his first

---

[64] Adams to Abigail Adams, August 28, 1774: Butterfield, ed., *Adams Family Correspondence*, I, 144.

[65] Adams to Abigail Adams, September 18, 1774: *Ibid.*, pp. 157-58.

[66] *Autobiography of Benjamin Rush*, George W. Corner, ed., (Princeton, 1948), p. 110.

Appearance."[67] There were many who showed more promise. Thomas Lynch, Jr. of South Carolina Adams believed to be "a solid, firm, judicious Man."[68] And there was, finally, Charles Thomson, "the Sam. Adams of Phyladelphia [*sic*]—the Life of the Cause of Liberty" in the city.[69] The job of opening up the characters and principles of so many men was not an easy one. There was such a "quick and constant Succession of new Scenes, Characters, Persons, and Events" that Adams found it difficult to keep any regular account.[70] He stayed at it, however, until by Congress' end he felt master of both men and measures.

The first Congress did not do everything just as Adams wished. It frittered away in deliberation a great deal more time than he thought necessary.[71] At the urging of Joseph Galloway, James Duane, and others, the Congress sent off a fresh petition to the King and an address to the people of England. Before his arrival in Philadelphia, Adams had expressed strong opinions on the ineffectuality of further petitions. Americans had tried them repeatedly without result. He had hoped Congress would do something "a little more Sublime and Mettlesome."[72]

Before reaching Philadelphia, Adams had been undecided what that something should be. The objects before him had seemed almost "too grand, and multifarious" for his comprehension.[73] He had concluded, however, that all of the colonies must together make clear by statement and action their joint intention to defend

---

[67] Diary, August 22 and September 1, 1774: *Diary and Autobiography*, II, 106-107, 119.

[68] Diary, August 31, 1774: *Ibid.*, p. 117.

[69] Diary, August 30, 1774: *Ibid.*, p. 115.

[70] Diary, September 11, 1774: *Ibid.*, p. 131.

[71] Diary, October 10, 1774: *Ibid.*, p. 150.

[72] Adams to James Warren, July 25, 1774: "Warren-Adams Letters," LXXII, 32.

[73] Diary, June 25, 1774: *Diary and Autobiography*, II, 97.

their liberties. He had come to Philadelphia seeking confirmation of his hope that Americans in all of the colonies
would regard the attack upon Massachusetts as an attack
upon themselves and be ready to join with her in mutual defense. By the time the Congress was over, his
hopes had been justified. His contact with the representatives of the other colonies demonstrated overwhelmingly to him that Americans in Virginia as in Massachusetts, in Pennsylvania as in Connecticut were united, if
not on the tactics of opposition, at least in the common
purpose of defending their liberties.[74] "The more We
conversed with the Gentlemen of the Country, and with
the Members of Congress," he recalled later in his Autobiography, "the more We were encouraged to hope for
a general Union of the Continent."[75] And to Abigail he
wrote while at Philadelphia that "the Esteem, the Affection, the Admiration" which had been shown toward
Massachusetts, had filled his bosom.[76] The gentlemen
from Virginia whom he had initially regarded with sus-
picion, proved upon acquaintance to be the most spirited
and consistent of any. Throughout the Congress, firmness of principle seemed to prevail.[77]

The determination and prudence of Massachusetts,
he reported, was "vastly applauded." Her citizens were
"universally acknowledged the Saviors and Defenders
of American Liberty."[78] Rumors that General Gage had
begun a bombardment of Boston had had a most wonderful effect upon the Congress. Every member seemed
to consider it an attack upon the capital of his own province. The immediate reaction was "WAR! WAR!

[74] "Novanglus": *Works*, IV, 98.

[75] *Diary and Autobiography*, III, 308.

[76] Adams to Abigail Adams, September 18, 1774: Butterfield, ed.,
Adams Family Correspondence, I, 157.

[77] Diary, September 2, 1774: *Diary and Autobiography*, II, 120.

[78] Adams to Abigail Adams, September 14, 1774: Butterfield, ed.,
Adams Family Correspondence, I, 155.

WAR!" pronounced "in a Tone which would have done Honour to . . . a Roman."[79]

On October 26, 1774, the first Continental Congress adjourned *sine die*, with provisions for a second assembly to gather on May 10 following, unless the requested redress of grievances be granted before that time.[80] "This Day the Congress finished," Adams noted thoughtfully. "Spent the Evening together at the City Tavern— all the Congress and several Gentlemen of the Town."[81] There must have been much to talk about around the now familiar tables of the City Tavern that final evening. Adams assuredly joined in the celebration, for he was quite pleased with the past seven weeks' work.

No doubt Adams reaffirmed his opposition to the petition sent by Congress to the King.[82] Adams had recommended that instead of petitioning, Congress declare their own position more forcefully; for example, to warn that the first English effort to remove any American elsewhere for trial under the recently resurrected statute of Henry VIII be regarded as an outright declaration of war upon all the colonies. In this, he had found himself overruled. On balance, however, Adams believed that Congress had done a great deal and done it well. Above all, it had presented a common front to England and demonstrated that all the colonies were ready to stand together. The delegates had represented "a diversity of religions, educations, manners, [and] interests."[83] Yet this group of men, previously unknown to each other, had managed to reach a consensus—in Adams' mind, no small accomplishment.

Twelve days after beginning, Congress had endorsed the Suffolk County Resolves declaring the Coercive Acts

[79] Adams to Abigail Adams, September 8 and 18, 1774: *Ibid.*, pp. 150, 159.
[80] Ford, ed., *Journals of the Continental Congress*, I, 102, 114.
[81] Diary, October 26, 1774: *Diary and Autobiography*, II, 157.
[82] Diary, October 11, 1774: *Ibid.*, p. 151.
[83] Adams to William Tudor, September 29, 1774: *Works*, IX, 346.

unconstitutional, urging all Americans to disregard them
and advising the people to arm and form their militia.[84]
This single act alone had done much to convince Adams
that American sentiments were right. "This was one of
the happiest Days of my Life," he exulted in his Diary.
"In Congress We had generous, noble Sentiments, and
manly Eloquence. This Day convinced me that America
will support the Massachusetts or perish with her." The
support which the other delegates demonstrated for the
people of Massachusetts, he confided to Abigail, and the
"fixed determination" to support them, "were enough
to melt an Heart of Stone."[85] Adams had earlier questioned the desirability of a new non-importation agreement. All previous efforts at embargoes had proved in-
effective if not downright harmful.[86] When, however,
Congress on October 18 established the Continental Association, Adams approved and gave it his firm support.

Congress' Declaration of Rights and Grievances,
adopted on October 14, Adams quite rightly recognized
as a major achievement.[87] The crucial fourth right,
claiming for the colonies the "free and exclusive power
of legislation in their several Provincial Legislatures"—
and thereby declaring publicly that Parliament had no
authority over the colonies other than what was allowed
by them upon sufferance for the general regulation of
Empire trade—Adams had personally drawn up.[88] The
protests in Congress over it were loud, but its passage
effectively committed all the colonies to an advanced
position.

[84] Ford, ed., *Journals of the Continental Congress*, I, 31-40.

[85] Diary, September 17, 1774: *Diary and Autobiography*, II, 134-
35. Also, Adams to Abigail Adams, September 18, 1774: Butterfield,
ed., *Adams Family Correspondence*, I, 157.

[86] Adams to James Warren, July 25, 1774: "Warren-Adams Letters," LXXII, 31-32.

[87] Ford, ed., *Journals of the Continental Congress*, I, 63-73.

[88] Diary, October 14, 1774: *Diary and Autobiography*, II, 152n.-
53n. Also, *Works*, II, 375n.-77n.

The people of Massachusetts, Adams realized, living as they did under the greatest danger, would wonder how firm continental support for them really was. Both during his stay in Philadelphia and after his return home, he took considerable pains to allay their fears. The actions which Congress had taken, he declared, were for the moment adequate. Even more importantly, he reported that the representatives of the other colonies had demonstrated their willingness to support Massachusetts, and had pledged themselves irrevocably to her.[89]

FROM September of 1774 on, Adams never seriously flagged in his belief that the American people would carry their efforts through to a successful conclusion. The Patriots, he believed, constituted "a vast majority of the whole continent."[90] During the course of the Revolution, the conduct of his fellow Americans continually reassured him that he was correct in his faith in American virtue. In the final analysis, he was convinced by the very success of the American venture. As he remarked several years after peace had been secured: "It is an Observation of one of the profoundest Inquirers into human Affairs, that a Revolution of Government, successfully conducted and compleated, is the strongest Proof, that can be given, by a People of their Virtue and good Sense. An Interprize of so much difficulty can never be planned and carried on without Abilities, and People without Principle cannot have confidence enough in each other."[91]

[89] Adams to William Tudor, September 29, 1774: *Works*, IX, 346-47. Also, *ibid.*, IV, 35, 92.

[90] "Novanglus": *Ibid.*, p. 106.

[91] Diary, July 16, 1786: *Diary and Autobiography*, III, 194. A careful reading of Adams' correspondence further suggests that his confidence in the American people and his conviction of their abiding virtue increased as the Revolution progressed. One can find in his earliest letters considerably more skepticism than during the 1770's. See, for example, Butterfield, ed., *Adams Family Correspondence*, I, 5, 25.

Out of his own Revolutionary experience, then, Adams fashioned an understanding of America's historical mission and of the character of the American people. He believed firmly that history (under the direction of divine Providence) was the story of man's search for liberty, and that America was destined to become the next and greatest in a continuing succession of empires—a land where both liberty and knowledge would flourish. Above all, he believed that the American people, conceived in virtue by the first settlers and refined yet further by the trials of revolution, would prove fully adequate to whatever was demanded of them. These conclusions, drawn by him out of the Revolutionary experience, formed, at least for the present, the basic assumptions of all his thinking about American society and the problems it faced.

Chapter III. "An Age of
Political Experiments"

With this understanding of the American Revolution in mind, Adams turned to the task of establishing new American governments. The importance for his political thought of his assumptions about American society is shown clearly in the recommendations he made about the forms which the governments should take; for he based his thinking directly upon a belief in the youthful simplicity of American society and the virtuousness of its people.

The unique opportunity that the Revolution offered the American people to reconstitute their governments, struck Adams with particular force. When, before the present epoch, he asked, had so many people enjoyed "full power" to establish the wisest and happiest governments their wisdom could contrive? "No people ever had a finer opportunity to settle things upon the best foundations."[1] Adams worked diligently to make these foundations secure.

In considering the problems of American society, Adams addressed himself both to the continental and state governments, though he accorded the states the preponderant role. He was fully aware of the need for a solidly based continental government—primarily to insure cooperation among the states in prosecuting the war. Troops and supplies had to be requisitioned, strategy coordinated, and joint approaches made to European powers. These tasks required the direction of a central, coordinating body. "The Cause must be supported as a

[1] "Thoughts on Government": *Works*, IV, 200. Also, Adams to Joseph Hawley, August 25, 1776: *Ibid.*, IX, 434.

Common Cause," Adams wrote to William Tudor in March of 1777, "or it must fall."[2] Adams' instructions to the Massachusetts leaders in 1774-1775 to move cautiously so that Southern fears of open fighting might be mollified, gave early indication of Adams' belief.

From the beginning, Adams worked to strengthen Congress. He served in it with but few absences from its first meeting in September of 1774 to his departure for Europe nearly three years later. The initial meeting of Congress, he believed, would be of the greatest importance in establishing a sound basis for continent-wide cooperation. Both during his first seven weeks in Philadelphia and after his return to Massachusetts, he urged everyone with whom he came into contact to give Congress their support. He served on numerous committees in it, perhaps the most important of them being the Board of War and Ordnance. In a variety of ways, he worked to strengthen Congress's influence. During the spring and summer of 1775, he urged the establishment of a continental army and presented the name of George Washington as commander in chief. Throughout his stay, Adams urged the strengthening of both land and sea forces. Earlier he played a major role in laying down guide lines for future contact between Congress and foreign governments. He was also on the committee named to draw up the Declaration of Independence, though he contributed little of substance to the document itself. And, as we shall see more fully, he took a leading part in urging Congress to sanction state action in establishing independent governments.[3]

Before he became convinced that independence was necessary, Adams was willing to go along with Congress's

[2] Adams to William Tudor, March 22, 1777: Adams Microfilm, Reel 91.

[3] W. C. Ford, "John Adams": *Dictionary of American Biography*, 20 vols. (New York, 1943), I, 72-82. Also, Carl Becker, *The Declaration of Independence* (New York, 1958), Chapter 4.

initial makeshift form. Congress, he acknowledged, should have specified powers during the remainder of the contest with England "to lay Taxes in certain Cases and make Laws in certain others."[4] Yet these he regarded as but a temporary delegation of authority by the separate colonies. He did not yet envision a permanent intercolonial government. The whole system of empire administration that he spelled out in his "Novanglus" essays over the winter of 1774-1775, was based upon a continuation of separate colonial "parliaments," each the equal of the English Parliament, not upon any single continental body. Each colony was to be governed by its own assembly and be joined with the other colonies, as with the people of England, in common allegiance to the King.[5] "Distinct states," Adams explained, "may be united under one king. And these states may be further cemented and united together by a treaty of commerce. This is the case." The King, as the unifying center of the British Empire, was to be "King of Massachusetts, King of Rhode Island, and King of Connecticut," as well as King of Great Britain and Ireland.[6] Once peace with England was restored, there would be no need for intercolonial organization in America except upon extraordinary occasions and for particular purposes.

With the decision for independence, however, Adams rapidly concluded that a more permanent and authoritative central organization would be necessary. As part of the plan for independence which he brought to the second Congress, he included the call for a formal confederation of all the colonies. On July 6, 1775, he wrote from Philadelphia to James Warren concerning the pro-

[4] "Notes on Measures to be Taken up by Congress, September-October 1774": *Diary and Autobiography*, II, 145, 145n.
[5] "Novanglus": *Works*, IV, 3-177. Also, R. G. Adams, *Political Ideas of the American Revolution*, pp. 107-27.
[6] "Novanglus": *Works*, IV, 113-14.

gram of action which he hoped Congress would follow: "We ought immediately to dissolve all Ministerial Tyrannies, and Custom houses," Adams advised, "set up Governments of our own, like that of Connecticutt in all the Colonies, confederate together like an indissoluble Band, for mutual defence, and open our Ports to all Nations immediately." This was the system that he had arrived at promoting "from first to last. . . ."[7] As the movement for a formal continental government gained momentum, Adams gave it his full support. By the end of July he was saying that America should have had in hand "a month ago" the "legislative, executive, and judicial power of the whole Continent, and have completely modelled a Constitution."[8] In January and February of 1776, he urged that a plan of confederation "in all its Paragraphs" be taken up by Congress. This apparently referred to the plan, "Articles of Confederation and Perpetual Union," presented to Congress by Benjamin Franklin on July 21, 1775, but not then considered or recorded in the official journal.[9] Establishing a central government, Adams now described as "the most intricate, the most important, the most dangerous and delicate Business of all."[10]

The evidence shows that Adams was not instrumental in drawing up the Articles of Confederation. Neither the scanty records of the debates on the continental government nor Adams' correspondence for the period (which in itself is quite extensive) shows that he played at all an important part. Nor were his thoughts about the central government extensively developed or con-

[7] Adams to James Warren, July 6, 1775: Burnett, ed., *Letters of the Continental Congress*, I, 152.

[8] Adams to James Warren, July 24, 1775: "Warren-Adams Letters," Massachusetts Historical Society, *Collections* LXXII, 88-89.

[9] "Memorandum of Measures to be Pursued in Congress, February (?) 1776": *Diary and Autobiography*, II, 231n.-32n., 233.

[10] Adams to James Warren, May 15, 1776: "Warren-Adams Letters," LXXII, 246.

sistent. He delineated with some precision the areas in which central direction was essential. The Confederation, for example, should have full authority in defense and foreign affairs. This was, of course, necessary during the period of conflict with England; it would be just as essential after independence had been secured. There would then be need for congressional supervision over such joint state concerns as tariff-making, treaty negotiations, defense, and Indian affairs.[11]

On the problem of which was supreme, the states or the Congress, however, Adams was less clear. There is evidence to suggest that he believed Congress to be national in character, and thus, in some matters at least, superior to the states.[12] During the debate over the method of voting to be followed in Congress, for example, Adams argued against allotting one vote per state, the standard position of individuals who believed the Confederation rested upon the states rather than directly upon the people.[13] Instead, he favored votes proportionate to population, a position consistent with a nationalistic point of view. The delegates, declared Adams in debate, did not represent the states, but stood "as the representatives of the people." In some states, the people were many, and in others, few; therefore, the state vote in Congress should be proportionate to the population it represented. The make-up of Congress, Adams continued, should be "the mathematical representation of the interests out of doors." In concluding, he made

[11] Adams to Abigail Adams, July 24, 1775: Butterfield, ed., *Adams Family Correspondence*, I, 255-56.

[12] For an excellent discussion of the question of sovereignty and nationalism during the Confederation, see Irving Brant, *James Madison, The Nationalist, 1780-1787* (Indianapolis, 1948).

[13] Jefferson's notes are perhaps the most important extant source of information on these debates. They are available in Julian Boyd, ed., *The Papers of Thomas Jefferson*, 17 vols. to date (Princeton, 1951-   ), I, 320-27. See also the notes kept by Adams (though they omit some of his own speeches) in *Diary and Autobiography*, II, 229 *passim*.

his point unmistakably clear. "The individuality of the colonies," he declared, "is a mere Sound." It had been said that Congress was a group of independent individuals making a bargain together. The question was what they should be when the bargain was made. "The confederacy," he explained, "is to make us one individual only; it is to form us, like separate parcels of metal, into one common Mass. We shall no longer retain our separate individuality, but become a single individual as to all questions submitted to the Confederacy."[14]

In other ways, as well, Adams voiced his affirmation of Congress's national character. He labored earnestly to secure a Congressional resolution calling upon all the states to set up new governments independent of the Crown. In seeking Congressional sanction for state action, he was at least by implication avowing Congressional supremacy.[15] In all probability, Adams sought this particular resolution more because it offered the most effective means of moving the colonies closer to independence than because it might be considered a declaration of national sovereignty. Yet the assumption which such action contained gave him no pause.

If Adams on some occasions talked about the Confederation as if it were a national government resting directly upon the people, however, he more typically described it as a creature of the states, created by them with only certain restricted authority, and ranking below them in importance. Adams never agreed with the notion, expressed by Patrick Henry, that the Confed-

---

[14] "Notes of Debates": *Works*, II, 499n.-500n. As Merrill Jensen points out, this was a common argument among representatives of the larger states who sought thereby to increase their own states' influence. No doubt, it figured into Adams' thinking. Merrill Jensen, *The Articles of Confederation* (Madison, Wisconsin, 1940), pp. 140-41.

[15] This is the argument that Lincoln made nearly a century later when he declared that "The Union is older than the States, and in fact created them as States." Roy Basler, ed., *The Collected Works of Abraham Lincoln*, 10 vols. (New Brunswick, 1953), IV, 434.

eration destroyed all distinctions between the colonies and marshalled all the people under one government. He denied Henry's assertion that Americans were living in a state of nature with all landmarks gone, all government dissolved. (Adams cited John Locke as authority that political revolution did not destroy the social compact.) Adams later recalled that he had "supposed no Man would think of consolidating this vast Continent under one Government. . . ." He had thought rather that the American states should, "after the Example of the Greeks, the Dutch and the Swiss, form a Confederacy of States," each of which should have a separate government.[16]

As we have seen, he was willing to accord the central government the leading role in matters of defense and foreign affairs and in the regulation of intercolonial disputes; but in the broader range of "domestic affairs," in the day-to-day regulation of American society that he was certain would be the central task of government after independence, he accorded the states a distinctly superior role. Upon the new state governments, rather than the Congress, would depend the ultimate success or failure of America's revolutionary venture.

When writing of matters of internal governance, Adams stressed the limitations rather than the capacities of Congressional jurisdiction.[17] Congress's authority, he insisted in 1776, came from the states and "should sacredly be confined" to a few areas: "war, trade, disputes between colony and colony, the post-office, and the unappropriated lands. . . ."[18] After the recent experience with a colonial administration far removed from control by the people, Adams was anxious that American governments in the future be kept closely accountable. The

[16] *Diary and Autobiography*, III, 352.
[17] Adams to Patrick Henry, June 3, 1776: Burnett, ed., *Letters of the Continental Congress*, I, 471.
[18] "Thoughts on Government": *Works*, IV, 200.

states were in most direct contact with the people and were subject to close supervision by them. In the states, therefore, should rest the preponderance of political power. The whole colonial protest, moreover, had initially developed in terms of conflict between the royal administration and the separate colonial assemblies. The sovereign rights of the people represented in their individual legislatures had been the objects of America's defense. Adams continued to think in these terms.

Even the powers which Adams acknowledged to fall within the legitimate sway of Congress, he usually described as derivative. In 1779, he composed a draft for the new Massachusetts Constitution. In it he spelled out in clear detail the supremacy of state governments in matters of internal regulation and the delegated nature of all Congress's authority. "The people of this Commonwealth," he wrote, "have the sole and exclusive right of governing themselves, as a free, sovereign, and independent state; and do, and forever hereafter shall, exercise and enjoy every power, jurisdiction, and right, which are [sic] not, or may not hereafter, be by them expressly delegated to the United States of America, in Congress assembled."[19]

Adams' emphasis upon the states rather than the Confederation continued nearly throughout the 1780's. His *Defense of the Constitutions of Government of the United States of America*, written in 1786-1787, was directed toward strengthening the state governments. Until his return to America in 1788, he continued to believe that the Confederation, weak as he knew it to be, was adequate and that the answer to America's problems lay in more energetic state administrations.[20] Indeed, he saw potential dangers in the powers which Congress did

[19] *Journal of the Convention for Framing a Constitution* . . . *For . . . Massachusetts Bay* (Boston, 1832), p. 193.

[20] For a discussion of Adams' disinterest in efforts to strengthen the Confederation up to November of 1787, see below, Chapter v.

possess. Congress, he feared, would attract men of ambition whose natural disposition would be to diminish the prerogatives of the states and the privileges of the people. Security against this danger would depend upon the accuracy with which the governments of the separate states had their own affairs arranged. In 1787, Adams wrote to Philip Mazzei, an Italian then under diplomatic commission from the state of Virginia, that if the states maintained inviolate their own governments, their liberty, good order, and prosperity would be the certain consequence, "whatever Imperfections may remain incurable in the Confederation."[21]

Throughout the 1770's and most of the 1780's, then, Adams believed that the preponderance of power should remain with the states. During normal times of peace, they rather than the continental government would provide the arenas in which the success or failure of America's experiment in self-government would be dedetermined. Consequently, from the meeting of Congress in May of 1775, until a general resolution calling on all states to establish new governments independent of the Crown was passed 11 months later, Adams fixed his attention upon the new state administrations. His most important activities during these months were directed toward securing their construction.

ADAMS came to the second Continental Congress in May of 1775 with a plan in mind: to establish governments in the states, form a continental agreement among them, and declare complete independence from all British control—preferably in this order. There would thus be no dangerous lapse of authority between colonial and independent governments.[22] In practice, Adams did not worry much about which step came first. A number of

[21] Adams to Philip Mazzei, June 12, 1787: Adams Microfilm, Reel 113.
[22] Adams to Patrick Henry, June 3, 1776: *Works*, IX, 387.

the colonial regimes had in fact been defunct for some time, yet the people had managed to get along well enough on their own.

Adams was not inclined, however, to leave the establishment of the new state governments to chance. From May on, he worked energetically in Congress to see that the American people recognized the need for new governments and took steps to meet it.[23] On June 2, the Massachusetts delegation laid before Congress an address from their Provincial Convention, dated May 16 and received June 1, asking advice on the future government of their state.[24] Without doubt, Adams was at least in part responsible for the introduction of the Massachusetts address. "This subject," he later recalled, "had engaged much of my Attention before I left Massachusetts. . . ." He had discussed it frequently with Professor John Winthrop of Harvard, Dr. Samuel Cooper, James Otis, Joseph Hawley, and others.[25]

Once the address was introduced, Adams took the opportunity to talk at considerable length about the necessity of taking up new governments, not only in Massachusetts but throughout the continent. As he recalled later in his Autobiography, when the letter was read, "I embraced the Opportunity to open myself in Congress, and most earnestly to intreat the serious Attention of all the Members and of all the Continent to the measures which the times demanded."[26] He said that he believed there was great wisdom in the adage: when the sword is drawn, throw away the scabbard; and that whether the Americans threw it away voluntarily or not, it was useless now.

The pride of England, Adams assured his colleagues,

---

[23] *Diary and Autobiography*, III, 315.
[24] *Ibid.*, p. 351. Also, Ford, ed., *Journals of the Continental Congress*, II, 78.
[25] *Diary and Autobiography*, III, 351.
[26] *Ibid.*

flushed with recent triumphs and nourished by a deep scorn of all the power of America, would force the states to call forth every resource of the country and to seek the friendship of England's enemies. These efforts could not safely be made without government in all the states. The case of Massachusetts, he continued, was only the most urgent. It could not be long before other states would have to follow her example. He concluded by saying that he now thought it the duty of Congress to recommend that every state call special conventions immediately to set up governments under their own authority. "These were new, strange and terrible Doctrines to the greatest Part of the Members," Adams recollected, "but not a very small Number heard them with apparent Pleasure. . . ."[27]

After Adams finished, Congress placed Massachusetts' communication on the table, and the following day (June 3) appointed a committee of five to take the request under consideration. None of the Massachusetts delegates were included. Adams and his colleagues, however, were called upon to testify.[28]

On June 7, the committee brought in its report. Two days later, Congress adopted the following resolution:

> *Resolved,* That no obedience being due to the Act of parliament for altering the charter of the Colony of Massachusetts bay, nor to a Governor or lieutenant-Governor, who will not observe the directions of, but endeavor to subvert that charter, the gov'r and lieutenant-gov'r of that Colony are to be considered as absent, and their offices vacant; and as . . . the inconveniences, arising from the suspension of the powers of Government, are intollerable . . . that, in order to conform, as near as may be, to the spirit and substance of the charter, it be recom-

[27] *Ibid.*, p. 352.
[28] Ford, ed., *Journals of the Continental Congress,* II, 79.

mended to the provincial Convention, to write letters to the inhabitants of the several places, which
are intituled to representation in Assembly, requesting them to chuse such representatives, and that the
Assembly, when chosen, do elect counsellors; which
assembly and council should exercise the powers of
Government, until a Governor, of his Majesty's
appointment, will consent to govern the colony according to its charter.[29]

Adams was not entirely satisfied with Congress's action, especially with the final clause stating that the Assembly and Council were to exercise the powers of government only "until a Governor, of his Majesty's appointment" would "consent to govern the colony according to its charter." This clearly implied eventual reconciliation, a possibility Adams by now thought extremely
remote, and indicated that the government to be established would be only temporary—precisely the notion
Adams was trying to erase. The resolution was an attempt to meet the need for new government but at the
same time to satisfy the protests of Congress's more conservative members that action was being taken in opposition to royal authority. This, of course, was the point
Adams now wished Congress to make openly and explicitly. The final, limiting clause of the resolution was
the work of the committee's two conservative members,
John Jay and James Wilson.[30]

In spite of his reservations, however, Adams thought
this first resolution an acquisition of some importance;
for, as he recognized, it provided a precedent for future
advice to other states to institute governments of their
own. And he believed that the other states would soon
have occasion to follow Massachusetts' example.

[29] *Ibid.*, pp. 83-84.
[30] *Diary and Autobiography*, III, 353. The report, Adams recalled
angrily, "was in great degree conformable, to the New York and
Pennsylvania System."

Adams had four months to wait, but on October 18 the delegation from New Hampshire placed before Congress a resolution similar to that of Massachusetts, again asking "the advice and direction of the Congress, with respect to a method for our administering Justice, and regulating our civil police."[31] The New Hampshire petition Adams believed to be mostly the work of General John Sullivan who had recently left Congress (where he had been a firm supporter of Adams) for home.[32] Again Adams "embraced with Joy the opportunity of harranguing on the Subject at large." Again he urged Congress to issue a general recommendation to all the states to call conventions and institute governments. And again he ran through his list of arguments: the "danger to the Morals of the People, from the present loose State of Things and general relaxation of Laws and Government"; the danger of insurrection in some of the most disaffected parts of the states; the necessity of preventing communication with the enemy; the fact that neither the people nor their friends in Europe would believe that America was united and determined in her own cause until governments were instituted; and the absurdity of carrying on war against the King while continuing to profess allegiance to him.[33]

The committee that Congress appointed this time to consider and report on the New Hampshire petition was "composed of Members, as well disposed to encourage the Enterprize as could have been found in Congress. . . ."[34] They were John Rutledge, Samuel Ward, Roger Sherman—and John Adams. The report that the committee returned on November 3, Adams remarked, was "a Tryumph . . . a most important Point gained."[35] This time there was no mention of conforming as nearly as possible to the colonial charter; nor was there any ex-

---

[31] Ford, ed., *Journals of the Continental Congress*, III, 298.
[32] *Diary and Autobiography*, III, 354.
[33] *Ibid.*, p. 355.   [34] *Ibid.*, pp. 356-57.   [35] *Ibid.*, p. 357.

pectation expressed that ultimately a governor "of his Majesty's appointment" would return and consent to govern the colony according to its charter. As a sop to conservative sentiment, the report declared that Congress's resolution was to hold good only "during the Continuance of the present dispute between Great Britain and the Colonies."[36] Yet even this concession was more illusory than real, for there was no statement of expectation that the end of the dispute would bring a return to the charter government.

The New Hampshire convention was urged to call "a full and free representation of the People," not just to carry on without benefit of governor the regular functions of assembly and council, but "if they think it necessary" (as Adams believed they would) "[to] establish such a form of government, as in their judgement will best produce the happiness of the people, and most effectually secure peace and good order in the province. . . ."[37] Most conspicuous by its omission was any reference to royal authority or the old charter government. Congress's resolution left the option completely open for the New Hampshire assembly to erect a government wholly independent of the Crown if it so wished.

As Adams (together with a good many of the more cautious members of Congress) realized, the New Hampshire resolution constituted a significant step toward "revolutionizing all the Governments"—precisely the thing he was attempting.[38] In spite of the retention in the resolution of the words "Province" and "Colonies" —and Adams had striven mightily to have them replaced with "States"—he was highly satisfied with Congress's work. The result was what he had expected. The same day, John Rutledge brought forward a petition from his own state of South Carolina similar to that of

[36] Ford, ed., *op.cit.*, III, 319.
[37] *Ibid.*
[38] *Diary and Autobiography*, III, 357.

New Hampshire. This time Congress wasted no time. At once another committee was named. (This time with Samuel rather than John Adams on it.) The next day, November 4, they brought in a report virtually identical to the one passed for New Hampshire the day before.[39] Again, as Adams recalled, he labored before the committee and before Congress to expunge the word "Colony" and substitute "State" and to change the word "dispute" to "war." But, he remarked, "the Child was not yet weaned."[40]

As yet, Adams' primary goal—securing from Congress a general recommendation to all the states to institute new governments openly independent of Crown and Parliament—had not been achieved. It was to wait a year for realization. In the meantime, the debate over state governments began to take on new importance. Over the winter of 1775-1776, American sentiment began to move more rapidly toward independence. It was now becoming increasingly apparent to all but the most stubborn individuals that a separation in the near future was probable. Great Britain seemed more than ever bent upon the total destruction of American liberties, and hopes of reconciliation were becoming increasingly dim. In January of 1776, Thomas Paine's *Common Sense* appeared, adding its force to the movement.

As sentiment both in Congress and out progressed toward independence, so did willingness to admit the necessity of establishing new governments free from all royal control. Even some of the persons most reluctant to see independence declared, were anxious once they became convinced it could not be avoided to erect governments capable of giving stability to public affairs.

During the first months of 1776, Adams took advantage of the increasing sentiment for independence to push his own interest in government. For a while, he

[39] Ford, ed., *op.cit.*, III, 319, 326-27.
[40] *Diary and Autobiography*, III, 388.

had been willing for Congress to issue specific instructions upon the petition of individual states. By 1776, however, he was declaring emphatically that this was no longer adequate, and he redoubled his efforts for a more decisive step—a Congressional resolution calling upon all the states to institute new constitutions explicitly independent from all British control.[41] Such a resolution would accomplish two things. It would encourage states still cautious about declaring a final separation to commit themselves to a joint American effort. And it would urge all the states to begin at once to plan for their future regulation. Within six months of the new year, Adams saw his goal realized.

From January to May, the debate in Congress continued. Part of the time (from December 8, 1775 to February 9, 1776) Adams was absent, having returned home to determine whether or not he should accept his recent appointment as Chief Justice of the Massachusetts Superior Court. The second week in February, however, he was back, again engaging in "almost dayley [*sic*] exhortations to the Institutions of Governments in the States and a declaration of Independence."[42] Shortly after his return, he drew up a "Memorandum of Measures to be Pursued in Congress." Listed prominently were two goals: "Government to be assumed in every Colony" and a "Declaration of Independency, [a] Declaration of War with the [English] Nation. . . ."[43]

From February to May, Congress moved step by step closer to both objectives. On March 23, a resolution passed calling for the outfitting of privateers "to cruise on the Enemies of these United Colonies," and making all ships belonging to the inhabitants of Great Britain

[41] *Ibid.*, p. 358ff. Also, Adams to William Heath, April 15, 1776: Massachusetts Historical Society, *Collections*, Series 7, IV (1904), 9-10.

[42] *Diary and Autobiography*, III, 360.

[43] "Memorandum of Measures to be Pursued in Congress, February (?) 1776": *Ibid.*, II, 231, 231n.

lawful prize.[44] This had also been a part of Adams' plan. During February, March, and April, Congress sat repeatedly as a committee of the whole house to debate the propriety of opening American ports to the trade of the world. The measure, noted Adams, "laboured exceedingly, because it was considered as a bold step to Independence." Adams had, indeed, "urged it expressly with that View. . . ."[45] On April 4, a resolution calling for the opening of American ports was laid before Congress and two days later it passed.

The general resolution on government was to wait another month. Early in May, Congress formed itself into a special committee of the whole to consider the state of the colonies. It continued to meet in this manner almost every day for the next several weeks. In the process, it considered a wide variety of matters: letters from General Washington, revenue problems, Indian affairs, naval arrangements, "and twenty other Things, many of them very trivial. . . ."[46] Adams could only harangue against the misapplication of time, he recalled with annoyance, and harangues but consumed more time. Only now and then could he "snatch a transient Glance at the promised Land."[47]

On May 9, however, the chairman of the committee of the whole, Benjamin Harrison, reported to Congress a resolution concerning state governments which, upon being read, was put off for decision until the following day. The Congressional Journal records what occurred next.

> Congress then resumed the consideration of the report from the committee of the whole, which being read was agreed to as follows:

[44] Ford, ed., *op.cit.*, IV, 229-32.
[45] *Diary and Autobiography*, III, 364.
[46] *Ibid.*, p. 381ff.
[47] *Ibid.*, p. 381.

> *Resolved*, That it be recommended to the respective assemblies and conventions of the United Colonies, where no government sufficient to the exigencies of their affairs have been hitherto established, to adopt such government as shall, in the opinion of the representatives of the people, best conduce to the happiness and safety of their constituents in particular, and America in general.
>
> *Resolved*, That a committee of three be appointed to prepare a preamble to the foregoing resolution.[48]

Adams had been largely responsible for the resolutions of the committee of the whole. They were "brought before the Committee of the whole House," he remembered, "in concert between R. H. Lee and me. . . ."[49] Now the first half, at least, of his goal had been realized. Congress had set the process of constitution-making under way. Recalling the matter some years later, Adams still accorded it great significance. "This Resolution," he wrote, "I considered as an Epocha, a decisive Event. It was a measure which I had invariably pursued for a whole Year, and contended for, through a Scaene [*sic*] and a Series of Anxiety, labour, Study, Argument, and Obloquy. . . ."[50]

The other half of Adams' program was yet to be attained. In the second of the resolutions—"that a committee of three be appointed to prepare a preamble"—Adams saw the opportunity to accomplish his other goal. "The members chosen," recounts the Journal for May 10, "were Mr. J[ohn] Adams, Mr. [Edward] Rutledge, and Mr. R[ichard] H[enry] Lee."[51] From the committee's make-up, the tenor of its report could have been anticipated.

[48] Ford, ed., *op.cit.*, p. 342.
[49] *Diary and Autobiography*, III, 383. See also the excellent editorial note in the same volume, pp. 240n.-41n.
[50] *Ibid.*, p. 383.   [51] Ford, ed., *op.cit.*, p. 342.

For the next three days the special committee met, and on May 13 reported its findings to Congress. The committee, Adams recounted, "thought it not necessary to be very elaborate, and Mr. Lee and Mr. Rutledge desired me as Chairman to draw something very short which I did and with their Approbation."[52] The preamble, as reconsidered and approved on May 15, was not particularly short (it outdistanced the resolution which it preceded, 194 words to 59), nor was it unelaborate. It declared, however, in unmistakable terms the separation of all colonial governments from any connection with royal authority. It read as follows:

> Whereas his Britannic Majesty, in conjunction with the lords and commons of Great Britain, has, by a late act of Parliament, excluded the inhabitants of these United Colonies from the protection of his crown . . . And whereas, it appears absolutely irreconcilable to reason, and good Conscience, for the people of these colonies now to take the oaths and affirmations necessary for the support of any government under the crown of Great Britain, and it is necessary that the exercise of every kind of authority under the said crown should be totally suppressed, and all the powers of government exerted, under the authority of the people of the colonies, for the preservation of internal peace, virtue and good order, as well as for the defence of their lives, liberties and properties . . . therefore. . . .[53]

To James Warren, Adams described this as "the most important Resolution that ever was taken in America."[54] If perhaps a bit excessive in his praise, he was nonetheless correct in asserting the preamble's importance. It

[52] *Diary and Autobiography*, III, 385. Also, *ibid.*, p. 335.
[53] Ford, ed., *op.cit.*, pp. 357-58.
[54] Adams to James Warren, May 1776: "Warren-Adams Letters," LXXII, 245.

was, as he claimed, a clear assertion of American independence, offered a month and a half before Jefferson's more famous document rendered the decision immortal. Adams recalled that "it was indeed on all hands considered by men of understanding as equivalent to a declaration of Independence. . . ."[55] The reaction of James Duane supported Adams' assertion. "Mr. Duane," Adams observed with relish, "called it, to me, a Machine for the fabrication of Independence. I said, smiling, I thought it was independence itself. . . ."[56] Carter Braxton, in a letter written two days after the preamble's adoption, said much the same thing. The resolution and preamble together, he wrote angrily, fell "little short of Independence." The assumption of government, he continued, was necessary, and to the resolution itself he made little objection. But when the preamble was reported, "much heat and debate did ensue for two or three Days."[57]

The resolutions and preamble together represented unquestionably the most radical step toward independence that the American states had yet taken. Little remained to be said after Congress had declared the Crown and Parliament "Enemies" of the American people, proclaiming that "the Exercise of every Kind of Authority under the . . . Crown should be totally suppressed," and that "all the Powers of Government" should be exerted "under the Authority of the People of the Colonies. . . ." What was left, was to set more clearly before the eyes of the world the manifold reasons which had made such a step necessary. In July, this final task was completed.

[55] *Diary and Autobiography*, III, 335.
[56] *Ibid.*, p. 386. See also the comments of John Jay in Adams' notes on the Congressional debates for May 13 to 15, *ibid.*, pp. 238-40.
[57] Carter Braxton to Landon Carter, May 17, 1776: Burnett, ed., *Letters of the Continental Congress*, I, 452-54.

ADAMS paid careful attention to the forms which the new state governments assumed. Decisions of this sort, he emphasized, were of the greatest importance, for upon them rested America's future happiness. "It is the Form of Government which gives the decisive Colour to the Manners of the People, more than any other Thing," he informed Mercy Warren in January of 1776.[58] Pope, cautioned Adams, flattered tyrants too much when he wrote:

> For forms of government let fools contest,
> That which is best administered is best.[59]

Nothing was more fallacious. Form had everything to do with a government's effectiveness; "the blessings of society" depended entirely upon it.[60]

It was thus essential to the success of the American venture to have the new governments set out initially on the right path, "to begin well." For misarrangements now made would have "great, extensive, and distant consequences. . . ." Americans were now employed, Adams reminded his countrymen, however little they might realize it, in making establishments which would affect the happiness of millions of inhabitants in the future. The constitutions now being formed, he believed, would last for "many generations."[61] If they proved ineffectual, the resulting confusion would make constructive alterations all but impossible. If they set out wrong, Adams believed, they would be able to return only with difficulty to the correct path. For the new governments to prove capable of taking up the authority once exercised by the colonial regimes, they would have

[58] Adams to Mercy Warren, January 8, 1776: "Warren-Adams Letters," LXXII, 202.

[59] "Thoughts on Government": *Works*, IV, 193.

[60] Adams to Mercy Warren, April 16, 1776: "Warren-Adams Letters," LXXII, 221.

[61] "Thoughts on Government": *Works*, IV, 193.

to be established quickly and permanently, and upon correct principles.

Adams had quite definite notions about the new governments. There were certain "laws" of politics which made the matter clear to him. Governments, he explained, were based upon general principles of operation much akin to the laws of nature which regulated the motion of the heavens and other of nature's machines. Just as he had always thought an army to be a piece of clock-work to be governed by principles as fixed as any in mechanics, Adams explained, so from all he had read in history and in authors who had speculated upon government and society, he was inclined to think a government must manage a society in the same manner, and that this was machinery too.[62] Just as Newton "figured out a mathematical-physical system for the heavens," so could equally valid laws be derived for politics too.

These laws, as Adams perceived them, declared that there were certain very definite relationships between governmental systems and the societies they were meant to regulate. If governments were to be successful, their constitutional structure could not be drawn at random, but only with careful reference to the peculiar circumstances of the society involved.

Adams developed the outline of his ideas in his "Thoughts on Government," published with his approval by R. H. Lee sometime during the first four months of 1776. In a letter to James Warren of April 20, 1776, Adams described the events that had led to the publication of his views.[63] Between his return to Congress from a brief trip home on January 9, and

[62] Adams to James Sullivan, May 26, 1776: *Ibid.*, IX, 376.
[63] Adams to James Warren, April 20, 1776: "Warren-Adams Letters," LXXII, 230-32. The background of this first effort of Adams at constitution-making still remains somewhat obscure. It has been best described in an admirable, short note by Adams' most recent editors: *Diary and Autobiography*, III, 331n.-32n.

April 20, several people had approached him asking advice on the form of government their states should adopt. The first request—at least the first to bring tangible results—came from two North Carolina delegates, John Penn and William Hooper. Sometime before May 27, the day they left Congress to attend the North Carolina provincial convention, Penn and Hooper acting separately asked Adams' advice.[64]

The time was short, Adams recalled to Warren, but thinking it an admirable opportunity for "communicating some Hints" upon a subject not sufficiently considered, especially in the southern colonies, he "concluded to borrow a little Time from his Sleep" and wrote out a sketch, giving a copy to each man.[65] Before the North Carolina delegates left for home, George Wythe saw Adams' document and desired a copy, which Adams obligingly "made out from his Memory as nearly as he could."[66] Shortly after this, Jonathan Sargeant of New Jersey requested another copy which Adams again wrote off from memory, this time "enlarged and amplified a good deal."[67]

Apparently, Adams' efforts were gaining in reknown, for almost at once R. H. Lee requested of him the same favor. Wearying of his task, Adams borrowed back Wythe's copy and lent it to Lee who had it printed in pamphlet form. Unfortunately, the printed copy was not so extensive as the Sargeant draft. The Wythe copy, however, constitutes what has become known as Adams' "Thoughts on Government."

In addition to the "Thoughts" (and his correspond-

[64] Adams to John Penn, January 1776: *Works*, IV, 203.

[65] Adams to James Warren, April 20, 1776: "Warren-Adams Letters," LXXII, 231. A copy of this earliest draft of what was to become the "Thoughts on Government" may be found in Adams' *Works*, IV, 203-209.

[66] Adams to James Warren, April 20, 1776: "Warren-Adams Letters," LXXII, 231.

[67] *Ibid.* No copy of the Sargeant draft seems to exist.

ence for the period), there was another place where Adams spelled out in detail his ideas about the state governments: his draft of a new constitution for Massachusetts, written in 1779. Adams was in Europe for most of the decade following 1778, with the exception of several months during the fall of 1779 when he briefly returned home. While at home, he attended the Massachusetts Constitutional Convention as delegate from Braintree (the dates were September 1 to 7 and October 28 to November 11). Here he found an opportunity to develop his ideas further and put them into practice.[68] On September 4, the convention named a committee of thirty, of which Adams was one, to draft a constitution. The committee, Adams later recalled to Edmund Jennings, placed him upon a subcommittee and by this group he was made "a Sub Sub Committee" of one, so that he "had the honour to be principal Engineer."[69] The convention adopted with but a few changes the draft Adams submitted.[70]

There are differences of detail between the forms of government suggested in the "Thoughts" and laid out in Adams' constitutional draft. This is primarily because he drew up the "Thoughts" with the Southern states in mind, while the constitution he intended for the quite different conditions of Massachusetts society. Yet both of them contain principles which Adams thought relevant to all of the American states.

[68] There are, unfortunately, no records of the debates inside the convention. Nor are there any entries in Adams' Diary for this brief but crucial period. He halted his Diary upon reaching the banks off Cape Cod on July 31, 1779 and began it again on November 13, the day he boarded ship once more for Europe.

[69] Diary, November 13, 1779: *Diary and Autobiography*, II, 400n.-401n.

[70] See S. E. Morison, "Struggle Over the Adoption of the Constitution of Massachusetts, 1780," Massachusetts Historical Society, *Proceedings*, L (1917), 353-411. Also, *Journal of the Massachusetts Constitutional Convention* (Boston, 1821), pp. 142-215; and *Works*, IV, 219-67.

The most important of these declared that the new state governments must all be popular republics. That is, they must all be responsible in every part to the will of the people. The supreme power of every government, Adams repeatedly proclaimed, resided in the body of the people; and the people should keep effective control of their governments in their own hands. This seemed to Adams the most obvious lesson of America's struggle to preserve her liberties against an absentee and ultimately unaccountable colonial administration.

Throughout the period in which the new state governments were under construction, Adams warned against political experimentation. He urged that the governments be made as much like the colonial regimes as circumstances and the guarantee of American liberties would allow, both because he believed there was much that was good in the colonial regimes and because this would facilitate a smooth changeover from the old governments to the new. Yet he insisted upon one essential change: that every vestige of monarchical and hereditary influence be erased and that the new governments rest directly upon the people.

Adams rejected out of hand the notions of American monarchy that were proposed.[71] He was too familiar with the threats to American liberty made by the British Crown to substitute an indigenous monarchy for it. Nor was it conceivable to him that there should be hereditary, aristocratical branches in the new governments similar to the House of Lords under the British constitution. Americans, Adams declared, could easily lop off both monarchy and royalty; "Kings We never had among Us, Nobles We never had. Nothing hereditary ever existed in the Country: Nor will the Country require or admit of any such Thing. . . ."[72] The "only valuable

[71] Louise B. Dunbar, *A Study of "Monarchical" Tendencies in the United States, from 1776 to 1801* (Urbana, Illinois, 1922).
[72] *Ibid.*, p. 356.

part" of the British constitution, Adams declared to Patrick Henry in 1776, was that which was republican.[73] In England, national happiness had been achieved only when the administration had "leaned to the democratical Branch as in the reign of Elizabeth, in the Interregnum, and from the Revolution to the Commencement of the present Reign."[74] By this, of course, he meant the popular part, the Commons with its representation of the people.

The emphasis that Adams placed upon the popular qualities of the new governments was quite remarkable. Adams' overriding concern was to expand and guarantee the role of the people in the political process. Trouble had arisen under the colonial administration, he affirmed, because the governors, and behind them Parliament and Crown had been outside the control of the American people. This had been the "tyranny" of the British: they had claimed to govern without giving Americans a full voice in their own affairs. They had, in fact, tried to reduce popular influence over the governments by taking from the assemblies control of executive and judicial salaries, and expanding the influence of juryless admiralty courts. Against the dangers made explicit by England's actions, Adams asserted forcefully the theory of popular sovereignty.

"All power," he wrote in 1779, "residing originally in the people, and being derived from them, the several magistrates and officers of government, vested with authority, whether legislative, executive, or judicial, are their subordinates and agents, and are at all times accountable to them."[75] Where annual elections ended, he warned, there slavery began. Authority was derived

[73] "Thoughts on Government": *Works*, IV, 194.

[74] Draft of a Reply to a "Friendly Address": Adams Microfilm, Reel 344.

[75] "Report of a Constitution for Massachusetts": *Works*, IV, 224.

from the people and was to be periodically returned to them through regularly held elections.[76]

In his draft of the Massachusetts Constitution, Adams made careful provision for continuous and effective popular control over public officials. Senators, assemblymen, and the two chief executive officers were all to be annually elected.[77] In 1779, he opposed the popular election of militia officers because experience had convinced him that popularity and military proficiency did not always coincide.[78] The same reasoning, however, did not apply to political leadership.

Popular participation in the new governments was to be broad. The voting requirements which he wrote into his 1779 draft were more stringent than the ones included in the abortive constitution of 1778, but were still quite unrestrictive. According to Adams' recommendation, every (white) male, twenty-one years of age and resident in any town for one year preceding an election, having a freehold estate within that town of "the annual income of three pounds, or other estate, real, or personal or mixt, of the value of sixty pounds" should have the right to vote.[79] As Robert Brown has demonstrated, the property requirements Adams suggested would have prevented very few people otherwise qualified from using their franchise.[80] In a letter of May

[76] "Thoughts on Government": *Ibid.*, p. 197. Also, Adams to John Hughes, June 4, 1776; Adams Microfilm, Reel 89.

[77] *Journal of the Massachusetts Convention*, pp. 199, 201, 204. Earlier, Adams had shown some reluctance to have the state executives elected directly by the people, until affairs got into "a more quiet course." *Works*, IV, 186-87.

[78] Adams to Joseph Hawley, August 25, 1776: *Ibid.*, IX, 434-35. Also, Burnett, ed., *Letters of the Continental Congress*, II, 269, 300-301.

[79] *Journal of the Massachusetts Convention*, pp. 199, 203, 204.

[80] Robert Brown, *Middle Class Democracy and the Revolution In Massachusetts* (Ithaca, New York, 1955), pp. 393-96. Robert Taylor, *Massachusetts, Colony to Commonwealth* (Chapel Hill, 1961), p. 53.

1776 to James Sullivan, Adams made it clear that he
regarded the franchise requirement as anything but narrow. It was most desirable, he wrote, "to make the
acquisition of land easy to every member of society; to
make a division of the land into small quantities so
that the multitude may be possessed of landed estates."[81]
This was the only way of preserving equal liberty, of
assuring consideration of the "liberty, virtues, and interest" of the people in all acts of government. Already
he believed the property distribution in America to be
broad, especially outside of the South; yet he wished to
expand it even further.[82]

Adams was anxious to withhold the vote only from the
ragtag part of society not capable of maintaining its own
economic independence. To be trusted with the vote,
he remarked, a person need only have some small property by which he might be supposed to have a certain
economic independence and thus a judgement and will
of his own. "A Fountain of Corruption" would result
from making voters of the propertyless, for their votes
would be determined by whoever controlled their means
of subsistence.[83] With this one limitation, Adams was
in full sympathy with broad popular elections "founded
in equality." "The Dons, the Bashaws, the Grandees,
the Patricians, the Sachems, the Nabobs . . . sigh and
groan," he remarked, yet "a more equal Liberty than

[81] Adams to James Sullivan, May 26, 1776: *Works*, IX, 376-77.

[82] Adams was convinced that the ideas of equality so congenial to
New England were disapproved by the delegates from the South.
He encountered Virginia "aristocrats" in Congress and heard Southerners demand greater distinctions between officers and troops in the
Continental Army. Consequently, he expected government there to be
less popular. Some elections might be held only every three or even
seven years without any inconvenience. The "usages, and genius,
and manners of the people" would have to be consulted. *Ibid.*, pp.
386, 398.

[83] Adams to James Warren, July 7, 1777: "Warren-Adams Letters," LXXII, 339. Also, *Works*, IV, 239.

has prevailed in other Parts of the Earth must be established in America."[84]

The relationship between distribution of property and the franchise was to Adams a clear and natural one. A major postulate of eighteenth-century political thought (deriving from Harrington but also from Filmer and Hobbes), declared that the balance of political power in any society must follow the balance of property. This Adams believed "as infallible a Maxim, in Politicks, as that Action and Re-action are equal, is in Mechanicks."[85] In America, the balance of property was "nine tenths on the side of the people." It was logical, then, that political power should reside with the people also. Property was not concentrated in the hands of a few, as in Europe. In America there was "but one order." There was not, therefore, any economic basis for privileged political classes. As the people had "the whole property of land," the right of sovereignty resided with them.

If the broad distribution of property in American society made popular government necessary, the prevalence of virtue among the people made it possible. Not only did the balance of property declare that governments based squarely upon the will of the people should be established; the character of the people convinced Adams that their will could be trusted. At this point, he took a page out of Montesquieu. With him, Adams agreed that not every form of government was suited to every society. Each system of government was suited to a particular characteristic or "spirit" predominant among the people it was meant to regulate. Thus the operative "spirit" of tyrannical governments was fear, of monarchies, honor—and of republican governments, virtue. The political system, moreover, as Montesquieu explained, helped to foster the "spirit" upon which it was

[84] Adams to Patrick Henry, June 3, 1776: Adams Microfilm, Reel 89.
[85] Adams to James Sullivan, May 26, 1776: *Ibid.*

based; tyrannies, for example, further extended the rule of fear, and monarchies emphasized the trappings of honor. With this, Adams agreed. Yet in his mind the relationship worked most forcefully in the opposite direction. The form of government had to be adapted to the "spirit" of the society it was meant to regulate, and when the "spirit" changed, the government necessarily did also.[86] "The foundation of every government," Adams repeated, "is some principle or passion in the minds of the people."[87]

Especially was Adams struck by Montesquieu's discussion of virtue. A republic with its great emphasis upon the people and its limited dependence upon authority, required that its citizens be capable of using their power wisely and be ready to sacrifice their own immediate interests when necessary for the public good. And, conversely, a virtuous people would be content only in the permissive atmosphere of republican government. "The only foundation of a free constitution," Adams declared in 1776, "is pure virtue. . . ."[88] To Mercy Warren, he repeated the point: "public Virtue is the only Foundation of Republics." There had to be among the people a positive passion for the public good, superior to all private passions. Men had to pride themselves in sacrificing private pleasures when they stood in competition with the welfare of society. In short, he concluded, "the only reputable Principle and Doctrine must be that all Things must give Way to the public."[89] Convinced as he was of American virtue, it seemed all the more natural to Adams that the new state governments should assume a popular, republican form.

If Adams during the 1770's was impressed by the

[86] Montesquieu, *Spirit of the Laws*, 2 vols. (London, 1777).
[87] "Thoughts on Government": *Works*, IV, 194.
[88] Adams to Zabdiel Adams, June 21, 1776: *Ibid.*, IX, 401.
[89] Adams to Mercy Warren, April 16, 1776: "Warren-Adams Letters," LXXII, 222-23.

egalitarianism and virtue of the American people and hence by the need for broadly popular governments, he was not blind to the fact that precautions were needed in setting the new governments up. His dominant mood as he looked upon American society was unquestionably optimistic; but his optimism never concealed from him certain political realities posed by human nature. Adams had little patience with the people who dismissed lightly any need for taking care with the new governments as long as they were popular. Careful consideration of political forms was important, he insisted, not only to insure that they corresponded with the structure and "spirit" of the society, but that they took into consideration the disorderly qualities common to all human nature.

As we have seen, Adams, while praising American virtue, recognized that Americans like other men were also creatures of passion, and if left uncontrolled would too often act selfishly against each other. Provision had to be made for this, even in the American political system. Recall that much of the urgency with which he called for the rapid establishment of state governments grew from a concern that the American people, unless subjected to the discipline of fixed political institutions, would become unused to orderly behavior. To William Gordon, he explained the importance of giving "energy enough to our governments, and discipline enough to our armies, to overcome . . . [the] base principle of selfishness, to make citizens and soldiers feel themselves the children of the commonwealth, and love and revere their mother so much as to make their happiness consist in her service. . . ."[90] Care in the construction of the new governments needed to be taken to foster virtue and control men's passions. Especially was this true, considering that the governments now being established would in the future have to regulate generations decidedly less

[90] Adams to William Gordon, April 8, 1777: *Works*, IX, 461-62.

virtuous than the present one. Even among Americans, popular influence had to be ordered.

The problem as Adams described it, was essentially the control of political power. However virtuous, men could not be trusted with unlimited political power. "Power in any Form . . . when directed only by human Wisdom and Benevolence," he observed, "is dangerous. . . ."[91] Once gratified, the lust for power fed upon itself and increased. Throughout his life, Adams uttered his warning. It applied to the American people as well as to others. As much as he trusted the wisdom of Americans, he recognized that even among them popular powers must be regulated. This could be accomplished, he emphasized, only by balanced governments.

Under every form of government, liberty was constantly threatened by men's love of power. It was, therefore, essential to any stable political system that no man or group of men be permitted to gather a preponderance of power into its own hands. Care must be taken to check and control this tendency. The only maxim of a free government, Adams cautioned, ought to be to trust no man living with power to endanger the public liberty.[92]

The way to control power, Adams explained, was to see that society was regulated for the good of all by fixed, impartial laws. Over and over again throughout the whole course of his career, Adams repeated his advice: Americans must establish over themselves "governments of laws and not of men." Only under a rule of law, protected against violation by personal ambitions, could freedom for the individual and stability for society be maintained. He had seen this demonstrated time after time in his own legal practice, and, most forcefully of all, in America's revolutionary experience.

[91] "Sui Juris" (John Adams), *Boston Gazette*, May 23, 1768: in *New England Quarterly*, XXXI (1958), 97.
[92] "Notes for an Oration, 1772": *Diary and Autobiography*, II, 59.

Laws defined the relationships between men and provided the ligaments which held society together. This was particularly true of popular governments, forced as they were to get along without the sanctions of special privilege.

If popular governments depended especially upon the rule of law for stability, it was equally true, and of even greater moment to Adams, that only under governments in which the people had full voice could impartial laws replace individual ambition as the governing principle. "The very definition of a republic," Adams insisted, "is 'an empire of laws, and not of men.'"[93] All governments other than those of permanent, known laws were governments of mere will and pleasure. Republics were founded upon equal laws, established by common consent for the common good.

By the rule of law, Adams meant two things. He meant on one hand, the development of a written constitution, closely delineating the rights of citizens and circumscribing the powers of officials. The dangers of political power when not measured against a firmly established fundamental law, clearly defining political rights and duties, had become clear to him during the years following 1765. Adams, as we have seen, had been active in encouraging the states to create written constitutions, drawn up and ratified by the people in special convention.

Of equal importance was the problem of statute law; of insuring that regulations passed by state legislatures would not violate the written constitutions and would represent the interests of society as a whole rather than of special groups. The solution to this, in Adams' thinking, lay in the proper structure of the constitution itself. "That particular arrangement of the powers of society, or, in other words, that form of government which is best contrived to secure an impartial and exact execu-

tion of the laws," Adams explained, "is the best. . . ."[94]
One word signified the characteristic of government that
Adams had in mind—*Balance*.

In discussing the new state governments, Adams
stressed no theme more insistently than their need for
an internal separation and balance of power. He was
quite willing to allow the state governments differences
of detail in their structure. There was an inexhaustible
variety of republics because the possible combinations of
the powers of society were capable of innumerable varia-
tions. Yet he insisted that each of them be balanced.

On occasion, Adams seemed willing to let the states
try out unicameral governments. He never approved of
such experiments as Georgia or Pennsylvania tried;
neither state, he warned, could long be happy with
them. Yet he admitted that their governments represented the choice of the people. And, he declared, "if
they please themselves they will please me."[95] The
political confusions which soon troubled Pennsylvania
bore out his forebodings. In spite of everything, Adams
seemed to think, however, that the people of Pennsylvania would see the error of their ways and correct
the situation before permanent damage was done. Pennsylvania's difficulties, he hoped, would be evidence
enough for the other states that a balance was necessary
for stability.

The supreme test of government in America, he observed, was whether it could be popular and yet balanced. The people in each state had more real authority
than had the citizens of ancient Athens. The elections
of senators and governors as well as representatives were
popularly determined. This would be a fair trial whether
a government so popular could preserve itself. If the
American governments were adequately balanced,

[94] *Ibid.*, p. 194.
[95] Adams to Francis Dana, August 16, 1776: Adams Microfilm,
Reel 89.

Adams was sure, their popularity would prove a blessing.

Only by balancing men's ambitions against each other in the political system could the yearning for power be controlled and the supremacy of law upheld. Power, declared Adams, "must be opposed to power, force to force, strength to strength, interest to interest, as well as reason to reason, eloquence to eloquence, and passion to passion."[96] The whole "mystery of a commonwealth" consisted in "dividing and equalizing forces."

As Adams described it, the political balance signified several things. First, it involved a separation among the three branches of government. "A legislative, and executive, and a judicial power," he wrote to R. H. Lee, "comprehend the whole of what is meant and understood by government. It is by balancing each of these powers against the other two, that the efforts in human nature towards tyranny can alone be checked . . . and any degree of freedom preserved in the constitution."[97] The threat to Massachusetts' liberties that had arisen when Governor Hutchinson, the Olivers, and others of "the Junto" controlled the executive, the council, and much of the judiciary was still fresh in Adams' mind.[98] In his 1779 draft of the Massachusetts Constitution, he placed the legislative, executive, and judicial powers in separate departments, "to the end that it might be a government of laws and not of men."[99]

Yet there was a second and more important kind of balance than this—one wholly within the legislative power and formed by the upper and lower houses and the executive acting in his legislative capacity. In any

[96] Quoted in Adrienne Koch, *Power, Morals, and the Founding Fathers* (Ithaca, New York, 1961), p. 82.

[97] "Thoughts on Government": *Works*, IV, 186.

[98] "Novanglus": *Ibid.*, pp. 62-63.

[99] *Journal of the Massachusetts Convention*, p. 197. The matter of the separation of powers had figured prominently in Adams' controversy with William Brattle in 1772-1773 over the royal payment of judicial salaries. *Works*, III, 513-74.

government, Adams observed, power derived from control of the legislative process. The authority to make and repeal laws constituted the real source of political influence. Under tyrannies, the legislative power rested with one man; under oligarchies, with a few. In republics, it was controlled by representatives of the people. Control of the legislative process, being the source of political power, became the primary object of personal ambition. Individuals seeking to advance their own standing turned to the legislature, since they could find there the means of satisfaction. Given too great an influence over the legislature, one man or group of men would inevitably use it for the gratification of their own passions at the expense of society as a whole.

In a popular government, then, the legislative power had to be rendered impartial; that is, be fragmented among several sources. A single assembly was liable to all the vices and frailties of an individual and had to be corrected by some controlling power. By separating the legislature into several parts and balancing them off against each other, care could be taken that no one person or group would gain undue influence.

During the 1770's, Adams paid virtually no attention to the opposition that might arise between opposing social or economic interests even within a single assembly. He did not deny that such interests existed; but his emphasis was upon the homogeneity of American society, and so he minimized the conflicts out of which a balance of specific classes or interests might be fashioned. The balance of which he wrote involved the distribution of power between constitutional bodies rather than specific social interests.

Under popular governments, Adams believed, the strongest element in the legislative balance, the one that threatened most often to override the other two, was the lower house. In the day-to-day operation of government, the assemblies tended to dominate both senate and executive. In his discussion of the state constitutions, Adams took care to warn against this. The reasons for the assemblies' tendency to predominate were clear. Their simple superiority of numbers was one thing. More important was the fact that they were the most popular branch of the new governments and consequently offered the best opportunity for the gratification of personal interests. Representation in the legislative assemblies, Adams remarked, should recapitulate as nearly as possible the interests and wishes of the people. The end to be aimed at in the formation of a representative assembly was "the sense of the people, the public voice." The perfection of the portrait consisted in its likeness. In 1776 Adams wrote to John Penn that the assembly should mirror the structure of society; should be "an exact portrait, in miniature," should "think, feel, act, and reason like the people."[100] The branch of government largest in size and offering the most direct opportunity for the gratification of personal ambition, then, tended naturally to predominate over the other two. In the assemblies also rested control of financial matters. Adams remembered quite vividly the effective use made of this power by the colonial legislatures against the royal governors. All the force of the governors and councils backed up by fleets and armies, had not been sufficient to gain the advantage. Adams had read the lesson well.

As one counterweight to the popular assembly, Adams insisted that the new constitutions provide for upper legislative houses. In his own 1779 draft, he included a senate; and by basing its representation upon the amount of taxes paid in special senatorial districts rather than simply upon population as in the house, he sought to give it a slightly different basis.[101] He also raised the property requirements for senators from the £100 free-

[100] Adams to John Penn, January 1776: *Ibid.*, IV, 205.
[101] *Journal of the Massachusetts Convention*, p. 199.

hold necessary for assemblymen to £300.[102] The senates' influence, however, he would restrict. There still remained in his mind the relatively minor role that the governors' councils had played under the colonial regimes. The powers he provided the Senate in his constitutional draft were few.[103]

For a more effective counterweight to the assembly, Adams turned instead to the executive. Given the natural tendency of the assembly to predominate, he took considerable pains to stress the importance of providing for a strong chief magistrate in the new governments. Especially with the governor's former bulwark, the authority of the Crown, now removed, Adams thought it particularly necessary to strengthen the executive's influence. A strong executive power became the keystone of his political system.

The executive was, of course, to be elective. As the choice of all society, he was to represent the people as a whole and be spokesman for the public welfare. If there was one truth to be collected from the history of all ages, Adams believed it was that the people's rights and liberties could never be preserved without a powerful executive. "The dignity of the commonwealth," he explained, must be maintained "in the character of its chief magistrate."[104] The governor, wrote Adams to Elbridge Gerry, ought to be "the Reservoir of Wisdom."[105]

To be an effective counter to the assembly, the governor had to be given power adequate for his own protection. Once "stripped of most of those badges of domination called prerogatives," Adams remarked, the executive should be given substantial authority. Adams

[102] *Ibid.*, pp. 201, 203.   [103] *Ibid.*, pp. 199-201 *passim.*
[104] "Report of a Constitution for Massachusetts": *Works,* IV, 251, 290.
[105] Adams to Elbridge Gerry, November 4, 1799: Adams Microfilm, Reel 93.

made careful provision for this in his constitutional draft of 1779. The executive he provided for was remarkably strong—more so, by a good bit, than in most other states.[106] So that he might maintain his independence of the legislature, the Massachusetts governor was to have a salary established by law. "As the public good requires, that the Governor should not be under the undue influence of any of the members of the General Court by a dependence on them for his support," wrote Adams, "that he should, in all cases, act with freedom for the benefit of the public—that he should not have his attention necessarily diverted from that object to his private concerns . . . it is necessary that he should have an honorable stated salary, of a fixed and permanent value, amply sufficient for those purposes, and established by standing laws. . . ."[107]

In order that the governor might make his influence sufficiently felt in the legislative process, Adams provided him with an absolute veto. "The first magistrate," Adams wrote simply, "shall have a negative upon all laws. . . ." He added no qualifications.[108] Adams had had some doubts earlier (in 1776) whether the people of New England would accept an absolute veto. He had no desire, he wrote to James Warren, to force such a measure upon them. Yet he continued to urge it, and in 1779 included it in his constitutional draft.[109]

[106] Note, for example, the relatively weak executive power established by the early constitutions of Pennsylvania (1776) and Georgia (1777). F. N. Thorpe, ed., *American Charters, Constitutions, and Organic Laws,* 7 vols. (Washington, D.C., 1909), V, 3,084-3,092, and II, 777-85. Also the constitutions of New York (1777) and Virginia (1776): *Ibid.,* V, 2,633-2,634, and VII, 3,817-3,818.

[107] *Journal of the Massachusetts Convention,* pp. 207-208.

[108] *Ibid.,* p. 197. The absolute veto was not retained by the Massachusetts convention, one of the few changes of importance made in Adams' draft. As finally decided, the governor's veto could be overridden by a two-thirds vote of both houses. *Ibid.,* pp. 228-29.

[109] Adams to David Sewall, June 12, 1776: Adams Microfilm, Reel 89.

In other ways, as well, Adams strengthened the executive authority. He accorded the governor extensive powers of appointment. All officers of the militia were subject to executive nomination with the advice and consent of the council, as were "all judicial officers, the Attorney-General . . . all Sheriffs, Registers of Probate, and Registrars of Maritime Courts. . . ."[110] Control of these offices would remove them from the assembly and add to the governor's influence. Adams also spelled out with great care the executive's control of the militia. The Massachusetts governor, as commander in chief, was to have "full power . . . to train, instruct . . . and govern the militia and navy"; to assemble "in martial array" the inhabitants and conduct them in repelling any persons attempting the destruction of the Commonwealth; and to wield over the army and navy "the law-martial in time of war, invasion, or rebellion, as occasion shall necessarily require."[111] Further, the governor, with the advice of the council, was to grant pardons and control the disposition of all money.[112]

The governor, then, was the capstone of Adams' political system. His function was to serve as spokesman for the public welfare against the appeals of special interests, and to act as a balance to the assembly. Adequate safeguards against the abuse of his broad powers could be provided by requiring him to submit to annual election by the people, and by placing a limit upon the length of time one individual might hold office.[113]

During the whole period of the Revolution, Adams never retreated from his belief in the unique virtuousness of the American people. The legislative balance was

[110] *Journal of the Massachusetts Convention*, p. 207.
[111] *Ibid.*, p. 206.
[112] *Ibid.*, pp. 206, 207.
[113] *Ibid.*, p. 208. In his constitutional draft, Adams limited eligibility for one man to no more than four years in any seven. *Ibid.*, p. 207.

simply the minimum safeguard needed to protect against the weaknesses inherent in all human nature. Uncontrolled power corrupted both good men and bad, and had to be guarded against among both. Though Americans did not need—and would not abide—the heavier controls of monarchy or aristocracy, they did require discipline to encourage them in their virtuous conduct. And this, Adams explained, would be provided by an unobtrusive system of checks and balances. With these limited guarantees, he believed the American experiment would prove a resounding success. The problems standing in the way of the new governments, he realized, were many. That the American states could govern themselves effectively without the familiar sanctions of Crown and Parliament would have to be proved. At times, he worried that the "popular principles and maxims" upon which the governments were founded would prove abhorrent to "the Barons of the South."[114] There seemed ample reason to doubt that the Southerners, who had made him so uneasy at the first Congress, were devoted to republican principles.[115] In the other states, the problem threatened to be just the opposite, that republicanism might be carried too far. The plans by which the people of New England and some of the other states had constituted their governments he found "remarkably popular, more so than I could ever have imagined, even more popular than the 'Thoughts on Government.'" In the early elections, the people seemed at times to have based their choice of officials upon "Capacity, Spirit and Zeal in the Cause" rather than "Fortune, Family, and every other Consideration, which used to have

[114] Adams to Horatio Gates, March 23, 1776: Force, ed., *American Archives*, Series 4, V, 472-73.

[115] Adams to Joseph Hawley, November 25, 1775: Burnett, ed., *Letters of the Continental Congress*, I, 260. But see also, Adams to James Warren, June 16, 1776: Adams Microfilm, Reel 89, where Adams expresses his surprise at the strength of republican sentiment demonstrated in the Southern states.

Weight with Mankind."[116] The new members of Congress in 1776 were of this mold. Many of the old leaders, "notwithstanding all their vast Advantages in Point of Fortune, Family, and Abilities," men like John Dickinson and Robert Morris, had been left out either because they opposed or were lukewarm about independence. Adams was inclined to wish that they might be restored at the next election; "altho mistaken in some Points," he explained, their abilities could contribute "to strengthen America, and cement her Union."[117]

To James Warren, Adams wrote with the impending Massachusetts election in mind, of the danger that men would gain influence "by Noise not Sense, by Meanness not Greatness, by Ignorance not Learning, by contracted Hearts not large Souls."[118] Writing home from Philadelphia, he urged that everyone unite upon two men of note for governor and lieutenant governor. Both officials, he insisted, should be respectable in their fortune, abilities, and integrity. Above all, he warned that dangerous contests be avoided. Caucus beforehand, he urged; "don't divide. Let the choice be unanimous, I beg." Division would split the province with factions. "I dread the Consequence of Electing Governors," he concluded, "and would avoid every Appearance of and Tendency towards Party and Division, as the greatest Evil."[119]

In the end, however, Adams saw the crisis come and go and the people once more prove themselves capable of virtuous behavior. The Massachusetts election turned out as well as he could have wished. He had been fearful before seeing the returns, but was relieved to see so many able men in each house; enough, indeed, to pre-

[116] Adams to Abigail Adams, July 10, 1776: Butterfield, ed., *Adams Family Correspondence*, II, 42.

[117] *Ibid.*, p. 42.

[118] Adams to James Warren, April 22, 1776: "Warren-Adams Letters," LXXII, 234.

[119] Adams to James Warren, May 12, 1776: *Ibid.*, p. 243.

vent dangerous innovations and yet carry through "necessary and useful improvements."[120] Just a year later,
he confided to Abigail his continuing persuasion that the
people possessed "a Fund of Wisdom, Integrity, and
Humanity, which will preserve their Happiness. . . ."[121]
And to James Warren yet a year after that, he affirmed
his conviction that notwithstanding all dissensions, there
was "a Mass of Prudence and Integrity" among the
people that would finally conduct them aright.[122]

For the moment, Adams remained convinced that the
American people would prove equal to the opportunities that the Revolution had opened to them. There was
among the inhabitants of the various states enough of the
republican spirit, nourished by their form of government, that they would neither submit to tyranny from
abroad nor, by failure to provide for their own affairs,
bring it upon themselves. As the 1770's came to an end
and the 1780's began, Adams could see in the orderly
behavior of the people convincing evidence that they
would make the American experiment a success. In the
years that lay immediately ahead, he would call his revolutionary faith sharply into question; but for the moment, it was enough.

[120] Adams to John Lowell, June 12, 1776: *Works*, IX, 393.
[121] Adams to Abigail Adams, June 2, 1777: Butterfield, ed., *Adams
Family Correspondence*, II, 253.
[122] Adams to James Warren, July 26, 1778: "Warren-Adams
Letters," LXXIII, 36.

Chapter IV. "Sea Change"

Between the 1770's and 1793, Adams carried through a major reevaluation of American society. The changes in his thinking were of fundamental importance, for they involved his most basic assumptions concerning the character of the American people and their capacity for orderly self-government; the make-up of American society, its egalitarianism and cohesiveness; and the nature of American political institutions, their popularity and permanence. Moreover, the ideas he now developed were to serve him throughout the remainder of his life. By 1793, he had become considerably more pessimistic; more like the John Adams of written history. He believed that since the 1770's America had undergone both moral and political decline. American virtue seemed to have faded. Established republican principles of honesty, thrift, industry, frugality, and simplicity had been replaced with their opposites. Personal gain, rather than disinterested concern for society had become the American hallmark. The earlier cohesion of American society, fostered by an egalitarian social order, had given way before the growth of special interests bent solely upon their own gratification.

Such changes seemed to Adams doubly ominous because of the speed with which they had occurred. At one moment, America's future had seemed promising; she had carried through a successful revolution and established effective new governments without serious internal confusion. Within a short time, however, her prospects had darkened. The task Adams set for himself was to determine what changes had taken place, how they had come about, and what they portended for America's future. The remainder of his political career constituted an effort to come to grips with these problems.

The changes in Adams' political thought were again a consequence of his observation of American society. During the 1780's, he found alterations in both the structure of society and the character of the people reflected in American behavior. Except for a few months during the winter of 1779-1780, Adams was abroad throughout the decade of the 1780's, first in France where he shared in negotiating the treaty of peace, and the Netherlands where he secured badly needed loans from the Dutch bankers, and then in England as first American ambassador to the Court of St. James. His absence from the American scene made more difficult the watch he kept upon American society. "One loses at a distance the thread of affairs," he observed at one point, "and frequently a true Judgment depends upon little Circumstances which we are not acquainted with."[1] But he kept track as well as he could of the course events were taking. He wrote constantly to his friends at home, lamenting his lack of information and imploring them to write him. His official public correspondence as well was full of questions about American policies and behavior.

Adams was not as isolated during his years abroad, however, as he occasionally made out; for his situation involved him directly in public business and offered him an excellent vantage point from which to gain insight into the behavior of the American people. As one of the American representatives abroad, he had many of the problems confronting the Congress, at least those involving America's relations with other powers, forced upon his attention. And from observation of Congress's treatment of these problems, he was able to reach certain

[1] Adams to Elbridge Gerry, April 25, 1785: Adams Microfilm, Reel 107.

conclusions about American society—conclusions which required a sharp reappraisal of his earlier beliefs.

There was, in addition, a further dimension to Adams' experience during the 1780's; another way in which the events of his own life compelled him to reconsider his understanding of American society. Put most simply, he found his own personal situation much less satisfying during these years, much less certain and untroubled than it had been in the years preceding. For one thing, his physical absence removed him from active participation in political affairs and his name from general public consideration. For a man so concerned with his own prominence, this was a substantial loss. He would be forgotten, he lamented to Abigail; he would "lose all opportunity of being a man of Importance in the World by being away from home. . . ."[2] Events would pass him by. New men would arise, eroding his former position of leadership. By 1788, when he finally returned, he was extremely anxious to get home, and preceded his arrival with nervous letters inquiring what his political future was likely to be.

From May of 1778 to August of 1784, moreover (with the exception of the few months between his two tours abroad), he was separated from his wife and family. (Abigail joined him finally in 1784 to finish out his stay abroad with him.) This was no small loss, for Adams depended heavily upon Abigail for counsel and support. The bond between them, intellectual as well as physical, was lasting and intense.[3] The physical separation they were forced to endure was a burden of considerable proportions for them both, as their letters clearly attest. In addition, Adams' health was substantially depressed during much of his stay abroad. Though he lived to be

[2] Adams to Abigail Adams, September 25, 1780: *Ibid.*, Reel 352; Adams to Abigail Adams, December 30, 1778: *Ibid.*, Reel 349.

[3] Page Smith, *John Adams*, pp. 923-25. Smith dwells on the intimacy of their relationship throughout his biography.

ninety, evidence enough of a hardy constitution, his health was never strong. He suffered throughout his life, and never more than when abroad, from a succession of aches and pains, most of them not serious enough to endanger his life, yet together serving to keep him in an almost constant state of ill-health. During his whole stay in Europe, he complained continually of colds and leg pains, boils and fevers. Discontent over his isolation from America, anxiety because of separation from his wife and family, and weakness from recurring physical complaints: these were some of the personal conditions under which Adams labored during the 1780's.

In other and more important ways, his experience during the 1780's was significantly different from what had gone before. To be sure, his achievements during the 1780's were substantial: particularly the much needed Dutch loan of 1782 and the peace treaty with Britain the year following. Yet in distinction to the 1770's, he found his stay abroad for the most part tiresome and frustrating and often personally embarrassing. It had constituted, he reflected in April of 1789, "an experience of ten years . . . too unhappy . . . to be ever forgotten."[4] Not his accomplishments, but the disappointments which surrounded them were what most impressed him.

The earlier years of his public life had provided him considerable gratification. His role during the Revolution and the early period of political reconstruction had been an important and satisfying one, and had persuaded him that he commanded the trust of the American people. In a thousand ways, he later recalled, he had had intimations during those years "that the hopes and Confidence of the People, were placed on me, as one of their Friends. . . ."[5] As a leading figure in the successful movement toward independence, he had developed a

[4] Adams to John Jay, April 30, 1789: Adams Microfilm, Reel 364.
[5] *Diary and Autobiography*, III, 290.

deep sense of correspondence with the ambitions of the American people. "I have hitherto had the Happiness," he remarked in 1778, "to find that my Pulse beat in exact Unison with those of my Countrymen."[6]

During the 1780's, however, his relationship with the American people was of a different sort. He became less confident of American virtue and of the approbation which his own virtuous conduct would bring him. No longer did he seem as able to command the esteem of the people or to speak with authority for them. During the 1780's, he began to experience a feeling of estrangement that was to grow until, in 1801, he would leave public life for good, confused and angry and blaming the society for his misfortunes.

The consequence of this change was not simply personal frustration. In his own mind, his mistreatment reflected most importantly upon the society that effected it. Each episode he read as an homily on the condition of American morals. Being a man both of great personal ambition and intense dedication to the public service, his concern over what he deemed his increasingly ambiguous relationship to American society was quite profound. And convinced unshakably of his own rectitude, he found the cause of his discomfiture not in his own doing, but in the actions of an unappreciative people. American society during the 1770's had proven virtuous—and given him praise. It could hardly be the same virtuous society now, he thought, that treated him so carelessly.

The immediate inspiration for Adams' reassessment of American society was the outbreak of Shays' rebellion in western Massachusetts during 1786. Curiously enough, his correspondence at the time contained little about this episode; yet in the first volume of the *Defense* (as well as later on in recollection) he acknowledged the importance of the Shays affair in redirecting his own think-

[6] Adams to James Warren, August 4, 1778: "Warren-Adams Letters," Massachusetts Historical Society, *Collections*, LXXIII, 39.

ing. The troubles in Massachusetts, however, had not sprung on him unexpectedly. During the year or so preceding, friends at home had written to him warning of growing unrest in several of the New England states. In New Hampshire, he was told, an armed mob had surrounded the state house declaring that no one could leave until the legislature voted a new paper issue, and had scattered only when forced to by the local militia.[7] Rhode Island, as always, was likewise in distress: her trade, he heard, was stagnated, her money valueless, her people breaking open stores and seizing grain.[8] Even Massachusetts had not been free from civil commotion. There was reason to fear, Charles Storer wrote Adams in September of 1786, that the state would soon be in a state of anarchy. Government no longer had energy enough to enforce the laws. Mobs were forming in the western counties protesting taxes, unfair representation, and excessive public salaries, and in some places even preventing the courts from sitting.[9] The lesson of all this was clear to Adams. The American people seemed ready to give themselves up to "Chance and Accident, factious rages . . . delerious enthusiasm." American liberties, Adams feared, could not long be preserved under such conditions.[10]

The changes in Adams' thinking, however, did not come about all at once during the winter of 1786-1787.

[7] Charles Storer to Adams, September 26, 1786: Adams Microfilm, Reel 368. For a brief description of this "Exeter Riot," see James D. Squires' *The Granite State of the United States, A History of New Hampshire from 1623 to the Present*, 2 vols. (New York, 1956), I, 156-58.

[8] Cotton Tufts to Adams, July 18, 1786: Adams Microfilm, Reel 368. Peter Coleman's book on *The Transformation of Rhode Island, 1799-1860* (Providence, 1963), however, suggests that by the late 1780's the Rhode Island economy was booming. See Chapter One of Coleman's book.

[9] Charles Storer to Adams, September 16, 1786: Adams Microfilm, Reel 368.

[10] Adams to Rufus King, June 14, 1786: *Ibid.*, Reel 113. Adams to Benjamin Hinchborn, January 27, 1787: *Ibid.*, Reel 368.

His experience during the whole decade preceding contributed directly to the process, for it prepared him finally to accept the conclusions which the Shays outbreak forced upon him: that virtue in America had declined alarmingly, and that the people were apparently no longer able to live peaceably under the gentle rule of popular government.

The first significant occurrence took place in 1778, during Adams' initial venture abroad. In November of 1777, Congress elected him commissioner to the court of France, replacing Silas Deane and joining Arthur Lee and Benjamin Franklin. His task was to help negotiate treaties of alliance and commerce with the French government. Upon his arrival in Paris, he found diplomatic recognition secured and preliminary articles of amity and commerce already signed. With the central objects of his mission thus accomplished, Adams found little to do but attempt to secure additional loans for the American cause and keep the flow of supplies uninterrupted. For these purposes, Franklin and Lee with their longer acquaintance in France were better suited. For lack of anything more substantial to do, Adams turned to the task of straightening out the tangled records of the commission—just the sort of busy-work he disliked. Within a short time, he was writing his friends in Congress explaining that one commissioner could handle American affairs easily enough (he recommended Franklin for the post) and letting it be known that he was willing to return.[11]

The changes which Congress effected, however, were hardly what Adams had bargained for. On February 11, he received word that Congress had decided to dissolve the commission. Franklin was to stay on as sole ambassa-

[11] Adams to Samuel Adams, February 14, 1779: Wharton, ed., *Revolutionary Diplomatic Correspondence*, III, 47-48. Adams to Congress, May 24, 1778 and to John Jay, February 27, 1779: Adams Microfilm, Reel 93.

dor to France, while Arthur Lee was transferred to the
Spanish court at Madrid. Adams' status was left unclear.
His commission to the French court was revoked, but
Congress in their instructions made no further provision for him.[12] There were intimations from several of
his friends in Congress that other duties were under
consideration. Yet how soon new instructions would
come, or whether they would come at all he did not
know. Nor, as he thought about it, was it clear whether
the lapse was an oversight or had been intentional. One
thing rapidly became certain: he found himself stranded
with nothing to do and nowhere to go—a situation which
rapidly became intolerable.

In recommending that Franklin alone be retained,
Adams had not anticipated being left hanging so awkwardly in mid-air. The more time that passed without
indication of what he was to do, the more restless he
became and the more convinced that he had been will-
fully mistreated. To John Jay, then the Congress's secretary for foreign affairs, he fired off a strong complaint.
He had entertained hopes, he declared irritably, that
when the change was made his own duty would have
been marked out either to return home or go elsewhere.
Congress's decision had been made in September, and
yet by February (when Adams wrote) they still had not
taken notice of him. The only inference he could draw,
he concluded tartly, was that Congress had no further
use for him.[13] To Samuel Adams, he expressed his disappointment still more sharply. He found the whole

[12] "Election of Franklin as Minister to France": Wharton, ed.,
Revolutionary Diplomatic Correspondence, II, 709.
[13] Adams to John Jay, February 27, 1779: Adams Microfilm,
Reel 93. In a communication of October 28, Congress hinted that
fresh arrangements for their foreign affairs were under way, and
that in the meantime Adams should exercise his "whole extensive
abilities" on the subject of finances; hardly a prospect that enthralled
him. Wharton, ed., *Revolutionary Diplomatic Correspondence*, II,
815.

subject of his "disgrace" one about which he could not easily write. "I would not feel another such sensation," he assured Samuel, "to be made a prince."[14]

He had been made to look ridiculous before all of Europe, and in spite of the embarrassment he hardly knew how to extricate himself. Should he stay on, hoping that new instructions would soon arrive? Or should he go home without clear warrant, taking the chance that a commission might arrive with no one to execute it? His first impulse was to go. Yet he was reluctant to leave without permission—and without receiving the new instructions that alone could free him from his predicament.[15] The scaffold, he complained, had been cut away and he left kicking and sprawling in the mire in "total Neglect and Contempt." If he deserved being struck down for all Europe to see, he at least merited being told why. Then he would have known his duty to return. As it was, he hardly knew what to do. Despite the rumors of future appointments, he decided sourly, Congress seemed determined upon leaving him in his present "ridiculous" situation.[16]

By mid-February, Adams had decided that he could stay on no longer. To Vergennes, the French foreign minister, Adams wrote that by the change of instructions he had been "restored to the character of a private citizen." After paying his respects to the King, he intended to quit the country.[17] The same day he wrote the French

[14] Adams to Samuel Adams, February 14, 1779: Wharton ed., *Revolutionary Diplomatic Correspondence*, III, 47-48. Adams to Abigail Adams, February 27, 1779: C. F. Adams, ed., *Familiar Letters of John Adams and his Wife* (Boston, 1875), p. 360.

[15] Adams to Abigail Adams, February 21, 1779: Adams Microfilm, Reel 350.

[16] Adams to Abigail Adams, February 28, 1779: *Ibid*. Adams to Abigail Adams, February 27, 1779: *Ibid*.

[17] Adams to Vergennes, February 16, 1779: Wharton, ed., *Revolutionary Diplomatic Correspondence*, III, 50-55.

minister of marine, Sartine, requesting passage on the first vessel sailing for America.[18]

In August of 1779, Adams returned to America, his discontent still unrelieved. He had suffered "the Neglect and Contempt of Congress," he complained; the world had been left to conjecture what had brought upon him "this Vengeance" of his sovereign. And this, he continued, after he had undertaken to obey the commands of Congress "at many Hazards" to his own life and property.[19] Once home, he lost no time asking his friends in Congress to send him copies of both the public and private journals so that he could determine the true cause of his misfortune. To John Jay, he wrote formally demanding the particulars.[20]

Anticipating his reaction, Adams' friends had written assuring him that Congress still maintained a high regard for his services and that no disrespect had been intended. Samuel Adams and R. H. Lee urged patience, and James Lovell declared unequivocally that there had been no plot against him.[21] Adams, however, remained unconvinced. From Lovell and others he learned about the criticism of him for his part in the quarrel that had

[18] Sartine to Adams, February 28, 1779: *Ibid.*, p. 71. Adams was not to escape so easily, however. Not until June 18, more than 13 weeks after leaving Paris, did he finally set sail on the *Sensible*. Adams found the delay "a cruel Disappointment" and imagined it to be the work of Franklin, scheming to delay him in the hope of facilitating his capture by the British during the longer summer passage. Diary, April 28, 1779: *Diary and Autobiography*, II, 363. Adams to Edmund Jennings, June 8, 1779: Adams Microfilm, Reel 93. (This letter was not sent.)

[19] Adams to William Whipple, September 11, 1779: Adams Microfilm, Reel 93.

[20] Adams to John Jay, September 10, 1779: *Ibid.* Adams' letterbook contains a number of angry passages which he omitted in the final draft.

[21] Samuel Adams to John Adams, October 25, 1778: H. A. Cushing, ed., *The Writings of Samuel Adams*, 4 vols. (New York, 1904-1908), IV, 79-81. James Lovell to Adams, June 13, 1779: *Works*, IX, 480-82.

developed among the American commissioners between Arthur Lee on the one hand and Deane and Franklin on the other. (After brief pretensions of neutrality, Adams had firmly sided with Lee.) Actually he had been handled more lightly in Congress than he imagined; his name was not included among the commissioners formally reprimanded for the "suspicions and animosities" that had existed among them.[22] He remained unhappy, though, that his name had been considered at all.

During the fall of 1779, Adams' temper gradually calmed. For one thing, he was busy virtually all of the time in the Massachusetts Constitutional Convention. In late September, moreover, the vindication he had sought finally came in the form of two new commissions to negotiate treaties of peace and commerce with Britain. From Congress, Elbridge Gerry wrote urging Adams to accept, arguing that the appointments constituted full exoneration of the charges formerly made against him.[23] Whether or not Adams needed Gerry's careful urging, he accepted the appointment—and with considerable relief. When he considered the remarkable unanimity with which he had been chosen, he confessed, and recalled how recently Congress had been divided over their representatives, he was "penetrated with a sense of the honor" done him.[24] Momentarily, his sensitive feelings had been assuaged.

In November of 1779, Adams set out again for Europe. His experience this time, however, was not to be

[22] Ford, ed., *Journals of the Continental Congress*, XIII, 484-87 For tactical reasons, Samuel Adams and James Lovell had voted for the inclusion of his name, and he wrote them curtly demanding to know why. Elbridge Gerry to Adams, September 29, 1779: Adams Microfilm, Reel 350.

[23] Elbridge Gerry to Adams, September 29, 1779: *Ibid.* James Lovell to Adams, September 28, 1779: Wharton, ed., *Revolutionary Diplomatic Correspondence*, III, 345-46.

[24] Adams to Luzerne, October 17, 1779: *Ibid.*, p. 383. Adams to Henry Laurens, October 25, 1779: *Works*, IX, 503-504.

substantially different than before. Within a short while, he found himself once more in an awkward position, one commission and set of instructions changed and another peremptorily cancelled. His troubles this time he attributed with considerable reason to French influence working against him in Philadelphia (abetted by Franklin's maneuverings in Paris).

There were difficulties endemic to the Franco-American alliance of 1778 and these provided the context in which Adams' troubles arose.[25] From the first, he had been an ardent supporter of Franco-American cooperation. The two countries, he recognized, different as they were in language, government, and religion, had a common interest in promoting American independence. If Adams found value in the French alliance, however, he saw a danger in casting off one colonial authority only to fall unwittingly prey to another. Gratitude for French assistance was warranted; yet Americans should realize that French aid was a function of her national interest and not give control of their own affairs into French hands. Following his return to Europe, however, this is precisely what Adams sensed was happening, and he set himself to the task of preventing it.

Adams' anxiety about America's independence was well considered. For France, while wishing America separate from Britain, did not want to see her so strong as to become a threat to French commercial or territorial interests. Moreover, France as the senior member of the partnership regarded the American states with a certain condescension. She believed they should follow her direction, especially in matters that involved European affairs. France was determined that cooperation in the

[25] The story of Adams' disagreements with Vergennes and of the French foreign minister's largely successful effort to have Adams recalled has been told and need not be fully repeated here. (Two studies of Adams' foreign policy and experience abroad are being done by other scholars, and should shed additional light on the problem.) A brief recapitulation of events will be adequate.

American venture should not compromise her own prior European commitments. Finally, the royal government of Louis XVI was not entirely comfortable in alliance with rebellious colonies, even someone else's.

The opposition of French and American policies was dramatically played out in the relations between Adams and Vergennes. Differences of temperament made co-operation between them difficult at best. The French foreign minister, suave, arrogant, adept in the circuitous ways of European diplomacy and dedicated only to the advancement of French interests, had little patience with Adams' bumptious assertions of independence. The short, intense, presumptuous New Englander, Vergennes found not only ungrateful but tiresome. Adams, for his part, equated the Frenchman's sophistication with dishonesty, and his restrained enthusiasm for the American cause as readiness to sell America short. During Adams' previous stay, moreover, Vergennes had sympathized with Franklin and Deane, while Adams had supported Lee. The Frenchman, finally, suspected correctly that Adams would be little inclined to follow France's lead in matters of diplomacy, and might even send out peace overtures to Britain on his own.

When Adams returned to France in 1779, opposition between him and Vergennes rapidly developed. For one thing, Adams wanted to make public announcement of his full powers to treat with Britain. Vergennes demurred, asking Adams instead to keep the purpose of his mission secret. The disagreement continued through the spring and into the summer of 1780, reaching a climax on July 25 when Vergennes in a sharply worded letter urged Adams to send on their correspondence to Congress and suspend in the meantime all thoughts of communicating with the British ministry. Vergennes also promised to transmit his own views to Congress through the French ambassador, Luzerne, and assured Adams that Congress would "think the opinion of the ministry of France worthy of some attention" whatever Adams' own attitude might be.[26]

About the same time, there arose the matter of Congress's devaluation of the continental currency, an issue that brought relations between Adams and Vergennes to an open break. In an effort to shore up its uncertain finances, Congress in 1780 declared that all loan office certificates were to be called in and replaced with new issue at the exchange rate of forty to one.[27] Adams was pleased with this indication of Congressional responsibility; sound finances he believed essential to sound government. Vergennes, however, was less than enthusiastic. He expressed dismay at the heavy losses which Congress's action would impose upon French investors. Again the two diplomats carried on a spirited exchange, Adams arguing that many of the present holders had obtained the certificates at considerable discount and that few of these holders were Frenchmen anyhow, while Vergennes continued to protest the unfairness of expecting foreign investors to assume the losses with American citizens.[28] Angered by Adams' relentless barrage of letters (the final straw fell on July 27, when Adams declared that he intended to communicate his sentiments to Vergennes on every matter of importance to the two nations), the foreign minister finally broke off communication altogether. Franklin, Vergennes declared, was the sole American accredited to His Most Christian Majesty's court, and it was with Franklin alone that Vergennes

[26] Vergennes to Adams, July 25, 1780: Wharton, ed., *Revolutionary Diplomatic Correspondence*, III, 882-83. For this exchange between Adams and Vergennes, see *ibid.*, pp. 496-883.

[27] Edmund Burnett discusses the collapse of the Continental currency in *The Continental Congress* (New York, 1941), Chapter 22. See also Robert East, *Business Enterprise in the American Revolutionary Era* (New York, 1938), Chapter 9.

[28] Adams to Vergennes, June 20, 1780: Wharton, ed., *Revolutionary Diplomatic Correspondence*, III, 805. Vergennes to Adams, June 21, 1780: *Ibid.*, pp. 805-807.

would in the future do business.[29] Adams, as might be expected, was infuriated at being so brusquely turned aside.

By 1781, moreover, Vergennes was anxious to accept the offer of mediation posed in October of the year before by Russia and Germany. The war in America was going badly, and at home domestic unrest and trouble with France's neighbors was looming. One thing, Vergennes sensed, stood in the way: the detailed conditions Congress had earlier spelled out concerning acceptable conditions of peace—with regard to boundaries, access to the Canadian fisheries, treatment of Tories, the return of American slaves, the collection of Tory-held debts, the prior recognition of American independence, and the prior removal of British troops from American soil—and the tenacity with which he knew Adams would adhere to them in any negotiation. The mediating powers, Vergennes realized, had no sympathy with such conditions for negotiation.[30]

Knowing from earlier experience the difficulty of dealing with Adams, Vergennes decided to bypass him and turn directly to Congress instead in an effort to get the American position changed. Acting through Luzerne in Philadelphia (and with the concurrence of Franklin), Vergennes worked carefully to clip Adams' diplomatic wings. Within a short while, he had done so quite effectively. First, Vergennes pointedly reminded the Congress of their continuing dependence on French aid. He next wondered whether in fact they "still wished to leave

[29] Adams to Vergennes, July 27, 1780: *Ibid.*, IV, 12-14. Irving Brant appears to be correct in maintaining that Adams was trying to squeeze Franklin aside; a blunder, as Page Smith has suggested, into which Adams was probably led by his restlessness under his own commissions. Brant, *Madison, the Nationalist, 1780-1787*, pp. 134-36. Page Smith, *John Adams*, I, 478. Vergennes to Adams, July 29, 1780: Wharton, ed., *Revolutionary Diplomatic Correspondence*, IV, 16-17.

[30] Samuel Flagg Bemis, *The Diplomacy of the American Revolution* (New York, 1935), p. 185.

it [the commission] in his [Adams'] hands." At the least, he suggested that Congress should issue instructions placing Adams under French guidance. As Vergennes made clear, his first choice was Adams' removal.[31]

In Philadelphia, Luzerne pressed the case in masterful style. He proffered an additional loan, then announced that because of France's own difficulties such help might not be so readily available in the future.[32] Allowing time for the message to sink in, Luzerne next explained that France intended to accept the offer of mediation and expected Congress—and their representatives—to agree. In line with this, Congress should "draw a line of conduct" for Adams, of which he "might not be allowed to lose sight."[33] Luzerne left little to Congressional imaginations. If they accorded any value to the King's friendship, he observed, they would see the necessity of prescribing for Adams "a perfect and open confidence in the French ministers, and a thorough reliance on the king. . . ." After giving Adams "the most important outlines for his conduct," they would order him "to receive his directions from the Count de Vergennes. . . ."[34] He again reminded the Congress how essential to America French sponsorship was, and how unfortunate it would be if Adams "by aiming at im-

[31] Vergennes to Luzerne, August 7, 1780: Henri Doniol, *Histoire de la participation de la France à l'établissement des Etats-Unis d'Amérique*, 5 vols. (Paris, 1886-1892), IV, 423-24. At Vergennes' urging, Franklin forwarded to Congress on August 9 the file of correspondence between Adams and Vergennes with a covering letter of his own, noting how Adams had offended the French court. Franklin concluded that it was his own intention to procure what advantages he could for America "by endeavoring to please this court. . . ." His task would be facilitated, he assured Congress, if other Americans were instructed to say nothing that might complicate it. Vergennes to Franklin, July 31, 1780: Wharton, ed., *Revolutionary Diplomatic Correspondence*, IV, 18-19. Franklin to Congress, August 9, 1780: *Ibid.*, pp. 21-25.

[32] Ford, ed., *Journals of the Continental Congress*, XX, 556-71.

[33] *Ibid.*, pp. 560-63.

[34] *Ibid.*, pp. 563-64.

possible things" forced France to proceed in the peace negotiations alone.[35]

Luzerne's observations had the desired effect, for in the early summer of 1781 Congress made major changes in their diplomatic establishment—changes that were precisely in line with French wishes. As early as January 10, after Vergennes' first communication, Congress had issued Adams a reprimand. Recognizing that his correspondence with Vergennes resulted from zeal in the service of his country, Congress nevertheless informed him that the French minister's judgment against the communication of Adams' instructions was well-founded, and that Adams should "be very cautious" about acting without French concurrence.[36] By June, Congress was ready to move more decisively. To Adams' commission for negotiating peace were added Franklin, Jay, Thomas Jefferson, and Henry Laurens. At the same time, a new commission was issued instructing all of them to accept "in concurrence with His Most Christian Majesty" the mediation proposals of Russia and Germany. To accompany the commission, Congress drew up a series of instructions, the significant points of which directed the commissioners 1) to regard as no more than the "desires" of Congress the earlier instructions sent to Adams concerning American *demands* for territorial and fishing arrangements in any treaty of peace, and to avoid any "absolute and peremptory Directions" on these matters; 2) to make "the most candid and confidential communication upon all subjects" to the French ministry, undertaking nothing in the negotiations without the ministry's "knowledge and concurrence," and "ultimately" to govern themselves by the ministry's "advice and opinion"; and 3) to agree to a truce "or to make such other concessions" as did not affect Congress's two *sine qua non*

[35] *Ibid.*, p. 564.
[36] Congress to Adams, January 10, 1781: Wharton, ed., *Revolutionary Diplomatic Correspondence*, IV, 229.

(American independence and the sanctity of all Franco-American treaties), providing only that Britain not be left in possession of any part of the United States.[37] Several days later Congress acted once more, this time to cancel Adams' commission for a commercial treaty with Britain.[38]

When news of the changes reached Adams in the fall, he was dismayed. Congress seemed willingly to have placed itself and America's future under French control. He had warned constantly against this very thing; he had labored tirelessly to keep America from compromising its independence, yet his efforts seemed to have been in vain.

Whatever the causes of Congress's action—and Adams clearly did not fully comprehend the difficulties Congress at that moment faced—he was justified in criticizing the departures Congress had made from their earlier positions. Instead of any longer rejecting the concept of a long-term truce, Congress now put the commissioners at liberty to agree to any truce and to make such "other concessions" as were necessary, demanding only that the ultimate goal of independence be maintained.[39] Again, Congress dropped as essential points of negotiation its insistence upon compensation for private American property wantonly destroyed by the British, and upon certain specifically described boundary lines, explaining that these now represented only the "desires" of Congress.[40] Moreover, Congress specifically directed their commissioners "ultimately" to gov-

---

[37] "Instructions for the Commissioners for Peace": *Ibid.*, pp. 504-505.

[38] Ford, ed., *op.cit.*, XX, 746-47. Adams heard of the decision in a letter of July 21 from James Lovell. Lovell to Adams, July 21, 1781: *Works*, VII, 453.

[39] Resolution of Congress, October 18, 1780: Wharton, ed., *Revolutionary Diplomatic Correspondence*, IV, 100-101, 505.

[40] Resolution of Congress, October 18, 1780: *Ibid.*, pp. 100-101. Instructions to the Commissioners, June 15, 1781: *Ibid.*, pp. 504-505.

ern their actions by the "advice and opinion" of the French foreign minister. To Adams, this was the most disturbing development of all. To Arthur Lee, Adams expressed disbelief that Congress would chain itself to a foreign power.[41] It would be a "humiliation that would astonish all the World," he later commented to James Warren, if the world knew that Congress had instructed their commissioners to obey French officials.[42]

Not only did Adams judge Congress's action a grave dereliction of responsibility, he regarded the changes in their diplomatic arrangements as a direct attack upon him. The additions to his peace commission he found embarrassing enough, though he acknowledged to Edmund Jennings that there might be some value in the move. (Negotiations conducted by representatives from several states, he thought, would be more likely to gain approval.)[43] And he was somewhat assuaged by being placed first in rank among the commissioners. The more he considered his situation, however, the more dissatisfied he became with it. "I am weary, disgusted, affronted, and disappointed," he confided to his Diary. "I have been injured, and my Country has joined in the Injury. It has basely prostituted its own honour by sacrificing mine."[44] Congress had been "plaid upon like Children, trifled with, imposed upon, deceived."[45] Did Congress no longer give consideration to the individuals who served them best? A triumph, he declared extravagantly, had been given "to Wrong against Right, to Vice against Virtue, to Folly against Wisdom to Servility against In-

[41] Adams to Arthur Lee, October 10, 1782: Adams Microfilm, Reel 107.

[42] Adams to James Warren, April 16, 1783: "Warren-Adams Letters," LXXIII, 214.

[43] Adams to Edmund Jennings, October 9, 1781: Adams Microfilm, Reel 355.

[44] Diary, February 18, 1783: *Diary and Autobiography*, III, 108.

[45] Diary, May 2, 1783: *Ibid.*, p. 118.

dependence, to base and vile Intrigue against inflexible Honour and Integrity."[46]

Vergennes and Franklin, Adams was convinced, had been the architects of the plot; the first because of Adams' intrepid independence of spirit and the second out of "base Jealousy ... and ... sordid Envy" of Adams' two commissions. Franklin, Adams declared, had committed "an assassination upon my Character."[47] (His feelings were not helped out by the fact that he first heard of the changes from Franklin rather than directly from Congress.) Because there had not been more men of honor in Congress to defend him, Adams had been discomfited, left "under a fearful looking for of Judgment" from Philadelphia.

By the cancellation of his commission for a commercial treaty with Britain, he had once again been left dangling before all Europe, with no reason given except the implied one of Congressional disapproval. Did the Congress intend by this that he should resign all his commissions, he demanded angrily of Abigail? The thought of doing so was not entirely displeasing. The revocation of his commercial mission had been "an affront to me and a Stain upon my Character." He would not wear it "one moment longer," he warned, than was "indispensably necessary for the public Good."[48] He had certainly never asked to come to Europe, to leave behind his wife and family and friends, and an increasingly lucrative profession. At great sacrifice he had done so; and yet repeated wrongs had been his only reward.[49]

Knowing full well what Adams' reaction would be, James Lovell wrote from Congress assuring him that his difficulties arose from Congressional folly, not animosity.

[46] Adams to Abigail Adams, July 1, 1782: Adams Microfilm, Reel 357.

[47] Adams to Edmund Jennings, July 20, 1782: *Ibid.*

[48] Adams to Abigail Adams, February 4, 1783: *Ibid.*, Reel 360. Adams to Abigail Adams, February 27, 1783: *Ibid.*

[49] Adams to Abigail Adams, July 1, 1782: *Ibid.*, Reel 357.

No dishonor had been intended, Lovell insisted; the changes, however ill-judged, had been matters of policy, not politics.[50] Adams was not convinced. "When a Man sees entrusted to him the most essential Interests of his Country," he observed righteously, "sees that they depend essentially upon him, and that he must defend them against the Malice of Enemies, the Finesse of Allies, the Treachery of a Colleague, and sees that he is not to be supported even by his Employers," it was "enough to poison the Life of a Man in its most secret Sources."[51]

In several other ways, as well, Adams' experience during the 1780's persuaded him of America's change. One involved the pressing need for European loans during the Revolution and the years immediately following. Because of his initial success with the Dutch bankers in 1782, Adams remained one of Congress's primary agents for securing further badly needed credits. Throughout 1783 and 1784, Congress bothered him continually with reports of America's dire financial condition. Adams accordingly turned again to the Dutch financial interests. He soon found out, however, that before granting further loans, the bankers insisted upon evidence that Congress intended to pay back the first ones. Yet neither Congress nor the states seemed willing to set their houses in order and make provision for meeting their existing responsibilities. Adams thus found himself caught in the middle between a demanding Congress on the one side and reluctant Dutch bankers on the other. And because he was in the middle, he bore the brunt of both their complaints.

From home, James Warren, James Lovell, Tristram Dalton and others reported Congress's sad financial plight. Dalton wrote Adams in December of 1783 that

[50] James Lovell to Adams, July 2 and 21, 1781: *Ibid.*, Reel 355.
[51] Adams to James Warren, April 9, 1783: "Warren-Adams Letters," LXXIII, 206.

the states were refusing to provide for the public treasury and that as a consequence Congress found itself unable to meet its obligations.[52] Alexander McDougall wrote about the same time warning that the people seemed indifferent to the public credit, upon which, McDougall warned, hung the very continuation of American independence.[53]

Adams responded angrily to the reports of financial disrepair and to the exhortations he received to do something about it. The people, he insisted, must meet their obligations. By not providing for payment of their debts, they were breaking faith with other nations as well as themselves. Had they forgotten every principle of private and public honesty, he wondered? Americans had to become strictly honest, he affirmed to Cotton Tufts, before they could claim the confidence of anyone either at home or abroad.[54] They were fully capable of providing for their needs. This made their failure all the worse. Their resources were adequate if they would but discipline themselves and set themselves to the task of financial repair.[55] The first step was for Congress to remedy the depreciation of the continental currency. The cry for more paper money, Adams insisted, was downright wickedness and dishonesty. Never would faith in America's word be restored as long as such "Systems of Villainy" were continued.[56] The only way to get the economy going effectively and to restore a sense of public honesty, was to stop the issue of paper money, tax the people heavily, and use the funds to pay off existing obligations.[57] The conduct of Americans in both Congress and the states, Adams lamented to Elbridge Ger-

[52] Tristram Dalton to Adams, December 5, 1783: Adams Microfilm, Reel 362.
[53] Alexander McDougall to Adams, November 29, 1783: *Ibid.*
[54] Adams to Cotton Tufts, July 4, 1786: *Ibid.*
[55] Adams to Cotton Tufts, March 23, 1786: *Ibid.*
[56] Adams to Richard Cranch, July 4, 1786: *Ibid.*
[57] Adams to James Warren, July 4, 1786: *Ibid.*

ry, "discovers a Depravity of Heart that I could scarcely have believed, of so many to their disgrace."[58] Until public credit was restored, Adams explained, his own efforts to contract further loans would prove futile. Much to his disgust, he was repeatedly forced throughout the remainder of his stay abroad to arrange stop-gap measures just to provide interest payments on previous loans.[59]

Another experience that revealed to Adams alarming tendencies in American society, involved his efforts to secure a commercial treaty with England. The only way that his honor might be restored after his troubles in 1781, he had insisted, was to be appointed first American ambassador to the Court of St. James. In February of 1785, Congress proffered him the nomination. (Not, however, until after heated debate and a certain amount of his own embarrassed maneuvering.)[60] When news of the appointment arrived, he set out from the continent armed with instructions to smooth relations between the two nations, and a commission to negotiate if possible a treaty of commerce. Difficulties began immediately upon his arrival. From Crown and court, he received a studiously correct but cool reception. He was treated with "dry decency and cold civility," he informed John Jay. This had been "the premeditated plan from the beginning. . . ."[61] Unofficially, his greeting was even less enthusiastic. Refugee Tories labored to arouse feeling against him, and much of the press handled him roughly. "There is a general Disposition," he reported sourly, "to prevent any American character and Work from

---

[58] Adams to Elbridge Gerry, December 13, 1785: *Ibid.*

[59] Page Smith, *John Adams*, II, 616-17, 708, 709, 727-30.

[60] Adams to Abigail Adams, February 4, 1783: Adams Microfilm, Reel 360. Adams to Abigail Adams, February 27, 1783: *Ibid.* Adams' satisfaction at the appointment was marred by both developments. Adams to Elbridge Gerry, May 2, 1785: *Ibid.*, Reel 364.

[61] Adams to John Jay, February 14, 1788: *Works*, VIII, 476.

acquiring Celebration."[62] Apart from several leading Whigs such as Joseph Priestley, Adams developed few personal friends. There were but "four or five Persons" with whom he could hold friendly intercourse, he complained to Thomas Jefferson; he was "not at home in this Country."[63]

More importantly, his commercial mission met with complete frustration. This in itself was disturbing enough. Yet he found himself blamed for accomplishing nothing when, as he protested, his failure was not at all his fault. The responsibility for his ineffectiveness, he rapidly concluded, lay with Congress and the states. As American representative, he suffered embarrassments because of their follies, yet they turned around and accused him of inattention to duty.

Adams quickly realized that there was no real chance for a commercial treaty. He would be able to do nothing, he commented irritably to Jay; his communications to the court would not even be answered. "In Short, Sir, I am Like to be as insignificant here as you can imagine."[64] In part, he attributed this to prevailing commercial conditions. English merchants, he explained, were understandably reluctant to make concessions when they already commanded so much of American trade.

Yet the real problem, he soon concluded, was not British intransigence, but the irresponsibility of the

[62] Jonathan Sewall to a friend, 1787: *Ibid.*, I, 58n. Adams to Dr. Williams, June 3, 1786: Adams Microfilm, Reel 113. The London *Public Advertiser* greeted Adams as "His Excellency John Adams (honest John Adams), the Ambassador of America. . . . An ambassador from America! Good heavens, what a sound! The Gazette surely never announced anything so extraordinary before. . . . This will be such a phenomenon in the *corps diplomatique* that 'tis hard to say which can excite indignation most, the insolence of those who appoint the character, or the meanness of those who receive it." Page Smith, *John Adams*, II, 627.

[63] Adams to Thomas Jefferson, March 1, 1787: Cappon, ed., *Adams-Jefferson Letters*, I, 177.

[64] Adams to John Jay, January 4, 1786: Adams Microfilm, Reel 112. Adams to John Jay, December 3, 1785: *Ibid.*

American states. Their inability to stand up to Britain, to cooperate in commercial measures that would force an agreement upon her he identified as the true source of America's difficulties. From America, Adams heard frequently of the troubles caused by the absence of effective commercial regulation. Merchants, warned Richard Cranch, were suffering severely. Gold was being drained off to pay for British shipping and goods and the resultant scarcity of specie was causing a decline in the prices of land and stock and an increase in land forfeitures. Firmer control over America's commercial affairs, Cranch warned, was urgently needed.[65]

Adams heard with some satisfaction that various states were making efforts to meet the need by laying their own embargoes and tariffs. Given the different interests of the states, however, cooperation was difficult, especially between north and south. The result was that people turned more and more to Congress for direction.[66] In February of 1781, Congress passed a general impost on British goods. For a few months the situation seemed to improve, as, one by one, the states agreed to the plan. Ultimately, however, with several of the states restive under it and New York holding out altogether, the scheme collapsed. Gradually, Massachusetts and other states withdrew their earlier ratification and, in an effort to regain British trade, even dropped their own restrictions.

Adams watched the situation with dismay. He approved of the state navigation acts, hoping that these alone would be sufficient. Increasingly, however, he came to see the need for a continental impost; and though he expressed some concern about giving the Congress substantial new powers, he soon concluded that Congressional action was necessary.[67] Forceful action had to be

---

[65] Richard Cranch to Adams, October 13, 1785: *Ibid.*, Reel 366.
[66] Rufus King to Adams, November 2, 1785: *Ibid.*
[67] Adams to Richard Cranch, April 9, 1784: *Ibid.*, Reel 362.

taken against the commercial restrictions of England. America could have no recourse, he maintained, but in a navigation act of her own. There would never be a commercial treaty until the states banded together and forced England to make concessions.[68]

Americans, however, seemed blind to the situation. Merchants deviled him with tales of their hardships and called upon him to do something for their relief.[69] In response, Adams protested that he was helpless until they were ready to take control of their own affairs and fight back. His own involvement in the situation made him sensitive to the states' inability to join in defending their interests. And their failure he found appalling.[70]

A final index of America's condition, Adams found in the argument between Congress and the English over fulfillment of the peace treaty of 1783. Upon Adams' appointment as American minister to St. James, Congress informed him that they were concerned about England's failure to live up to certain of the treaty agreements, namely: evacuation of the western posts, return of "stolen" Negroes, and restitution for other American property wantonly destroyed during the Revolution. Adams was to confer with the English ministry and secure immediate compliance with their obligations.

Upon his arrival, Adams informed Lord Carmarthen, the British foreign secretary, of his instructions. In reply, Carmarthen told Adams in no uncertain terms that Britain would give no satisfaction to American complaints until the United States also fulfilled their agreements; that is, until they allowed the return of Tories and the recovery in sterling money of bona fide debts contracted before the Revolution.[71] Adams suspected at first

[68] Adams to Cotton Tufts, March 11, 1786: *Ibid.*, Reel 113. Adams to Tristram Dalton, May 26, 1786: *Ibid.*

[69] Stephen Higginson to Adams, August 8, 1785: *Ibid.*, Reel 365.

[70] Adams to James Bowdoin, May 9, 1786: *Ibid.* Adams to Stephen Higginson, February 18, 1786: *Ibid.*

[71] Carmarthen to Adams, February 28, 1786: *Ibid.*, Reel 367. See

that Carmarthen's countercharges were largely an excuse for Britain's doing what she intended to do anyway: retain possession of the posts. Yet it rapidly became clear to Adams that there was no chance of agreement until America fulfilled her part of the treaty. Because Britain defaulted on her obligations was no reason America should do likewise.

From the spring of 1786 on, Adams wrote home belaboring both Congress and the states for their failure to abide fully by the treaty. The various state laws against the collection of British-held debts, he declared, constituted "a direct Breach" of the treaty agreement. In all probability, he continued, turning his attention increasingly from British to American failures, the state laws had "prevented the evacuation of the Posts . . . the payment for the Negroes and even a treaty of Commerce. . . ." He found it difficult, he confessed to Cotton Tufts, to believe that his own state by its restrictions against British debts meant to betray the public faith. Yet Massachusetts was one of the offenders. Even setting aside matters of honor, it was bad policy to persecute the Tories; for this alone gave them influence in Britain and gave the British government an excuse to retain possession of the western posts and frustrate the collection of American claims. Adams longed to see his countrymen acting as if they felt their own greatness—that is, with dignity, generosity, and spirit—not as if guided by little prejudices. Americans had too long trifled with the public faith. They should repeal at once every law at odds with the peace treaty, and then demand Britain's fulfillment of her side of the agreement. Until this was done, he explained, he would "labour in vain."[72]

H. C. Allen, *Great Britain and the United States* (New York, 1955), p. 269ff.

[72] Adams to Cotton Tufts, May 26, 1786: Adams Microfilm, Reel 113. Adams to Samuel Austin, May 25, 1786: *Ibid.* Adams to John Jay, May 25, 1786: *Ibid.*, Reel 112.

In this matter also, the people seemed not to recognize either their own failures or the impossible position they put him in. They expected him to do something to secure agreements, he observed to Samuel Austin, yet failed to provide the means of doing it. Why did Congress not realize this, and at least stop harping upon his ineffectiveness? Were his dispatches, he wondered, being kept secret so he might be blamed for the faults of others?[73] "High Language" from him to the British Court, he warned, would not work. It would meet only contemptuous silence. Britain was in too strong a position and America too weak. No step he could take would have any effect. Congress and the states must act first: to regulate effectively their own commerce, support their finances, and fulfill their treaty engagements. Only by forcing Britain to respect the United States, could a meaningful agreement be reached. It had been his lot, he complained to Elbridge Gerry, to be expected to make brick without straw. "A more disagreeable situation," no man had ever experienced.[74]

On February 3, 1787, Adams sent a letter to John Jay explaining his desire to return home the following year. "A life so useless to the public, and so insipid to myself, as mine is in Europe," he declared, "has become a burden to me, as well as to my countrymen." He would sail by the first convenient ship in the spring a year hence, unless Congress should see fit to recall him sooner—an eventuality, he confessed to Jay, he would find quite satisfactory. It was important, he urged in conclusion, "that arrangements should be made as early as possible. . . ."[75] After a substantial delay, he finally received Congressional approval of his decision to return home.[76] He still had one

[73] Adams to Samuel Austin, May 25, 1786: *Ibid.*, Reel 113.

[74] Adams to Elbridge Gerry, May 24, 1786: *Ibid.* Adams to Mercy Warren, May 24, 1786: *Ibid.*

[75] Adams to John Jay, February 3, 1787: *Works*, VIII, 429.

[76] Congress voted to relieve Adams of his commissions on October 5, 1787. Ford, ed., *Journals of the Continental Congress*, XXXIII, 612-

final inconvenience, however, to endure. Congress failed to include in its communication a formal letter of recall from his post in the Netherlands. Much to his irritation, he had to make a trip to The Hague in the midst of winter to take personal leave.[77] At last, in April of 1788, he set sail with Abigail for America.

Adams carried back with him a set of attitudes toward American society considerably different from those with which he had set out a decade or so before.

In the failure of the American people to maintain their independence from French influence, to set their economic affairs in order, to band together and compel Britain to respect them, and to continue the orderly regulation of their society, he saw evidence of a disturbing decline in public morality. He began to doubt whether he could any longer assume so confidently that Americans were capable of popular self-government. Reports from home had reinforced his own observations. In June of 1786, John Jay had lamented to him that the American people were too much interested in private gain and too little concerned with their public responsibilities.[78] And from James Warren, Adams had received frequent complaints about the "total change in Principles, and Manners" among the people. In spite of Warren's known exaggerations, his comments gave Adams pause.[79] Rumors of the dissolution of the Confederation had flooded in upon Adams. Jay warned of Congress's weakening condition.[80] Arthur Lee told of a growing rage for emigration to the new territories beyond the mountains, and the absence of careful consideration of the political con-

---

13. Jay's letter informing Adams of the decision arrived in London in mid-December.

[77] Adams to John Jay, February 6, 1788: Adams Microfilm, Reel 112. Abigail Adams to Thomas Jefferson, February 26, 1788: Cappon, ed., *Adams-Jefferson Letters*, I, 227.

[78] John Jay to Adams, June 6, 1786: Adams Microfilm, Reel 368.

[79] James Warren to Adams, October 22, 1786: *Ibid.*, Reel 369.

[80] John Jay to Adams, October 14, 1785: *Ibid.*, Reel 366.

sequences.[81] Various sections of the country, Tristram Dalton had reported in alarm, including the territories of Franklin and Kentucky and even Vermont and Maine, were threatening to declare themselves independent.[82] From James Sullivan, Adams heard about Tory merchants in Maine forming close ties with Nova Scotia and refusing to pay commercial duties to Massachusetts.[83] Rufus King had written grumblingly that if the southern states did not better cooperate in a system of joint commercial regulation, the northern and eastern states would form "a sub confederation" to remedy their own embarrassments.[84] Public virtue seemed no longer to characterize the behavior of the American people. And Adams' own observations as American representative in France and England, as we have seen, provided strong evidence that the reports were essentially true. Secondly, his growing doubts about the American people were reinforced by his own unhappy experience. In his anger over his mistreatment, he tended to develop a simple equation between his personal interest and the well-being of American society. "The Honour the Dignity and the future Safety of the United States," he declared extravagantly in soliciting appointment to the British court, were involved in his nomination.[85] When he suffered embarrassment, the American interest suffered as well. A society, moreover, which cared so little about its virtuous servants could hardly any longer be characterized by virtuous sentiments itself. Among Americans, Adams protested, virtue seemed less and less esteemed. Only ambition and intrigue any longer promised success (he obviously had Franklin in mind); "greatness" was

[81] Arthur Lee to Adams, March 6, 1785: *Ibid.*, Reel 364.
[82] Tristram Dalton to Adams, October 18, 1785: *Ibid.*, Reel 366.
[83] James Sullivan to Adams, October 24, 1785: *Ibid.*
[84] Rufus King to Adams, November 2, 1785: *Ibid.*
[85] Adams to Abigail Adams, February 4, 1783: *Ibid.*, Reel 360. Adams to Abigail Adams, February 27, 1783: *Ibid.*

now obtainable by "little Tricks and low Devices."[86] Perhaps most importantly of all, his unhappy experiences abroad, his dissatisfaction with the treatment accorded him by Congress, his growing uncertainty about his relationship with the American people—he could serve no country with dishonor, he protested to Edmund Jennings—predisposed him to accept the lesson taught by his own observations and the warnings from home: that there had been a declension in the moral character of the American people and the effective cohesion of American society.[87] The difficulties this raised for problems of social regulation were many and severe.

[86] Adams to Edmund Jennings, May 22, 1779: *Ibid.*, Reel 350.
[87] Adams to Edmund Jennings, May 4, 1779: *Ibid.*

Chapter V. "Disaggregation"

Adams began the systematic reevaluation of American society and of the American political order during the last part of his stay abroad and continued it through the first years after his return. (He reached Boston finally in the spring of 1788.) His ideas were contained in his second major body of political writings: the three-volume *Defense of the Constitutions of Government of the United States* (1787-1788), the "Discourses on Davila" (1790), and his personal correspondence with Samuel Adams, Roger Sherman, and others.

Again, Adams drew upon his understanding of the cyclical theory of historical change to provide context for his analysis of the new developments in American society.

The cyclical view of history which Adams had used as a framework within which to arrange the events of the Revolution had postulated the rise and fall of successive political empires. History demonstrated that in the past each empire had risen to a position of supremacy, achieved maturity, and then begun a course of decline. Theory postulated as well that every future empire would do the same. The process was irresistible; each nation must pass through a cycle of birth, youth, maturity, old age, and death. In any given case, the pace of development might be extended somewhat by prudent action or foreshortened by folly, but ultimately each nation was destined to pursue the same course.

As he examined America's condition around 1790, Adams concluded that she was moving rapidly through her cycle of development. Logically, Adams had from the first been forced to assume that America could not escape her common fate. Yet because of her special situation—established on a broad, rich continent, inhabited by a peculiarly virtuous people, and removed physically from European corruptions—he had expected that America's course of development would be slow. Now, however, he found evidence that she was rushing ahead faster than he had anticipated. America seemed, in fact, to be already moving toward social maturity. The process was not yet complete; even in his gloomiest moments Adams acknowledged this. The tendency, however, was unmistakable. It remained but for history to play out its inexorable course.

Adams found visible signs of America's development all about him. There was the rapid growth of population. From 1754 to 1790, the thirteen original states increased from about one and one half to over three million people, leaving aside the settlers in areas not yet admitted to the union.[1] Adams watched the expansion of American society with wonderment. Every prospect, he remarked in late 1786, was that at a time not very distant, America would have "a hundred millions of inhabitants. . . ."[2] Already the states individually had become "large and populous nations. . . ." Even over the past decade, during an "impoverishing and destructive war," Americans had increased rapidly in number.[3] Adams found pleasure in contemplating the fact, yet he was aware of the difficult problem of regulation posed by this growth. Such "enormous Masses of Mankind," he advised grimly, were not easily to be managed. Looking back upon the trials of the Revolution, he found it fortunate that the separation from England had come when it did, before a large and heterogeneous population had developed. With added millions of people, the continent might easi-

[1] E. B. Greene and V. P. Harrington, *American Population before the Federal Census of 1790* (New York, 1932), pp. 3-8.

[2] "Defense": *Works*, IV, 587. Adams to Matthew Robinson, March 4, 1786: Adams Microfilm, Reel 113.

[3] "Defense": *Works*, IV, 387. Adams to Matthew Robinson, March 4, 1786: Adams Microfilm, Reel 113.

ly have crumbled into twenty warring divisions. By
1786, the American states contained more people than
any other nation that had ever experimented with popular government; and they were growing every day more
"disproportionate"—more diverse and less capable of being held together by simple governments. Countries that
increased as rapidly as the states of America, Adams concluded, "are not to be long bound with silken threads;
lions, young or old, will not be bound by cobwebs."[4] History had demonstrated that with increased numbers the
problem of regulation grew as well, that popular governments could thrive only where population was sparse.
The implications of this for American society were obvious.

Even more significant as an index of social development, was the rate of economic growth. By the mid-
1780's, the American states had begun a general economic recovery from the dislocations of trade and agriculture caused by the war.[5] By 1789, commerce and ship-
building were reviving as trade routes opened again. As
a result of poor European harvests, there was a large
demand for American agricultural products. Signs of returning prosperity were numerous. By 1789, three new
bridges were under construction in Massachusetts; a
Potomac canal had been begun; and American merchantmen were again sailing to the East Indies and on
to China. From 1790 to 1795, the per capita circulation
of money rose from $3.00 to $7.77.[6] During the first
years of the 1790's, Hamilton's financial program speed-
ed the movement toward recovery. "Since the federal
constitution has removed all danger of our having a paper tender," observed one Philadelphia newspaper in
1789, "our trade is advancing fifty per cent. . . . Our

[4] "Defense": *Works*, IV, 287.
[5] Merrill Jensen, *The New Nation* (New York, 1950), pp. 194-
234.
[6] Dauer, *The Adams Federalists*, p. 73.

monied people can trust their cash abroad, and have brought their coin into circulation."[7]

Adams was by no means opposed to America's economic growth. Throughout the 1780's, he had urged the states to expand their commerce and manufacturing in order to make themselves economically independent of Europe. He was aware, in addition, that an active economy was essential if America was to repay her Revolutionary debts. Constantly he urged thrift and industry upon the American people. Yet he had misgivings about the consequences of economic development if carried too far, too fast. Both trade and manufacturing created wealth, and wealth tended inevitably to corrupt republican society.

The increase of wealth, moreover, not only fostered the decay of republican virtue, but tended to divide society into two great interests set off economically and therefore socially and politically against each other. Here again, Adams' historical theory put the issue in perspective. According to theory, youthful societies were simple in structure, egalitarian in nature. Maturing societies, however, were characterized both by greater numbers and greater wealth, and the wealth tended to become concentrated in the hands of a few. As a consequence, the society became increasingly disparate. Characterized no longer by a great middle grouping of independent yeomen, but by extremes of wealth, it lost social cohesion. Adams' word for the process was "disaggregation." From the late 1780's on, he began to describe America increasingly in these terms.

The two groups into which Adams believed American society was settling, he described variously as the few and the many, the gentlemen and the commonalty, the "haves" and the "have-nots"—but most often as the aristocracy and the democracy. The distinguishing criteria

[7] *Pennsylvania Gazette*, December 16, 1789.

between the two were several; but the most important was wealth.

Throughout his life, Adams had recognized the philosophical arguments for a "natural aristocracy." Even before the Revolution, when he was so impressed with the egalitarianism of American society, he had acknowledged the legitimate preeminence of certain individuals. Sometime around 1760 he copied into his literary notebook the observation that "although there is a moral and political and a natural Equality among Mankind, all being born free and equal, Yet there are other Inequalities which are equally natural. Such as Strength, Activity, Industry, Genius, Talents, Virtues, Benevolence."[8] Certain persons, he had affirmed, were clearly more competent to lead and should be listened to. He had counted himself one of them. From the Continental Congress, he had urged his friends in Massachusetts to see that able and experienced men were chosen to public office. Adams acknowledged that in most states a relatively few families displaying special talents had monopolized public office. Even in Massachusetts, the people had returned a select number of individuals year after year to positions of leadership. At times, he confessed, he thought this went too far. The people had gotten into trouble by placing their trust too uncritically in the names of Oliver and Hutchinson. But there had been a select number of families—Winthrops, Sewalls, Warrens, and others—who had served Massachusetts with particular distinction.

In the "Defense," Adams went further in describing the natural sources of aristocracy in every society. There must always be superiors and inferiors, he explained, "because God has laid in the constitution and course of nature the foundations of the distinction."[9] Moral and

---

[8] "Literary Notes and Papers": Adams Microfilm, Reel 118.

[9] "Defense": Works, IV, 427. Adams to T. B. Hollis, June 11, 1790: Adams Microfilm, Reel 115.

political equality Adams always stood ready to admit and defend; equality of ability, however, was another matter. "It is only in point of rights," he observed, "that men are born or created either equal or independent."[10] This was true even in America. Here as well there were "great inequalities of merit, or talents, virtues, services, and what is of more moment, very often of reputation." Sources of inequality were "common to every people" and could "never be altered by any," because they were "founded in the constitution of nature." In support of his argument, he cited writers from Theognis to Bolingbroke.[11]

In writing of an American aristocracy, Adams insisted that he was not referring to formalized class distinctions or privileges sanctioned by law. These could be found in Europe; in America the process had not gone so far. "You seem to think aristocracy consists altogether in artificial titles . . . garters, ribbons . . . exclusive privileges, hereditary descents, established by kings or by positive laws of society," Adams protested to John Taylor. "No such thing! Aristocracy was, from the beginning . . . and ever will be . . . independent of all these artificial regulations."[12] This observation was given in 1814, but it represented his thinking around 1790 as well.

What constituted aristocracy in Adams' sense of the word was not special privilege, but influence gained from certain "talents." Influence—this was the key word in his definition. Inequalities of influence created and established by civil laws, might be said to constitute an

[10] Adams' marginal comments in his copy of Gabriel Bonnot de Mably's *de la Legislation*, pp. 68, 69: Adams Collection, Boston Public Library. Also Adams' marginalia in his copy of Rousseau's *Discourse sur l'Inegalite*, p. 73: Adams Collection, Boston Public Library.

[11] "Defense": *Works*, IV, 397, 411-12, 413-14. There was, of course, a theoretical basis for the doctrine of human inequality in the Chain of Being rationale. Adams knew of it, though he never wrote much about it. "Defense": *Ibid.*, VI, 285.

[12] Adams to John Taylor, 1814: *Ibid.*, 457.

"artificial" aristocracy. These, however, were not the sort of distinctions that Adams had in mind. He differentiated between them and the "natural" aristocracy based upon "those superiorities of influence . . . which grow out of the constitution of human nature."[13]

The sources of influence were many: wealth, family name, reputation, virtue, intelligence, even beauty or physical strength. Inequalities in any one of these might give one person an advantage over another. For this reason, they could all legitimately be used as indices of natural aristocracy. Jefferson later agreed with Adams that aristocracy, at least in terms of American society, might be defined broadly as influence. But he affirmed that to be "natural," it must be based upon either talents or virtue, and that all other forms of influence should be suppressed. Adams thought Jefferson's definition unrealistic. Every aristocracy, Adams agreed, was based upon "talents." But "Education, Wealth, Strength, Beauty, Stature, Birth, Marriage, graceful Attributes and Motions, Gait, Air, Complexion, Physiognomy" were talents as well as virtue or learning. Any one of these that in fact commanded influence in society gave to the man who possessed it the character of an aristocrat in Adams' sense of the word.[14]

In its most important sense, aristocracy meant the ability to influence someone else's vote. By an aristocrat, Adams explained, he meant anyone who by any means could "command or influence *two votes; one besides his own*."[15] In America's republican society, this was the focus of aristocratic influence.

If Adams thought in terms of an American leadership aristocracy throughout his life, however, he described

[13] "Defense": *Ibid.*, 451.

[14] Adams to Thomas Jefferson, November 15, 1813: Cappon, ed., *Adams-Jefferson Letters*, II, 398. "Defense": *Works*, IV, 391-92.

[15] Adams to John Taylor, 1814: *Ibid.*, VI, 456. Adams to John Taylor, June 4, 1814(?): Washburn Papers, Massachusetts Historical Society.

it in significantly different terms during the late 1780's and 1790's than he had in the decades preceding. Before, he had never identified the natural aristocracy as a distinct faction, with interests separate from the rest of society. The elite had embodied values which all the people held dear. Now, however, he did describe the aristocracy as a separate body, one opposed to another interest which he called the democracy, and bent upon its own selfish advantage.

Moreover, he had originally believed that in American society influence in practice attached to individuals possessing such talents as intelligence and exemplary virtue. This had been the reason why even in his most egalitarian days he had looked with favor upon the election and reelection to office of a select group of individuals. By the mid-1780's, however, Adams perceived that influence seemed to be gathering in the hands of individuals who could make no legitimate claim to leadership; whose prominence was based not upon virtue or ability, but wealth and family name alone. Philosophy might equate aristocracy with "The Wise and Good," he announced to Jefferson; but the world identified them by their practice—the rich and the wellborn.[16] This was the conclusion at which Adams arrived after 1786.

Certain families seemed to be taking great pains to trace back their ancestral lines and make ostentatious claims of their descent. There arose, he thought, "a more general anxiety to know their originals . . . from the easier circumstances and higher spirit of the common people."[17] And all the while, the people seemed ready to accord certain individuals whatever honors they claimed.

Increasingly important as a basis of aristocratic influence, Adams believed, was the factor of wealth. He feared, as we have seen, not only that wealth was grow-

[16] Adams to Thomas Jefferson, September 2, 1813: Cappon, ed, *Adams-Jefferson Letters*, II, 371.
[17] "Defense": *Works*, IV, 395. *ibid.*, VI, 236.

ing in American society, but that it was gathering in the hands of a small part of the population. American society did not yet manifest the great economic distinctions of European societies, yet Adams believed that the movement toward economic inequality in America was gaining momentum. As evidence, he cited the accelerating rush of speculation both in land and securities that occurred during the 1780's. In the "Defense," he complained repeatedly of the prevailing mania for land, warning that America would face real danger when great quantities of it came to be held by a few people.[18] "Paper wealth has been a source of aristocracy in this country, as well as landed wealth, with a vengeance," he later recalled to John Taylor. "Witness the immense fortunes made *per saltum* by aristocratical speculations, both in land and paper."[19]

Most significantly the concentration of wealth meant consolidation of social and political power. From Harrington, Adams copied into his "Defense": "Men are hung upon riches; not of choice . . . but of necessity, and by the teeth. Forasmuch as he who wants bread, is his servant that will feed him. . . ." A noble discovery, Adams thought. If this balance between property and power was not the foundation of all politics, it was of so much importance that no man could be a master of the subject without having well considered it.[20] Property was thus "a natural and unavoidable" cause of aristocracy.[21] During the 1770's, Adams had assumed the broad distribution of property within American society. Now, however, new men of wealth were appearing, men who readily transposed their economic power into political influence.[22]

[18] *Ibid.*, IV, 359.
[19] Adams to John Taylor, 1814: *Ibid.*, VI, 508.
[20] "Defense": *Ibid.*, IV, 427, 428.
[21] Adams to John Taylor, 1814: *Ibid.*, VI, 512.
[22] More study needs to be done on the redistribution of wealth in the states during the Revolution and the 1780's, and its effects

Adams did not always describe the differences between the aristocratical and democratical elements of society solely in economic terms. We have seen that he recognized the importance of family name. And at times he used the terms "gentlemen" and "simplemen" to signify social differences. By the former, he explained at one place in the "Defense," he meant not "the rich or the poor, the high-born or the low-born," but "all . . . who have received a liberal education." By "simplemen," he meant "laborers, husbandmen, mechanics, and merchants in general" who pursued their occupations without any knowledge in "liberal arts or sciences. . . ."[23] When Adams used the terms "aristocracy" and "democracy," however, it was most often in terms of economic differences. Even education he acknowledged as usually the prerogative of the wealthy.[24] "It is wealth," he wrote simply, "that produces the inequality of conditions."[25] Wealth remained for him the touchstone of social division.

Adams described one other important attribute of a developing society besides the appearance of internal division. According to theory, one could expect to find definite correlations between the stages of an empire's growth and its moral condition. People still in the early stages

on the social and political structures. Some of the interesting possibilities of such an examination are suggested by a recent book on Newburyport, Massachusetts. Benjamin W. Labaree, *Patriots and Partisans, the Merchants of Newburyport, 1764-1815* (Cambridge, Massachusetts, 1962).

[23] "Defense": *Works*, VI, 185. It is curious that by the 1790's Adams regarded education as often a support of aristocracy ("there never can be, in any nation, more than one fifth—no, not one tenth of the men, regularly educated to science and letters"), whereas he had earlier regarded it as the great engine of equality. Adams to Taylor, December 26, 1814: *Ibid.*, p. 495.

[24] "Defense": *Ibid.*, p. 185.

[25] Zoltan Haraszti, *John Adams and the Prophets of Progress* (Cambridge, Massachusetts, 1952), p. 188.

of maturity were apt to be simple and thrifty, industrious and honest—in short, imbued with the private virtues which republican theory and Calvinist doctrine declared to be good. More than this, the citizens of a youthful nation could be expected to be concerned about society as a whole; even, if need be, at their own personal
expense. Young societies, simple both economically and
demographically, were held tightly together by a common adherence to social virtue. This, Adams had believed to be characteristic of America during the 1770's.

As a society developed, however, changes occurred in
its moral condition. People became more involved in
their own material interests and tended to ignore their
social responsibilities. Throughout history, every maturing society had experienced a gradual decline in public
virtue. David Tappan, Hollis Professor of Divinity in
Harvard College, spelled out the moral implications of
social maturity in an address of 1798. "Experience
proves," he declared,

> that political bodies, like the animal economy, have
> their periods of infancy, youth, maturity, decay,
> and dissolution. In the early stages of their existence
> their members are usually industrious and frugal,
> simple and hardy, united and brave. Their feeble,
> exposed, and necessitious [sic] condition in some
> sort forces upon them this conduct and these habits.
> The practice of these virtues gradually nourishes
> them to a state of manly vigor. They become ma-
> ture and flourishing in wealth and population, in
> arts and arms, in almost every kind of national pros-
> perity. But when they have reached a certain point
> of greatness, their prosperity inflates and debauches
> their minds. It betrays them into pride and avarice,
> luxury and dissipation, illness and sensuality, and
> too often into practical or scornful impiety. These,

with other kindred vices, hasten their downfall and ruin.[26]

As a nation grew in wealth and power, then, its moral strength declined. "The History of All Ages and Countries," Adams explained, "are uniform, that Luxury grows with Population Wealth and Prosperity."[27] And luxury was the cancer that destroyed republican moral fibre.

Adams faced a dilemma similar to one that had confronted his Puritan forebears. He urged Americans to apply themselves to the economic tasks of this world, yet he at the same time feared the material consequences of their endeavors. "Will you tell me how to prevent riches from becoming the effects of temperance and industry?" he asked Jefferson. "Will you tell me how to prevent riches from producing luxury? Will you tell me how to prevent luxury from producing effeminacy, intoxication, extravagance, Vice and folly?"[28] This was the problem Adams faced. Industry seemed incompatible with the equally important virtues of frugality and simplicity.

Adams was not an advocate of economic indigence for America. To expect the people to be long content under the stringent conditions imposed by the Revolution, he believed, was foolish. "The love of poverty" was "a fictitious virtue that never existed."[29] Such harsh discipline might be good for the character of the American people, but they loved commerce "with its conveniences and pleasures" too much to tolerate privation any longer than necessary.[30]

[26] Persons, *American Minds*, p. 125.

[27] Adams to John Watson, July 23, 1818: Adams Microfilm, Reel 123.

[28] Adams to Thomas Jefferson, December 21, 1819: Cappon, ed., *Adams-Jefferson Letters*, II, 551.

[29] "Defense": *Works*, V, 289.

[30] Adams to R. H. Lee, 1786: *Ibid.*, VIII, 374-76.

Luxury, Adams had warned while still abroad, had "as many and as bewitching charms" in America as in Europe.[31] Wealth alone, he recognized, made possible the enjoyment of many fine things: painting, beautiful homes, literature, and music. He had seen the truth of this in France, and anticipated something like it for America. His role, he explained to Abigail, was to study war and politics so that his sons might have liberty to study mathematics and philosophy, commerce and agriculture, and his grandsons the right to pursue painting and music, architecture and poetry.[32]

Yet wealth inevitably brought luxury, and luxury corrupted. "Luxury, wherever she goes," he had warned, "effaces from human nature the image of the Divinity."[33] It spurred the wealthy classes into a rage for material possessions, the marks of social status, and the poor into jealous dissatisfaction with their own lot. Adams' final conclusions about Europe had borne this out. In France, wealth provided the instrumentalities to "inform the understanding" and "refine the taste"; yet wealth served even more to "seduce, betray, deceive, deprave, corrupt and debauch" the heart.[34] The magnificence of France was a bagatelle, "introduced by time and luxury in exchange for the great qualities and hardy, manly virtues of the human heart."[35] Commerce, luxury, and avarice, he explained to Benjamin Rush later on, in 1808, destroyed every republican government.[36] The more wealth

[31] Adams to Abigail Adams, June 3, 1778: C. F. Adams, ed., *Familiar Letters*, p. 334.

[32] Adams to Abigail Adams, 1780: *Ibid.*, p. 381. See Wendell Garrett's illuminating discussion of "John Adams and the Limited Role of the Arts" in the *Winterthur Portfolio*, I (1964), 243-55.

[33] Adams to Abigail Adams, June 3, 1778: C. F. Adams, ed., *Familiar Letters*, p. 334.

[34] Adams to Abigail Adams, 1780: *Ibid.*, p. 380.

[35] Adams to Abigail Adams, April 12, 1778: *Ibid.*, pp. 329-30.

[36] Adams to Benjamin Rush, September 27, 1808: *Works*, IX, 602-603.

and elegance, the less virtue; this same formula held true in all times and places.

Throughout the 1780's, Adams warned America to avoid the mistakes of Europe. He had received frequent warnings from some of his more orthodox republican brethren, notably James and Mercy Warren and his cousin Samuel Adams, of the deplorable decline in American morality. "Money," James Warren had informed him gloomily in 1785, "is the only object attended to, and the only Acquisition that commands respect. Patriotism is ridiculed; Integrity and Ability are of little Consequence. . . . Luxury keeps pace with the manners of older and more affluent countries."[37] Luxury, dissipation, and extravagance, the mortal enemies of republics, lamented John Thaxter, were too visible in the country.[38]

Adams had been reluctant to admit that the reports of his friends could be true; after all, American virtue had seemed firmly established just a few years before. Some of the follies of his countrymen were too serious to be dismissed as frivolity, he admitted. But time and the perseverance of the virtuous, he had hoped, would produce a cure. "We shall find, by and by," Adams had observed, "that those who corrupt our Simplicity, will be restrained."[39] America was still overwhelmingly a nation of farmers, and for years agriculture would provide most Americans with their living. They would apply themselves to manufactures "only to fill up [the] interstices of time" in which they could not labor on their

[37] James Warren to Adams, January 28, 1785: "Warren-Adams Letters," LXXIII, 249. Samuel Adams to John Adams, July 2, 1785: Cushing, ed., *Writings of Samuel Adams*, IV, 315.

[38] John Thaxter to Adams, January 22, 1786: Adams Microfilm, Reel 367.

[39] Adams to Mercy Warren, September 1779: "Warren-Adams Letters," LXXIII, 120.

land, and to commerce only to carry raw materials to Europe.[40]

Evidence mounted, however, which convinced him that a major readjustment in American morality was impending. Speculation, ostentatious display, the breakdown of authority in the states, the failure of the people to meet their public obligations: all these were unmistakable signs of change. The "spirit of commerce," morally incompatible with the "purity of Heart and Greatness of soul" necessary for a happy republic, seemed to grip American society. The only safe principle of republican government was that "all Things most give Way to the public." Where commerce gave tone to the society, where wealth was the preeminent goal, the public interest suffered. Adams wished he could say that virtue and wisdom increased in proportion to wealth. The relationship, however, seemed to be inverse. Commerce was "more in honor in America than in England or even in Holland."[41] A disquieting number of magistrates and leading citizens were merchants. Adams believed this ominous for America's future.[42]

Less and less, then, was Adams any longer able to assume either America's youth or innocence. His earlier optimism about American society was gone. The American states had ceased to resemble their simple, virtuous selves. Instead, they were becoming stronger and more complex, wealthier and less cohesive, more luxurious and less virtuous.

In the reconstruction of his political thought, Adams continued to discuss human nature in terms of an internal balance between reason and the passions—only now with some essential differences. During the 1770's,

[40] Adams to Vergennes, July 26, 1780: *Works*, I, 326.
[41] Adams to George Morgan, November 21, 1791: Adams Microfilm, Reel 115.
[42] Haraszti, *Adams and the Prophets of Progress*, p. 127.

while acknowledging that men too often fell prey to their selfish affections, Adams had given considerable scope, at least among the American people, to the restraining influence of conscience, reason, and public virtue. Though all men were capable of violent and selfish actions, Adams had believed that Americans most often acted honorably and in the public interest. The important thing for Adams during the 1770's, had been not the fact that Americans shared a common humanity with other people and were thus subject to universal human passions, but that the unique circumstances of the American experience had modified their character and made them more rational and wholesome—in a word, more virtuous than other men.

By the 1790's, however, Adams was emphasizing not the uniqueness of America's moral condition, but its similarity to other nations'. He argued now that even among Americans the passions were unlimited, that they increased by exercise and were insatiable.[43] No longer did he feel able to invoke American virtue to counterbalance American passions. Though he allowed "benevolence and generous affections" to exist in every human breast, Adams observed in 1787, yet "every moral theorist" admitted the selfish passions "in the generality of men to be the strongest." Few persons loved the public better than themselves. "Self interest, private avidity, ambition, and avarice" existed in every society and under every form of government.[44] Adams made the point again and again, significantly omitting all distinctions between American society and any other.

Emulation, that is the desire for the esteem of one's fellow man, to be "observed, considered, praised, beloved, and admired," Adams now declared to be the key to all human nature. It lay "at the foundation of our

---

[43] Adams to Adrian Van der Kemp, February 27, 1790: Van der Kemp Papers, Historical Society of Pennsylvania.

[44] "Defense": *Works*, VI, 57.

whole moral system in this world. . . ." Every personal quality, every occurrence was cherished in proportion to its capacity for gratifying this universal affection. Conversely, contempt and neglect by society brought "as severe a pain as the gout or Stone." To resist the passion of emulation required a mind either "sunk below the feeling of humanity, or exalted by religion or philosophy far above the common character of men."[45] Emulation stimulated all of the selfish affections: jealousy, ambition, vanity. Adams now insisted that it also guided men's more honorable actions as well: the pursuit of knowledge, patriotism, and industry.[46]

Adams did not mean to deny the possibility of virtuous behavior. He continued to describe his own activities in such terms. Yet in his discussion of the American people, both reason and virtue now occupied distinctly secondary positions. He usually ascribed selfish motives to American conduct. Americans were no longer different from anyone else. To Benjamin Rush in 1789, Adams admitted that he saw "very little moral or political Preference" in the American people. As far as anyone could tell, there was as much vice and folly, infidelity and idleness, luxury and dissipation among Americans as among the inhabitants of London. Whatever advantages Americans possessed, were "chiefly geographical."[47] In his description of America's moral condition, he had come quite far since just a decade before.

ONE further circumstance needs mention in considering Adams' reevaluation of American society; that is the change in his focus of attention from the state to the continental scene. During the 1770's, Adams had carried on his discussion of politics and society in terms of the

[45] "Davila": *Ibid.*, pp. 232, 237, 234.

[46] "Davila": *Ibid.*, p. 240.

[47] Adams to Benjamin Rush, July 28, 1789: Alexander Biddle, ed., *Old Family Letters*, 2 vols. (Philadelphia, 1892), I, 48.

individual states. Even though he had been active in Congress and had urged the states to join together in a common effort against Britain, he had believed that the states provided the context in which matters of internal social regulation were to be decided. When he had talked of popular republican government being suited for American society, he had meant for the states individually with their limited population, economic development, and geographical area.

Through 1787, Adams continued to regard the state governments as the most important agencies of social control. "Our first object," he had declared back in 1783, "is to secure the liberties of our citizens in the separate States. Our second, to maintain and strengthen the Confederation."[48] Until 1788, this continued to be his system of priorities. Throughout the three volumes of the "Defense" (finally completed in December of 1787), he consistently kept his attention upon the states. Only in the closing paragraphs, and then quite incidentally, did he turn to prospects of a new continental government.

During the 1780's, he became increasingly anxious about the weaknesses of the Confederation, of its growing inability even to coordinate the foreign relations of the several states. His experience abroad convinced him that in such areas as commercial regulation, Congress should be granted added powers. Other than this, however, he remained reluctant to increase Congress's authority—especially concerning matters that involved domestic social regulation. If the states maintained inviolate their separation and balance of powers, he commented to Philip Mazzei in June of 1787 (and this was as well the chief burden of the "Defense"), liberty and good order would be the certain consequence, "whatever Imperfections may remain incurable in the Confedera-

[48] Adams to Elbridge Gerry, September 3, 1783: Wharton, ed., *Revolutionary Diplomatic Correspondence*, VI, 669-71.

tion."[49] Through 1787, he continued to believe that with certain specific powers added, the Confederation was adequate as it stood, and that the real answer to America's internal problems lay in a further strengthening of the state governments.[50]

Adams was kept informed of the various moves afoot for amending the Articles of Confederation. None of them, however, aroused his interest. From David Ramsay, he heard of the proposed commercial convention at Annapolis.[51] In reply, Adams expressed the hope that it would do some good by bringing the states into closer cooperation, but his enthusiasm went no further.[52] To the Marquis de Lafayette, he confided that he was "sorry" a convention was to take place, "because Congress would have done as well, at a less Expense and in a shorter time."[53]

Initially, at least, Adams was as unexcited about the Philadelphia convention. From John Jay in November of 1786 and again in February of 1787, he heard that efforts would be made in the new convention to alter the Confederation, perhaps decisively.[54] Isolated as he was, Adams knew nothing about the intentions of Madison, Hamilton, and others to reconstruct the continental government entirely. Had he suspected, he would certainly have been more fearful than sympathetic. He still

---

[49] Adams to Philip Mazzei, June 12, 1787: Adams Microfilm, Reel 113.

[50] "Defense": Works, IV, 580.

[51] David Ramsay to Adams, May 14, 1786: Adams Microfilm, Reel 367.

[52] Adams to David Ramsay, August 1, 1786: Ibid., Reel 113.

[53] Adams to Lafayette, June 26, 1786: Ibid. Adams to Rufus King, June 14, 1786: C. R. King, ed., The Life and Correspondence of Rufus King, 6 vols. (New York, 1894-1900), I, 144n.

[54] John Jay to Adams, November 1, 1786: Henry P. Johnston, ed., The Correspondence and Public Papers of John Jay, 4 vols. (New York, 1890-1895), III, 214-15. John Jay to Adams, February 21, 1787: Ibid., pp. 233-34.

thought of Congress in terms of a "diplomatic assembly" of sovereign states.[55]

By 1788, however, circumstances had combined to switch Adams' political perspective from the individual states to the continent as a whole, and to change his mind about the proposed new central government. The increasing paralysis of Congress made him vulnerable to the argument that basic changes in its structure were necessary. Moreover, his reports from home suggested a dangerously growing parochialism within the states, even in New England. William Gordon, for example, wrote in alarm of the efforts being made to strengthen the Union as "a violation of the Confederation and the great fundamentals upon which it was established."[56] Tristram Dalton, Adams' friend and classmate at Harvard, reported that the Massachusetts General Court was so jealous of the powers of Congress that it had instructed its delegates to work for the abolition of the treasury office and the substitution of a rotating board made up of representatives from all the states. "It appears to me impossible," Dalton concluded, "that the U. States can continue long, as such, in this unsettled situation."[57] Adams became convinced that America could neither command respect abroad nor remain long united at home unless important measures to insure continental unity were taken.

Conditions in Europe impressed upon Adams the importance of continental union. By 1788, war was threatening to break out between France and her neighbors. With Europe dividing into two armed camps, Adams feared that each of them would try to win the sympathy and support of the American states. The ultimate but very real danger was that the states, already quarreling

[55] "Defense": *Works*, IV, 579-81.
[56] William Gordon to Adams, August 14, 1787: Adams Microfilm, Reel 368.
[57] Tristram Dalton to Adams, April 6, 1784: *Ibid.*

among themselves, would divide over European loyalties and strike out against each other.

The union of the continent, Adams wrote to Jefferson in 1787, "is indeed an object of such Magnitude, that great Sacrifices ought to be made to its Preservation. The Consequences of a Division of the Continent, cannot be foreseen fully perhaps by any man."[58] With a European conflict coming on, Adams warned, America must determine to stay aloof. The greatest safeguard against involvement, he believed, was a strong continental government capable of holding the states together and enforcing neutrality upon them all. The magnitude of territory, population, and wealth, and especially the rapid growth of the states, he warned, had made the Confederation unequal to the task.[59] The newly proposed national government offered the firmest prospects of success.

In a letter of October 3, 1787, Adams received from Jay a copy of the proposed national constitution. From this moment on, his support swung away from the states in favor of the central government. The new constitution, unlike the old Confederation, Adams noted with approval, constituted a distinctly national government. He insisted that it be called "national"; "foederal" he thought "an improper word."[60] Unlike the Confederation, it rested squarely upon the people and possessed a definite legislative power of its own. Adams made yet more explicit his view that the new government derived its powers directly from the people and was supreme over the states in a letter to Cotton Tufts of June 1789. We learned in our youth, Adams began, that the *summa imperii* was indivisible; yet people seemed to be talking of the new constitution in opposite terms. There were

[58] Adams to Thomas Jefferson, May 8, 1787: *Ibid.*, Reel 112.
[59] "Defense": *Works*, VI, 219.
[60] Adams to William Tudor, June 28, 1789: Adams Microfilm, Reel 115. Adams to James Lovell, June 4, 1789: *Ibid.*

avowed efforts being made to make the central government sovereign in some cases and the states sovereign
in others. This was not possible; the central government
could not be partly national and partly federal. Either
it or the states was supreme. Both could not be. For
Adams, the correct choice was clear. The new government was "wholly national." It operated directly upon
the people and was intended to regulate many of their
domestic affairs. Its officials were responsible to the people, not to the various states.[61]

Given the need for a stronger central government to
regulate America's "great and various people" and to
fend off the threat of involvement in a European conflict, Adams found the proposed new government timely. He was dissatisfied with certain aspects of it; the
Senate he thought too strong and the Executive too
weak. Yet, in the main, he deemed it good—especially
its provision for an internal balance of power. It seemed
to him "admirably calculated to preserve the Union, to
increase Affection," and to bring Americans "all to the
same mode of thinking."[62] After reading the copy sent
him by Jay in late 1787, he wrote back urging its adoption by all the states.[63] After returning to America and
assuming a position under the new government, his
dedication to it increased.

As the focus of Adams' attention shifted from the
states to the continental government, the difficulties inherent in the problem of social control seemed to him
to increase correspondingly. One assumption of eight-

[61] Adams to Cotton Tufts, June 28, 1789: *Ibid.* Correa Walsh
argues that Adams remained even after 1787 "really a States'-rights
man," that he believed the Revolution had made the states independent of each other. Walsh offers no convincing evidence, however, citing only some observations Adams made in 1776. Correa
Walsh, *The Political Science of John Adams* (New York, 1915),
p. 268.

[62] Adams to Thomas Jefferson, November 10, 1787: Cappon, ed.,
Adams-Jefferson Letters, I, 210.

[63] Adams to John Jay, December 16, 1787: Adams Microfilm,
Reel 112. "Davila": *Works,* VI, 269.

eenth-century political thought was that only small, compact societies were suited for popular republican government. By 1787, Adams was having some doubts whether even the individual states would long continue to qualify. They now appeared to him "numerous and rich" with "territory capacious and commerce extensive."[64] He referred to several of them as "great populous nations." With his switch in attention to the continental scene, the problem was compounded. He was now thinking in terms of millions of people rather than several hundred thousand, of an area measuring thousands rather than hundreds of miles, and of a staggering array of economic and social interests. Passions, Adams observed, were never perfectly controlled by individuals, "still less by nations and large bodies of men, and less and less, as communities grow larger and larger, more populous, more commercial, more wealthy, and more luxurious."[65] The difficulties of bringing millions to agree in any measures or to act by any rule were overwhelming.[66]

By 1790, then, Adams' conception of American society had dramatically changed. No longer did he envision a society of unspoiled republicans, maintaining their own independence, and guiding their conduct by the strict standards of social virtue. Nor was he thinking in terms of a society small and egalitarian, simple and undisturbed by internal division. Rather, he now confronted a people moving with disarming speed in the direction of social maturity, already displaying ominous distinctions between "aristocratic" and "democratic" interests, and made up of individuals more passionate than rational, more selfish than virtuous. The remainder of his political career he spent in an effort to deal with the changes he had perceived; to insure, in the face of them, the continuing effective regulation of the American people.

[64] "Defense": *Ibid.*, p. 109.
[65] Adams to John Taylor, 1814: *Ibid.*, pp. 487-88.
[66] Adams to Richard Price, April 19, 1790: *Ibid.*, IX, 564.

Chapter VI. "A Balance of Opposing Interests"

Maintaining order and stability in a society no longer characterized by virtue and tending to divide into two antagonistic interests, posed a much more difficult problem for Adams than he had faced during the 1770's. In considering the matter of social regulation from the late 1780's on, Adams displayed none of the easy confidence that had characterized his discussion just a decade or so earlier. No longer did he emphasize the natural inclinations of the American people for orderly behavior. He now placed much greater emphasis upon the need for effective instruments of social control.

During the 1770's, of course, Adams had argued that firmly established governments were necessary in each state in order to insure that liberty did not degenerate into license. We have seen how actively he encouraged the formation of new state governments. During these years, however, he had approached the problem of social regulation confidently, and at times even casually. The American people, he had felt certain, would make all necessary arrangements. In their conduct, Americans were guided by a strict code of personal and social morality sanctioned by a wise Providence. This had seemed to Adams the ultimate guarantee of orderly behavior. "My Opinion of the Duties of Religion and Morality," he had written to Abigail in the 1770's,

> comprehends a very extensive connection with society at large, and the great Interest of the public. Does not natural Morality, and much more Christian Benevolence, make it our indispensible Duty to

lay ourselves out, to serve our fellow Creatures to the Utmost of our Power, in promoting and supporting those great Political systems, and general Regulations upon which the Happiness of Multitudes depends. The Benevolence, Charity, Capacity and Industry which exerted in private Life, would make a family, a Parish or a Town Happy, employed upon a larger Scale, in Support of the great Principles of Virtue and Freedom of political Regulations might secure whole Nations and Generations from Misery, Want and Contempt. Public Virtues, and political Qualities therefore should be incessantly cherished in our Children.[1]

In the promise of a future life where rewards and punishments would be dispensed in equitable measure, Adams had believed, lay perhaps the strongest sanction for moral conduct. God governed his whole creation "by proportioning Rewards to Piety and Virtue, and Punishments to Disobedience and Vice." In general, virtue carried its own reward and vice its own punishment, even in this world. But as there were many exceptions to this rule, "the Joys of heaven . . . and the Horrors of Hell [were prepared] in a future State to render the moral Government of the Universe, perfect and compleat."[2]

During the 1770's, moreover, Adams had stressed that men could be instructed in the value of social order through moral training and political education. Montesquieu explained that virtue must be taught. Adams

[1] Adams to Abigail Adams, October 29, 1775: Butterfield, ed., *Adams Family Correspondence*, I, 316-17.

[2] Diary, August 22, 1770: *Diary and Autobiography*, I, 365. Adams' religious faith was clearly in the Arminian tradition. He denied, for example, the reality or the necessity of modern-day miracles (though not their possibility). And he was strictly unitarian in theology. He continued throughout his life, however, to believe firmly in an afterlife, and to regard it as an essential support for any moral code. See H. I. Fielding, "John Adams: Puritan, Deist, Humanist": *Journal of Religion*, xx (1940), pp. 33-46.

had concurred. "Human nature with all its infirmities and deprivation," he had explained in 1775, "is still capable of great things. It is capable of attaining to degrees of wisdom and of goodness which, we have reason to believe, appear respectable in the estimation of superior intelligences. Education makes a greater difference between man and man, than nature has made between man and brute." The abilities to which men could be trained by early education and constant discipline, were "truly sublime and astonishing."[3]

By the 1790's, however, Adams' faith in the efficacy of both religion and education as effective guarantors of social order had weakened. He now stressed their limitations rather than their capacities and insisted that alone they were far from enough. The increase and dissemination of knowledge, he observed in 1787, instead of rendering strong controls over society unnecessary, increased the need for them. For bad men increased in knowledge as fast as good, and "science, arts, taste, sense, and letters" could be employed for the purposes of injustice and tyranny as well as law and liberty, for corruption as well as virtue.[4] As evidence, Adams cited the example of France. There the results of misguided reason were being terribly demonstrated. From the first, Adams distrusted French assertions of perfectibility. The dismal turn of events after 1789 not only convinced him of the futility of the French experiment, but caused him to question the ability of men in general to use their powers of reason constructively. The French tried making

[3] Adams to Abigail Adams, October 29, 1775: Butterfield, ed., *Adams Family Correspondence*, I, 317. Adams to Richard Cranch, August 29, 1756: Adams Microfilm, Reel 114. Adams' marginalia in his copy of Richard Hurd's *Moral and Political Dialogues*, p. 124: Adams Collection, Boston Public Library.

[4] "Davila": *Works*, VI, 276. The arts, he explained, promoted virtue only as long as virtue was in fashion; after that, they exalted luxury and corruption. Haraszti, *Adams and the Prophets of Progress*, p. 59.

reason a "natural Religion," he scoffed, and look at the result! His conclusion was simple and emphatic: "Reason [was] insufficient to govern Nations." The authority of reason was not stern enough to keep rebellious appetites under control.[5] The message was universally true. "The improvement, the exaltation of the human character, the perfectibility of man, and the perfection of the human faculties," Adams wrote in criticism of Mary Wollstonecraft's *French Revolution*, "are the divine objects which her enthusiasm holds in beatific vision. Alass, how airy and baseless a fabric!"[6] With Condorcet's easy dictum that knowledge enhanced human virtue, Adams now emphatically disagreed.

Nor would Adams any longer concede that virtue sanctioned by the Christian religion could do much to cure society's ills. "Moral and Christian, and political virtue," he still believed, could not be too much practiced or rewarded. But to place liberty on that foundation alone was not safe. He now maintained that no people had ever existed who loved the public interest better than their own. Virtue was "as precarious a foundation for liberty as honor or fear."[7] Few persons in any nation—and he included America in his observation—were enlightened enough either by philosophy or religion to prefer public duty over their own private concerns.[8]

Trusting less in the wisdom and virtue of man, then, Adams emphasized more the necessity for authority and control. "I have long been settled in my own opinion," he wrote to Jefferson in 1787 (though he had in fact reached the conclusion only recently), "that neither Philosophy, nor Religion, nor Morality, nor Wisdom, nor Interest, will ever govern nations or Parties, against

[5] Adams' marginalia in his copy of Conyers Middleton's *Works*, III, 166-67: Adams Collection, Boston Public Library.

[6] Haraszti, *Adams and the Prophets of Progress*, p. 187.

[7] Adams to John Taylor, 1814: *Works*, VI, 469.

[8] "Defense": *Ibid.*, p. 211.

their Vanity, their Pride, their Resentment or Revenge, or their Avarice or Ambition. Nothing but Force and Power and Strength can restrain them."[9]

During the 1770's, the danger he had perceived had been of excessive authority, of concentrated power, represented by the British Crown and Parliament, insensitive to the liberties of the American people and unresponsive to their wishes. By the 1790's, however, his definition of America's problem had changed. Now it seemed to him a distinct possibility that from an excess of liberty would devolve anarchy. His primary concern was to produce more stable guarantees of social stability. In little more than a decade, he had changed fundamentally the terms in which he discussed the problem of social control.

American society, Adams now emphasized, suffered increasingly the effects of conflict between its two great divisions. In America the many tried to plunder the few (Adams had Shays' Rebellion in mind), while men of power fleeced the poor.[10] Americans might claim to have no distinctions of rank, Adams observed, and therefore to be exempt from the disorders which spring from them. Yet in America there were laborers and yeomen and gentlemen; distinctions were sought as earnestly in the New World as elsewhere. And Americans had to take account of this in considering matters of social regulation.[11] The American people, he concluded, growing deficient in virtue and less cohesive in organization, needed as never before the guidance of firmly established authority, of stable institutions capable of mediating conflicts and ordering the society's activities.

The two institutions that Adams invoked were law and government. Throughout the late 1780's and 1790's,

[9] Adams to Thomas Jefferson, October 9, 1787: Cappon, ed., *Adams-Jefferson Letters*, I, 202-203.
[10] "Defense": *Works*, IV, 462.   [11] "Defense": *Ibid.*, V, 488.

Adams maintained with growing vigor that the only safeguard against "the Vices of Men" were permanent laws, established for the good of society as a whole and standing above the passions of the moment. The urgency with which he pressed this argument was distinctly new. "If the Common People in America lose their Integrity," he warned John Jay in 1787, "Laws alone and those political institutions which are the guardians of them" offered hope.[12] Repeatedly he made his point. Every citizen "must look up to the laws, as his master . . . and his friend." Only laws made jointly by the representatives of all the interests in society could be trusted with unlimited confidence. They alone provided the bond which gave unity to a commonwealth. Only under "a government of laws and not of men," could society flourish.[13]

Adams had made the point many times before. Impartial laws, established in the general interest and safe from the passions of the moment, he had always deemed essential to social order. His explanation of why he agreed to undertake the defense of Captain Preston and the British soldiers in 1770, was that justice had to be done and the laws upheld. Again in 1773, when the Crown had attempted to take over payment of judicial salaries from the General Court, Adams had deemed the move a serious threat against American liberties and had recommended impeachment as a recourse. He had felt uneasy, however, in doing so. The judges of the Superior Court had been "respectable and virtuous characters." To attempt impeachment might well encourage disrespect for men "who wore the Robes and bore the sacred Characters of Judges" and for the rule of law

[12] Adams to John Jay, September 23, 1787: Adams Microfilm, Reel 112.
[13] "Defense": *Works*, VI, 56. Adams' marginalia in his copy of the Abbé de Mably's *de la Legislation*, p. 122: Adams Collection, Boston Public Library.

they represented.[14] And in discussing the establishment of state governments, he had urged the importance of providing for the regular enactment and administration of equitable laws.

Yet by the 1790's his emphasis upon permanent laws, enforced by stable government, had became decidedly more shrill. He had earlier been instructing the people, expecting them to listen. Now he feared they would not and that the opposition of interests in society would excite passions to a point where legal restraints would be ignored. It was impossible to reconcile the "diversity of sentiments, contradictory principles, inconsistent interests and opposite passions," which America now contained, he explained, "by declamations against discord and panegyrics upon unanimity. . . ." The strict endorsement of impartial laws by "a government possessed of sufficient force" was the only way.[15] This was the lesson Adams had learned as he watched confusion grow during the 1780's; and it was the message he felt compelled to repeat again and again during the years following.

Adams was at times unclear as to exactly what he meant by "law." As a young lawyer, he had read widely in both the common and civil law—Justinian, Vinnius, and Montesquieu in the originals, as well as Coke and Wood in commentary. Before the Revolutionary troubles got under way, he had recognized the English Common Law as part of America's legal tradition. In one of his earliest published writings (1763), he had declared that long examination of the systems of legislators both ancient and modern, had convinced him that "the liberty . . . of men . . . [and] the grandeur and glory of the public" had never been so fully accommodated as in "that most excellent monument of human art, the common law of England. . . ."[16] And in 1765, he had argued the

[14] *Diary and Autobiography*, III, 299.
[15] "Defense": *Works*, V, 431.
[16] "On Private Revenge": *Ibid.*, III, 440.

sanctity of American rights under the Common Law against the Stamp Act.[17]

As the trouble with England deepened, however, Adams' position changed. In his "Novanglus" essays of 1775, criticizing the Tea and Coercive Acts, he argued that contrary to English assertions the Common Law prevailed only within the realm of England, that the realm did not extend beyond the ocean, and that therefore efforts of the Parliament to act upon the colonies under English law were without foundation. "The common law, and the authority of parliament founded on it," he insisted, "never extended beyond the four seas. . . ."[18] Under the press of circumstance, he found this affirmation now desirable. Englishmen, he explained, could be governed only by laws to which they had given consent; and the Englishmen living in America had never placed themselves under the common law.

Law was a function of sovereignty, and sovereignty rested with the people gathered of their own will into political associations. Prior to 1776, Adams explained that the sources of legal authority in America were the charters contracted between colonists and king. New England men derived their laws, he explained, not from common law, but from the law of nature, and "the compact made with the king in our charters."[19] After independence, the extension of this doctrine was obvious. The basis of all legal authority still lay in compacts among the people. This authority now found expression in the constitutions, both state and national, formed by the people acting in convention.[20] Here the sovereignty residing in the people was given form and substance. In the day-by-day operation of society, legal authority, under the constitutions, rested with the representative

---

[17] "Instructions of the Town of Braintree": *Ibid.*, pp. 465-68.
[18] "Novanglus": *Ibid.*, IV, 121ff.
[19] *Ibid.*, p. 122.
[20] "Defense": *Ibid.*, p. 293.

legislative assemblies.[21] That is, in the legislature rested the sovereign power, delegated by the people, to make laws. To a further elaboration of the legislative power, Adams around 1790 turned his attention.

The preservation of equitable laws as the basis of orderly social intercourse, Adams maintained, depended upon the nurturing care of certain political institutions: primarily the separation of government into executive, judicial, and legislative branches, with the latter separated further into three opposing parts—the executive acting in his legislative capacity and the two legislative houses. "The laws, which are the only possible, rule, measure, and security of justice," he declared, "can be sure of protection, for any course of time, in no other form of government. . . ."[22]

The outline of the balance was the same as that described by him during the 1770's. But the assumptions behind it, and therefore the significance of his discussion were now considerably changed. His comments, for one thing, were now based upon the assumption of human selfishness rather than virtue. "All projects of government, founded in the supposition or expectation of extraordinary degrees of virtue," he observed, "are . . . chimerical."[23] Increase of power, influence, and importance was the constant object of the human mind.[24] Human nature never rested; once in motion, it rolled like the stone of Sisyphus until some resisting force con-

---

[21] Adams advised in 1776 that "the system and rules of the common law" be formally adopted by the states as their own. The legislatures might then make specific alterations in it to suit their own condition. Adams to William Cushing, June 9, 1776: *Ibid.*, IX, 391. As late as 1811, however, he acknowledged that it was debatable whether the United States had any common law. Adams to Benjamin Waterhouse, December 12, 1811: Ford, ed., *Statesman and Friend, Correspondence of Adams with Waterhouse, 1784-1822*, pp. 71-72.

[22] "Defense": *Works*, IV, 295, 194.

[23] Adams to Samuel Adams, October 18, 1790: *Ibid.*, VI, 415.

[24] Haraszti, *Adams and the Prophets of Progress*, p. 70.

tained it. As a consequence, Adams made the argument over and over again that provision must be made in political institutions—he meant essentially the balance between aristocratic and democratic influences—"to compel all to respect the common right, the public good, the universal law, in preference to all private and partial considerations."[25]

The second new element in Adams' discussion, was his assumption that American society was dividing into two great opposing interests. This changed materially the nature of the balance which he invoked. During the 1770's, Adams had warned against allowing control of the legislative power to fall into the hands of any one man or group of men. For safety, he had insisted that this power be fragmented by dividing it between the two legislative houses and the executive. This was a separation of power among constitutional bodies, done simply for the purpose of separation—because it was by definition bad to allow power to become centralized—without serious consideration being given to what social or economic interests in society these bodies represented. In fact, he gave the executive and the two legislative houses no social or economic definition. (Check, for example, Adams' discussion of the balance in his "Thoughts on Government," where he describes the dangers of a single legislative house as arising from the inclination of any group of individuals, if given the opportunity, to vote themselves special advantages; i.e., perpetual power, legislative privileges, exemption from taxation.)[26]

By the 1790's, however, Adams was writing in terms of a legislative balance between specific and antagonistic social groups—the aristocracy and the democracy. The first was to be represented in the upper house, and the second in the lower. "The great art of lawgiving," he explained in 1789, "consists in balancing the poor against

[25] "Defense": *Works*, VI, 8.
[26] "Thoughts on Government": *Ibid.*, IV, 195-96.

the rich in the legislature. . . ."[27] The rich and the poor among the people, he repeated some years later, "so invidious at all times against each other," had to be opposed in the two houses of the legislature.[28] He now wrote of "orders of men" watching and balancing each other. This was society's only security. Only by "combining the great divisions of society in one system," could the laws be rendered secure and stability achieved.[29]

By the 1790's, then, Adams believed the need for a balance of the legislative power more urgent than ever. At the same time, he detected an alarming recrudescence of sentiment in favor of unbalanced governments. There continued to be some lingering American advocates of unicameral government; but the new impetus came from abroad, particularly France. Adams' three-volume "Defense" constituted an extended apologia of balanced governments, inspired largely by Turgot's letter of 1778 to Dr. Price, criticizing the United States for their adherence to British political forms.[30] The "Discourses on Davila," in which Adams defended the principle of balance in the national constitution, found its inspiration in Condorcet's later endorsement of Turgot's position.[31] Adams feared that the Frenchmen would gain a hearing in America. The mistakes of great men, when they countenanced the prejudices of numbers of people, he remarked, especially in a very young country and under new governments, could not be too fully confuted.[32]

And with American society developing so rapidly, the problem was compounded. In a wealthy and diverse

[27] "Davila": *Ibid.*, VI, 280.

[28] Adams to Timothy Pickering, October 31, 1797: *Ibid.*, VIII, 560.

[29] "Defense": *Ibid.*, IV, 557. Adams to Abigail Adams, March 14, 1788: C. F. Adams, ed., *Letters of John Adams Addressed to his Wife*, 2 vols. (Boston, 1898), II, 112. "Defense": *Works*, IV, 462.

[30] *Ibid.*, pp. 299-300.

[31] *Ibid.*, VI, 225. Adams to Richard Price, May 20, 1789: Adams Microfilm, Reel 115.

[32] "Defense": *Works*, IV, 302.

country, he insisted, a triple-headed legislature was "the best and the only remedy" against ruin. Unbalanced governments required "the utmost frugality, simplicity, and moderation" to make human life tolerable under them. Only a three-fold balance, on the other hand, was capable of governing "a great nation and large territory" or of preserving liberty "among great degrees of wealth, luxury, dissipation, and even profligacy of manners...."[33] The United States were becoming "large and populous nations," growing every day more disproportionate and less capable of being held together by simple governments.[34] With the awful lesson of France before him, Adams made it his task to drive this point home.

Control of the law-making process, that is of the legislative branch of government, then, must be kept out of the hands of either the aristocratic or democratic interests. They must be pitted against each other, in Madame de Staël's words, "like two wrestlers whom an equal degree of strength renders motionless."[35]

At first it was the aristocracy that concerned Adams most. During late 1786 and early 1787, as he was writing the first two volumes of the "Defense," he believed that the aristocratic power posed the greater threat to the legislative balance. History demonstrated clearly, he then affirmed, that when territory became large and commerce flourishing, the emergence of an aristocratic power was the inevitable consequence; an aristocracy "consisting of a few rich and honorable families; united against the people and the first magistrate, seeking to gather all political power to themselves."[36] Experience demonstrated, moreover, that the aristocracy were "the most difficult Animals to manage, of anything in the

[33] *Ibid.*, VI, 96.
[34] *Ibid.*, IV, 287.
[35] Adams' marginalia in Madame de Staël's *Influence of the Passions upon Happiness*: in *More Books, Bulletin of the Boston Public Library*, Sixth Series (Boston, 1926), I, 103.
[36] "Defense": *Works*, IV, 381.

whole Theory and practice of Government."[37] As long as human nature had passions and imagination, Adams observed, there was reason to fear that wealth and birth would have more influence than either reason or equity could justify.[38]

The emergence of an American economic and political aristocracy: this was the great change in America's condition that Adams detected. And herein lay the chief peril. "It is from the natural aristocracy in a single assembly," he asserted, "that the first danger is to be apprehended in the present state of manners in America. . . ."[39] Prospects were that the process would continue. The war now breaking out in Europe, he warned in 1787, whether America was forced into it or not, "will render our Country . . . great and powerful in comparison of what she now is." And "Riches, Grandeur and Power," he continued, "will have the same effect upon American minds as it has upon European minds."[40] America, he felt sure, would not profit from Europe's mistakes. A Covent Garden rake, Adams expostulated, "will never be wise enough to take warning from the Claps caught by his Companions." This was not melancholy, he concluded, but experience.[41]

The most striking evidence of the growth of an American aristocracy Adams found in the Society of the Cincinnati. In this organization, the American people demonstrated how susceptible they were to the same corruptions as Europeans. Americans might profess that their society contained no distinctions or titles and call such desires childish, he observed, yet the Cincinnati demonstrated that the disposition to them and even to their

[37] Adams to Thomas Jefferson, July 9, 1813: Cappon, ed., *Adams-Jefferson Letters*, II, 352.

[38] "Defense": *Works*, IV, 398.

[39] *Ibid.*, pp. 444-45.

[40] Adams to Thomas Jefferson, October 9, 1787: Adams Microfilm, Reel 112.

[41] Adams to Thomas Jefferson, October 9, 1787: *Ibid.*

hereditary descent was as strong in America as elsewhere. There was not a more remarkable phenomenon in universal history, he believed, than the Cincinnati. And the distressing thing about it was that officers once voluntarily engaged in service under the people, the moment the war was ended, instituted "titles and ribbons, and hereditary descents," by their own authority without the consent either of the people, or their representatives.[42]

In the face of an encroaching aristocratic power, Adams explained that the only recourse was to provide for its control before it became too strong. "You are afraid of the one," he replied to Jefferson in commenting upon the new national constitution; "I of the few. . . . You are apprehensive of monarchy—I of aristocracy."[43] The solution was to isolate the aristocratic influence in the upper house; "to all honest and useful intents, an ostracism."[44] Only in this way could the rising aristocratic power be controlled. The effort to isolate the aristocracy in one branch of the legislature constituted the main thrust of Adams' argument through 1786 and much of 1787. As part of a single legislative house, the aristocracy would inexorably extend its power until it dominated the entire assembly. "The rich, the well-born, and the able," Adams explained, "acquire an influence among the people that will soon be too much for simple honesty and plain sense, in a house of representatives."[45] They would soon overawe and destroy the public liberties; and then set about fighting for control among themselves. Civil conflict and the final resort by the people to a single tyrant for relief would be the inevitable result.

By surrounding "the rich and the proud" with the

[42] "Defense": *Works*, v, 488.
[43] Adams to Thomas Jefferson, December 6, 1787: Adams Microfilm, Reel 112.
[44] "Defense": *Works*, iv, 290, 354-55, 398.
[45] *Ibid.*, p. 290.

democratic power on one side and a strong executive on the other, the aristocracy could be kept within bounds. By this means alone, could society have "the benefit of their wisdom, without fear of their passions."[46] When a few great men began to exert too much control over the lower house, Adams explained, the voters could remove them into the Senate. There, confronted by men of his own kind, no one person could gain exclusive influence. Like fire, the aristocracy were good servants, but all-consuming masters. If adequately regulated, their talents could greatly benefit society, for they represented "the brightest ornaments and glory of the nations. . . ." If "judiciously managed in the constitution," they might be society's greatest blessing. If not, they would surely be its curse.[47]

While emphasizing the dangers of an uncontrolled aristocratic influence, Adams did not ignore the democracy. In the first volume of the "Defense," for example, he warned that the democracy if given full rein would demonstrate a "rapid tendency to abuse."[48] The balance, he pointed out, was intended to control both interests, to allow neither excessive power. The burden of his message throughout the first two volumes of the "Defense," however, was the preeminent danger from the aristocracy.

In the third volume, and with increasing vigor after his return to America (for example, in his "Davila" essays), Adams changed his message to emphasize not so much the danger of an American aristocracy, as first its ineradicable basis in human nature, and second its value to society when properly regulated. He now stressed more the dangers from an unbalanced democracy and urged provision for its control. Adams' shift in emphasis was noted by his contemporaries. Jefferson, Benjamin Rush, and Joel Barlow all greeted Adams' first volume with enthusiasm for its exaltation of the

[46] *Ibid.*, p. 414.   [47] *Ibid.*, p. 397.   [48] *Ibid.*, p. 488.

people and its warning against aristocratic influence. By the time the third volume appeared, however, they were criticizing him for abandoning republican principles.

The reasons for Adams' change are not hard to find. During 1787, as he composed the third volume of the "Defense," he continued to receive alarmed reports of the troubles in western Massachusetts and elsewhere. As already noted, he was at first reluctant to give them credence; but by mid-1787, evidence that property was being threatened and the law subverted had become overwhelming. Then, beginning in 1789, open social revolution broke out in France. Almost at once upon hearing of the French upheaval, he began his "Discourses on Davila," the most sustained presentation of his new point of view.

Adams reacted strongly to the "democratical hurricane" in France. Edward Handler has persuasively argued that before the French Revolution actually arrived, Adams had had no real understanding of the seriousness of the upheaval impending, nor any sympathy with the lofty ambitions of the French liberals.[49] Adams had been "astonished," he later recalled, at the explanation given him at the time by Lafayette of the broad plan to reform France.[50] During 1787 and 1788, at his post in England, Adams clearly became aware that something serious was impending in France—something unlikely to be good. "All Europe resounds with Projects for reviving States and Assemblies . . . and France is taking the lead," he remarked uneasily in December of 1787. The fermentation, he hoped, would bring improvements, a lessening of superstitions and tyranny. Yet vague as his fears were, he worried that with all the noble sentiments and enchanting eloquence,

[49] Edward Handler, *America and Europe in the Political Thought of John Adams* (Cambridge, Massachusetts, 1964), Chapter 3.
[50] Adams to Thomas Jefferson, July 13, 1813: Cappon, ed., *Adams-Jefferson Letters*, II, 355.

"essential Ideas" would be forgotten; that experiments in social levelling and unbalanced government which had always proved fatal would be tried again.[51]

Within a short time, his fears were confirmed. "War, pestilence, famine" ravished France, threatening all of Europe. Once the French Revolution began, Adams saw in it "no tendency to any thing but anarchy, licentiousness and despotism."[52] France was attempting something for which she was not suited; free republican government for twenty-five million people, twenty-four-and-a-half million of whom could neither read nor write, was "unnatural irrational and unpracticable. . . ." She was trying to eradicate all social distinctions and establish government in one center.[53] Disaster could be the only result.

Adams was most alarmed lest the spirit of innovation spread to America. The "lawless, tyrannical rabble" which followed Daniel Shays voiced doctrines of social levelling as dangerous, he came to believe, as those of the French Jacobins. Mobs, he warned, would never do to govern States. To talk of liberty in such a state of things was delusive. Was not a Shays as great a tyrant when he sought to "pluck up law and justice by the roots" as a Thomas Hutchinson who tried to overrun them partially?[54] Ties between France and America, Adams realized, were close. And therein lay the danger. Some Americans seemed to "pant for equality of persons and property" as ardently as Frenchmen.[55]

This was the theme that from 1789 on, Adams struck

[51] Adams to Thomas Jefferson, December 10, 1787: Adams Microfilm, Reel 112.
[52] Adams to Abigail Adams, February 9, 1794: C. F. Adams, ed., *Letters to his Wife*, II, 142.
[53] Adams to Thomas Jefferson, July 13, 1813: Cappon, ed., *Adams-Jefferson Letters*, II, 355.
[54] Adams to Benjamin Hinchborn, January 27, 1787: *Works*, IX, 551.
[55] Adams to Richard Price, April 19, 1790: *Ibid.*, p. 564.

with increasing force. Efforts at social levelling were foolish and dangerous. Inequalities of mind and body were so established in the constitution of human nature that no art or policy could ever "plain them down to a Level." Adams had never read reasoning more absurd nor sophistry more gross, even in proof of the Athanasian Creed, he declared, "than the subtle labours of Helvétius and Rousseau to demonstrate the natural Equality of Mankind."[56] Efforts to destroy "all decorum, discipline, and subordination" in society—the "wild idea of annihilating the nobility"—he vigorously condemned.[57] Adams aimed his message directly at America. Do not be misled by French claims of abolishing distinctions, he warned his countrymen; "impossibilities cannot be performed."[58] "Take but Degree away," he copied into one of his "Davila" essays; "untune that string/ And Hark! what discord follows! each thing meets/ In mere oppugnancy. . . ."[59]

Further, Adams now insisted that order was attributable primarily to the upper elements of society. The aristocracy, he proclaimed, provided the chief fund of wisdom, wealth, and virtue, and, once chastened, were "in general, the best men, [and] citizens . . . the guardians, ornaments, and glory of the community."[60] The "natural and actual aristocracy" of Europe, he commented in 1790 in direct reversal of his earlier views, had been essential parties to the preservation of liberty against the tyranny of kings. They might well serve a similar function in America.[61]

In volume three of the "Defense," Adams turned about and argued the special position of the American senates as the guardians of liberty. Were not senators

[56] Adams to Thomas Jefferson, July 13, 1813: Cappon, ed., *Adams-Jefferson Letters*, II, 355.

[57] "Davila": *Works*, VI, 275, 299.

[58] *Ibid.*, p. 270.   [59] *Ibid.*, p. 266.

[60] "Defense": *Ibid.*, p. 73.

[61] Adams to Samuel Adams, October 18, 1790: *Ibid.*, pp. 417-19.

under the influence of powerful motives, he wondered, "to be tender and concerned for the security of liberty?" What greater refuge could a people have than a council in which "the national maxims and the spirit and genius of the state" were preserved by "a living tradition?" The American senates should constitute "a living repertory of all the history, knowledge, interests, and wisdom of the Commonwealth. . . ." They had been the patrons of liberty "on many occasions" against the "giddy, thoughtless multitude. . . ."[62] How different was this from what he had written only a few years before!

Adams' views of the democracy changed as well. In the third volume of the "Defense" and in his "Davila" essays, he explained that the failure of the balance in government led usually to confusion at the hands of a mob. The democratic influence seemed now to have assumed for him the more darkly aggressive role; to represent less the protagonists of liberty than the creators of instability. "In proportion as a government is democratical in a degree beyond proportional prevalence of monarchy and aristocracy," he explained in a remarkable statement, was all authority prostituted.[63]

What now seemed noteworthy to Adams was the unruliness of the people, not their virtue. It was very easy to flatter the democracy by making distinctions based upon the supposed superiority in virtue between them and the aristocratical elements, he acknowledged. But he found no reason to believe one segment any more honest than another. "*Sobriety, abstinence*, and *severity*" were never remarkable characteristics of the democratical branch in any constitution. The people were easily inflamed, were seldom aware of the purposes for which they were set in motion or of the consequences, and when once heated and in full career could neither man-

[62] "Defense": *Ibid.*, pp. 93-94, 394.
[63] *Ibid.*, pp. 98-99, 97.

age themselves nor be regulated by others.[64] When unchecked, they were easily as cruel, unjust, and brutal as any king. To believe that they would fail to usurp other men's rights if given the chance was a delusion.[65] "Numbers have not the discernment of spirits," Bolingbroke had observed. "Aye!" agreed Adams, "here is the rub."[66]

As his views of the democracy darkened, Adams became increasingly sensitive to the rights of property. The necessity of a separate legislative body for the aristocracy he now emphasized because it offered a safeguard for property. "The property and liberty of the rich," he advised, must be given "a security in a senate, against the encroachments of the poor in a popular assembly."[67] Property was as much a right of mankind as political liberty. And the rich had "as clear and as *sacred* a right" to their property as did the poor.[68] Again Adams' devotion to the sacredness of property was not new. He had fought to protect American possessions from unjust taxation during the Revolution. What had changed, was Adams' belief that among some Americans property was no longer secure. Adams had earlier assumed that a people among whom property was so broadly distributed, would unfailingly respect its sanctity. The activities of Daniel Shays, of the states, and even Congress, now convinced him this condition no longer prevailed.

With American society dividing into two antagonistic interests, then, and American virtue counting every day for less, Adams by 1790 came to emphasize as never before the importance of authority and control. Especially did he stress the need for strong government, adequate-

---

[64] *Diary and Autobiography*, III, 299.
[65] "Defense": *Works*, VI, 10, 7.
[66] Haraszti, *Adams and the Prophets of Progress*, p. 57.
[67] "Defense": *Works*, VI, 89.
[68] *Ibid.*, pp. 9, 65, 280.

ly balanced and thus made safe against the passions either of the few or the many. He was now saying that in America, government could no longer afford to be as closely dependent upon the people as formerly. To be safe, government would have to be more independent, more free from continuous interference by either the aristocracy or democracy. Government, moreover, required new means of impressing its authority upon society. These conclusions were manifest in two controversies in which Adams became embroiled during the period 1789 to 1793—controversies involving his alleged "anti-republicanism."

Accusations that Adams had changed his principles and become an enemy of popular republican government flared up during the years immediately following his return from England. They revolved around two things: his advocacy of the use of titles and other ceremonials in the new national government, and his consideration of the possible need for substituting hereditary succession for the election of President and Senate.

To the charges of anti-republicanism, Adams loudly protested his innocence. And many of his critics were unfair, either intentionally or inadvertently misrepresenting some of the things he wrote. (By 1790 he could identify a significant number of enemies: the friends of Franklin and Deane, trading interests angered by his failure to secure a commercial treaty with England, sympathizers with France who differed from him in attitude toward the French Revolution.) Adams' critics, however, were correct in perceiving that basic changes had occurred in his outlook.

The controversy over the use of titles began in 1789. The first Congress to sit under the new constitution had to determine what form of address to use in communicating with the executive. With no precedent but British tradition as a guide and this largely out of favor, the problem was first whether Congress should reply to the

President's initial address at all, and if so, in what form? The House resolved the matter with dispatch, agreeing without serious dissent to address the chief executive simply as "George Washington, President of the United States."[69] In the Senate, however, things were not so simply done.

A controversy immediately arose, with Adams and R. H. Lee (strange political bedfellows, given their opposing positions on the adoption of the constitution— though they had, of course, worked together in the Continental Congress) urging in "great earnestness" that a more exalted form of greeting be employed.[70] Adams later maintained that he had simply inquired of the Senate whether a formal mode of address would be desirable. It seems clear, however, that he actually took the initiative in urging its adoption.[71] In all seriousness, he recommended that the President be hailed as either "His Highness" or "His most benign Highness."[72] The most modest title Adams thought suitable for the office of President was "His Majesty, the President."[73] A "Royal, or at least a Princely Title," Adams explained to William Tudor, would be found "indespensibly [sic] necessary" to maintain the dignity of the American people.[74]

At once, outraged republicans rose to the attack, with the acid-tongued William Maclay leading the way. From

[69] Irving Brant, James Madison, Father of the Constitution, 1787-1800 (Indianapolis, 1950), pp. 256-57.

[70] James Madison to Thomas Jefferson, May 23, 1789: Gaillard Hunt, ed., The Writings of James Madison, 9 vols. (New York, 1900-1910), v, 369n.-70n.

[71] William Maclay, senator from Pennsylvania (and no friend of Adams), reported that the Vice-President railed for forty-five minutes on the point. E. S. Maclay, ed., The Journal of William Maclay (New York, 1890), pp. 27, 1-3, 22-26, 63-137.

[72] Adams to William Tudor, May 3, 1789: Tudor Papers, Massachusetts Historical Society.

[73] Adams to Benjamin Rush, July 24, 1789: Biddle, ed., Old Family Letters, I, 46.

[74] Adams to William Tudor, May 3, 1789: Tudor Papers.

April to May 1789, the controversy monopolized much of the Senate's time; and its echoes, both inside Congress and out, continued for a long while after. Adams was accused of wishing to throw over the new government and replace it with an American monarchy patterned after the British Crown. Or, alternately, his critics credited him with a desire to provide titles for a whole aristocratic class and to set them over the people.

Adams complained that the charges were grossly unfair. And he had legitimate cause for complaint. For as ominous as his proposals seemed to be, they in fact cloaked no hidden desire to promote either an American monarchy or a formally established aristocracy. Though he was by this time impressed with the stabilizing influence of the aristocratic interest, he had no desire to give control of the government over to it. Adams was quite clear that his titles would be affixed to public offices (and only to a few) rather than to the incumbents of the offices or their assigns.[75] In fact, he argued that the selective use of titles for a few political offices would help control the aristocratic interest. The real opposition to a Presidential title, he explained, came not from the people, but from aristocrats who didn't want the executive strengthened against them.[76]

In substantial measure, Adams' endorsement of American titles was inspired by his concern to strengthen the national government against the divisive influence of state loyalties. As he set out for New York and his new position as Vice-President in April of 1789, he was impressed by the frailty of the new national government.

---

[75] Adams to Benjamin Rush, July 5, 1789: Biddle, ed., *Old Family Letters*, I, 42. John C. Miller's explanation that this resulted from Adams' disinclination to exalt Washington gives Adams less credit than he merits. John C. Miller, *The Federalist Era, 1789-1801* (New York, 1960), pp. 7-8.

[76] Adams to William Tudor, June 28, 1789: Adams Microfilm, Reel 115.

The people of America, he feared, would more readily institute the new government than yield obedience to it. The states, he wrote worriedly to Benjamin Rush, continued uppermost in the minds of the people, and would continue so until steps were taken to raise the national government in their estimation.[77] "The fate of this Government," he warned William Tudor, "depends absolutely upon raising it, above the State Governments."[78]

One of the most serious problems was that men of ability tended still to identify with the states. These people, Adams urged, must be wed to the national interest. (This was, of course, the same point, less cogently argued, that Hamilton used in defense of his fiscal policies.) What resource was there on which the new government might found its authority? Had it honor or profits? (Hamilton could readily have answered that.) Was a position in it desirable to men of fortune and ambition? Adams thought not. Men, he lamented, considered national posts only as stepping stones to promotion at home. Unless this was rectified, unless the national government amounted to more than a ladder on which to mount to higher positions in the states, it would soon go the way of the Confederation.[79]

The best recourse available, Adams believed, was the use of "decent and moderate titles" as distinctions of national office. It was certain, he declared to Benjamin Rush, "that we never shall have either Government, or Tranquility or Liberty, until some Rule of Precedency is adopted, and some Titles settled." One might depend upon it; the state governments would be uppermost in the minds of the people until superior titles were given national officials.[80] How, for example, could the Presi-

[77] Adams to Benjamin Rush, July 24, 1789: *Ibid.*

[78] Adams to William Tudor, May 9, 1789: Tudor Papers.

[79] Adams to William Tudor, May 28, 1789: Tudor Papers. Adams to William Tudor, June 28, 1789: *Ibid.*

[80] Adams to Benjamin Rush, July 24, 1789: Biddle, ed., *Old*

dent command respect if he enjoyed no loftier designation than "Excellency," the same title used by state governors?[81]

To the ready accusation that as Vice-President he expected a title of his own, Adams replied with something less than complete candor that he cared as little for marks of distinction as anyone. Titles, he insisted, were necessary to give dignity and energy to government; on this ground alone did he claim to be an advocate of them.[82]

Whatever Adams' personal ambitions, however, his critics were right in observing that his argument reflected rather dimly upon the American people. Titles Adams regarded essentially as instruments of control, as means of asserting governmental authority. His European experience had shown him the usefulness titles might have. Throughout Europe, the importance of "a certain Appearance in proportion to Rank" was evident in encouraging attitudes of respect for authority among the people.[83] According to what he had seen in England, France, Holland, and Spain, Adams exclaimed, there was nothing which "strikes and overawes the most abandoned of the Populace so much as Titles."[84] Something of the kind every government must have, American as well as European.

Adams' interest in titles derived immediately from his

Family Letters, I, 46. Adams to "A Recluse Man," January 19, 1792: *Works*, VIII, 513.

[81] Adams also argued from his own experience that the American President would command little respect in the courts of Europe as long as he held the title of a common diplomatic agent. Adams to James Lovell, July 16, 1789: Adams Microfilm, Reel 115. Adams to Benjamin Rush, July 24, 1789: Biddle, ed., *Old Family Letters*, I, 46.

[82] Adams to Benjamin Rush, July 24, 1789: *Ibid.* Adams to William Tudor, May 27, 1789: Tudor Papers.

[83] Adams to John Jay, May 13, 1785: Adams Microfilm, Reel 349.

[84] Adams to Benjamin Rush, July 28, 1789: Biddle, ed., *Old Family Letters*, I, 48.

prevailing view of the American people. No longer were appeals to reason and virtue enough to assure their orderly behavior. It was necessary now to appeal directly to the affections as well. The psychological basis of the appeal lay in his notion of emulation, the passion for distinction among men. This, as we have seen, he now identified as "the main spring of human nature"; the history of mankind was little more than "a single narration of its operation and effects."[85] Government had to take this into consideration and utilize this passion for its own advantage. This was "the only adequate instrument" of order and subordination. It alone commanded an effectual obedience to laws. Without it, neither human reason nor standing armies could prevail. "This is my philosophy of government," Adams explained. "The great art lies in managing this emulation."[86]

Whatever attracted attention and esteem was cherished, and marks and signs, stars and garters did this. Though there was nothing inherently respectable in them, they received more deference than did learning, virtue, or religion. The appearance of the Society of the Cincinnati offered evidence of this. All nations, Adams noted, "have endeavored to regulate the passion for respect and distinction, and to reduce it to some order in society, by titles marking the gradations of magistracy. . . ."[87] Thus, the visible language of signs might attract the attention of the people and attach them to their officials. This, Adams was careful to assure his readers, was "the true spirit of republics"; for in such governments, appeals either to the imagination or to force were the only methods of assuring submission to the laws.[88] By holding out the rewards of public distinction,

[85] Adams to Benjamin Waterhouse, July 19, 1789: Ford, ed., *Statesman and Friend*, p. 142. "Davila": *Works*, VI, 234.
[86] Adams to Timothy Pickering, October 31, 1797: *Ibid.*, VIII, 560.
[87] *Ibid.*, VI, 242.   [88] *Ibid.*, p. 243.

men of all sorts, even of least reason or virtue, could be "chained down to an incessant servitude to their fellow creatures. . . ." They could be "constituted by their own vanity," Adams explained, "slaves to mankind."[89]

The science of government, then, Adams reduced to the simple expedient of playing upon the passions of the people. On this turned "the whole system of human affairs."[90] The view of American character thus represented was distinctly unflattering. "Where virtue is lost," Adams observed, "Ambition succeeds then indeed Ribbons and Garters become necessary."[91] By the 1790's, he had concluded that in America this moment had arrived. No longer could the people be trusted to remain orderly. They needed to be persuaded, even to be tricked into respecting the authority that was set over them.

The second and more significant charge of anti-republicanism that Adams faced centered around his purported desire to replace the new national constitution with one more closely patterned after the British model; specifically, to substitute hereditary succession for popular election to high national office.

John Langdon of New Hampshire, recalling a conversation of 1794 with Adams, remarked that the Vice-President had expressed the belief that the American people would not long be happy without an hereditary executive and senate.[92] John Taylor, perhaps speaking of the same incident, claimed in 1796 that Adams had told him personally the day would come when America would be glad to accept an hereditary President.[93] And Benjamin Rush, one of Adams' firmest friends, told Adams directly in 1790 that both he and Jefferson

[89] *Ibid.*, p. 245.   [90] *Ibid.*, p. 269.

[91] Adams to Elbridge Gerry, April 25, 1789: Adams Microfilm, Reel 107.

[92] *Boston Independent Chronicle*, November 24, 1800.

[93] John Taylor to Daniel Brent, October 9, 1796: *John P. Branch Historical Papers*, 5 vols. (Richmond, Virginia, 1901-1918), II, 267.

agreed that Adams had changed his principles since
1776. Both of them, concluded Rush, deplored Adams'
new "attachment to monarchy."[94] The affair grew out
of Adams' concern over the danger of irregularities in
American elections. America, he explained, was not the
first experiment in popular republican government; and
with few exceptions, all earlier attempts had fallen
victim to the same enemy—corrupt elections. By corruption, he meant the "sacrifice of every national Interest and honour, to private and party Objects."[95] This
was now threatening America, and steps to guard against
it would have to be taken.

As long as Adams had kept his attention upon the
states, he had not manifested great concern over elections. In small districts where there were not great
offices at stake, the tendency toward corruption was
weak. When he switched his attention to the national
scene, however, the prospect of irregularities seemed
suddenly much greater. History and experience made
clear, he explained to Adrian Van der Kemp in 1790,
that elections "cannot be long conducted in a populous,
oppulent and commercial nation, without Corruption,
Sedition and Civil War."[96] As the population became
larger and more disparate, it divided into opposing political factions. In the resulting contest for power, each
of them resorted to whatever means were available to
promote its own interests. As a result, passions were
aroused, internal divisions deepened, and ultimately civil
conflict brought on.

Under the new national government, Adams feared

[94] Benjamin Rush to Adams, April 13, 1790: Lyman Butterfield,
ed., *Letters of Benjamin Rush*, 2 vols. (Princeton, 1951), I, 546,
522. See also F. B. Samuel, ed., Jefferson's *Anas* (New York, 1903),
pp. 36-37.

[95] Adams to Thomas Jefferson, November 15, 1813: Cappon, ed.,
Adams-Jefferson Letters, II, 401.

[96] Adams to Adrian Van der Kemp, February 27, 1790: Van der
Kemp Papers, Historical Society of Pennsylvania.

above all that the continent would divide into two great parties coinciding with the social divisions of aristocracy and democracy. As he looked about him, this seemed to be taking place. "Awful experience," together with reading and reflection, he remarked as early as 1790, combined to convince him that Americans were "more rapidly disposed to corruption in elections" than he had ever before thought possible.[97] Already he could cite contests and irregularities in the Congressional elections of 1790, and, even more personally, the efforts of Hamilton and others to hold down his electoral vote in 1788. During the first years under the new government, party faction seemed to be growing rapidly. "The tendency to civil war," he warned, "is rapid."[98] Elections, he lamented to Abigail four years later, were going the usual way in America. "O! that I had done with them."[99] Disenchanted as he was with the prospects of American political development, Adams made some incautious proposals about what should be done. They caused an uproar at the time and continued to plague him during the remainder of his life.

Once corruption had taken hold in a nation's elections, Adams affirmed, the only safe remedy was to do away with the most dangerous of them and resort instead to hereditary succession. To fail this was to invite certain disaster. America, Adams emphasized, had not yet reached this condition; but prevailing signs indicated that ultimately she would and that the problem of how to correct it would shortly have to be faced. How

[97] Adams to Benjamin Rush, April 18, 1790: *Works*, IX, 566.

[98] Adams to Adrian Van der Kemp, March 27, 1790: Van der Kemp Papers.

[99] Adams to Abigail Adams, May 17, 1794: C. F. Adams, ed., *Letters to his Wife*, II, 160-61. Jefferson recounted a story, probably apocryphal, told him by John Langdon, that Adams in a fit of rage over the votes given to George Clinton for Vice-President in 1792 had exclaimed: "Damn 'em, Damn 'em, Damn 'em, you see that an elective government will not do." Samuel, ed., Jefferson's *Anas*, p. 196.

soon, he never made clear. He never advocated the immediate implementation of hereditary succession in either state or national governments, as he was accused of doing. "I am by no means for attempting any such thing at present," he assured Benjamin Rush in 1789. "The experiment is made and will have fair play."[100] In 1789, he expected the change to become necessary at "no very distant period of time," though far enough away so that he would not live to see it. By 1813, he was projecting the crisis "many hundred years" into the future.[101] Adams continued to explain that America should do without hereditary government as long as she safely could. "As long as sense and virtue remain in a Nation in sufficient Quantities to enable them to choose their Legislatures and Magistrates," he declared, "elective Governments are the best in the world."[102]

What he said, and damned himself in the saying, was that given the present drift of American society, at some time in the future, popular elections would become sufficiently unstable to persuade the American people to choose the safer way of hereditary succession. "We have no government armed with power capable of contending with human passions unbridled by morality and religion," he explained. "Our constitution was made only for a moral and religious people. It is wholly inadequate to the government of any other."[103] When corruption did break in, a remedy would have to be found—and what that remedy was, everyone knew.[104] "Mankind have universally discovered that chance was

---

[100] Adams to Benjamin Rush, June 9, 1789: Biddle, ed., *Old Family Letters*, I, 38. "Defense": *Works*, VI, 25.

[101] Adams to Benjamin Rush, June 9, 1789: Biddle, ed., *Old Family Letters*, I, 37-38. Adams to Thomas Jefferson, November 15, 1813: Cappon, ed., *Adams-Jefferson Letters*, II, 399.

[102] Adams to Benjamin Rush, October 25, 1789: Biddle, ed., *Old Family Letters*, I, 245.

[103] "Reply to the Massachusetts Militia," October 11, 1789: Adams Microfilm, Reel 119.

[104] "Defense": *Works*, VI, 25.

preferable to a corrupt choice," he declared, "and have trusted Providence rather than themselves."[105] In answer to his critics, Adams explained that when the occasion arose, it would not be necessary to impose the new system by force. The people, he argued rather inconsistently, would be wise enough to see their danger and move to remedy it. They were familiar with conventions and would use them again when necessary.[106]

The elections most susceptible to irregularities were those for Senators and the President, in which electoral divisions (entire states) were large and the attractions of office great. Once corruption had set in, the first step to meet it would be to make the Senate permanent, thus denying to the aristocracy the opportunity (or the necessity) of interfering in elections.[107] This, however, would enhance the power of the upper house. In order to maintain the balance, it would then be necessary to make the executive permanent as well. The lower house could safely be left elective, as the true representative of the popular will. (Because of its small electoral districts and larger numbers, Adams explained, election to the House of Representatives did not inflame passions as much.)[108] Aristocratic, monarchic, and democratic powers, then, would be in perfect balance. For Adams, the parallel with the British constitution—"the most stupendous fabric of human invention"—was clear.[109]

Yet if Adams never spelled out precisely when he expected the changes to come, he continued to affirm to all who would listen that America would ultimately

[105] Ibid., p. 57. Biddle, ed., Old Family Letters, I, 37-38.

[106] "Defense": Works, VI, 57.

[107] This might be done, he speculated to one correspondent, by having permanent senators either elected by state conventions or named by the President. Adams to Adrian Van der Kemp, March 27, 1790: Adams Microfilm, Reel 115.

[108] Adams to Adrian Van der Kemp, March 27, 1793: Van der Kemp Papers.

[109] "Defense": Works, IV, 358.

confront them. "I am clear," he wrote in 1790, "that America must resort to them [two hereditary branches] as an Asylum against Discord, Seditions and Civil War. . . . Our ship must ultimately land on that shore or be cast away."[110] As early as 1787, Adams expressed to Jefferson his fear of the consequences of national elections. "Elections, my dear sir," he wrote, "Elections to offices which are great objects of Ambition, I look at with terror. Experiments of this kind have been so often tryed, and so universally found productive of Horrors, that there is great Reason to dread them."[111] As he projected American politics into the future, he saw ample reason to fear the worst.

For his endorsement of hereditary government, Adams reaped severe criticism—and he resented the fact bitterly. I have been "overborne by Misrepresentation," he complained.[112] He would forfeit his life, he later challenged Jefferson, if anyone could find one sentence in his writings which by fair construction could be made to favor the introduction of hereditary monarchy.[113] Technically, Adams' life was safe. It was true that he was always willing to be convinced that the American republic could work. And he hoped that it finally would.[114] Yet his critics were significantly right. His

[110] Adams to Benjamin Rush, July 9, 1789: Biddle, ed., *Old Family Letters*, I, 37-38.

[111] Adams to Thomas Jefferson, December 6, 1787: Cappon, ed., *Adams-Jefferson Letters*, I, 214.

[112] Adams to Thomas Jefferson, July 15, 1813: *Ibid.*, II, 357.

[113] Adams to Thomas Jefferson, July 13, 1813: *Ibid.*, p. 356. See also Adams' denial in his Inaugural Address: Richardson, ed., *Messages and Papers of the Presidents*, I, 229.

[114] Correa Walsh, while acknowledging that Adams never advocated the immediate introduction of hereditary government, asserts that "he had looked forward to it with pleasurable contemplation, that his spirit leaned toward it." Walsh, *Political Science of John Adams*, p. 283. Other commentators on Adams have mostly agreed. Yet the situation was just the opposite. Adams contemplated the introduction of hereditary elements with considerable disappointment, for it represented the frustration of the republican vision that he

view of the prospect of popular republican government in the United States had indeed changed. He now betrayed a disturbing lack of confidence in its long-term future. It was "impossible to say, until . . . fairly tried," he explained, whether an hereditary executive would not "be better than annual elections by the people."[115] The experiment had repeatedly failed elsewhere. Whether America could succeed could only "be proved by experience."[116] He remained essentially pessimistic. It was quite possible, even probable, that the popular election of Executive and Senate would ultimately prove unmanageable. As corruption crept in, these two branches at least would have to be removed from close dependence upon the people. Only then could they be made instruments of order rather than avenues of political intrigue.

THE vision of American society that Adams had fashioned by the 1790's, then, was quite different from his conception of twenty years before. His discussion of the problem of maintaining social order had changed correspondingly. He now emphasized the importance of strong institutions of social control—law and government. In distinction to his popular emphasis during the 1770's, he now stressed the dangers of popular government, and even warned that in order to avoid the evils of political corruption the most important elections would probably have to be done away with. His theme was the necessity of removing government from the direct influence of the people, of circumscribing their power rather than expanding it. The essential problem of society as he now defined it, was not to extend the area of individual freedom against irresponsible gov-

---

had fashioned during the 1770's. Not with pleasure but with regret did he conclude that the change would become necessary.

[115] "Defense": *Works*, VI, 122.

[116] *Ibid.*, p. 118.

ernment, but to prevent the enjoyment of liberty from degenerating into license. The danger to American society came not from excessive authority, but from conflict and anarchy.

For the first time, he sensed a divorce in the minds of considerable numbers of people between liberty and property. During the Revolution, he had emphasized the solidity of the people—their recognition of the fact that property rights underlay all human freedom, political as well as economic. Adams now postulated a split in society between an aristocracy of wealth who demonstrated little concern for the liberties of the rest of the people, and a democracy who in the name of liberty threatened the property of the wealthy. In order to prevent a clash between them, he called upon a vigorous government, able to control both interests by a mixture of force and cajolery.

His understanding of America's place in the sweep of history had also become considerably less clear. No longer did he so confidently talk of America as the beacon of liberty, showing the way for a benighted Europe. Now the similarities rather than the differences between the Old World and the New seemed to him most compelling. America had not yet reached Europe's stage of development; but she was on the way and moving fast. The United States enjoyed "no special Providence." The differences between America and Europe were no longer of kind, but only of time. In short, Adams' earlier vision of an untroubled future extending indefinitely after independence, had darkened considerably. From the late 1780's on, Adams was forced to adjust to this change; to admit to himself, however difficult it might be, that American society was now different, and to encourage Americans to realize this with him and plan accordingly.

Many of Adams' observations about American society remained vague and unsubstantiated. He certainly exaggerated the divisions among the people, especially the tendency toward an opposition of aristocratic and democratic interests. There were perhaps several reasons why Adams overstated his case. Part of it was his reckless use of terms. He often used such words as "aristocratic" and "monarchical" representatively rather than literally, without making the difference clear. "By kings and kingly power," he explained on one occasion, "is meant . . . by . . . me, the executive power in a single person." By aristocratical, he often meant "aristocratic-like."[117] Yet too often he failed to explain himself adequately. As R. R. Palmer has pointed out, Adams wrote casually about the three "orders" in American society, a term which in its more familiar European context signified legally established privileges, though he did not intend to give the term this meaning at all.[118]

Adams' use of the word "orders" betrayed still a greater confusion on his part—one between American and European society. It is important to remember that Adams was abroad from 1778 to 1788, a period of significant social unrest in Europe. Especially were conditions unsettled in France, the Netherlands, and England—the three countries in which he spent most of his time. In each of them, clearly defined social classes existed; and during the 1780's, the conflict between them became more sharp. At first, the aristocratic forces were in process of strengthening their hold upon the institutions of social control. Adams was markedly impressed by this development. "Monarchies and aristocracies," he observed, "are in possession of the voice and influence of every university and academy in Europe . . . [while] democratical mixtures are annihilated. . . ."[119]

[117] *Ibid.*, p. 186. Adams to James Lovell, July 16, 1789: Adams Microfilm, Reel 115.
[118] R. R. Palmer, *The Age of the Democratic Revolution: The Challenge* (Princeton, 1959), pp. 275-76.
[119] "Defense": *Works*, IV, 289-90.

Adams was in the Netherlands just as the struggle between the Stadholder and gentry broke into the open.[120]
By the late 1780's, it was evident that popular discontent with aristocratic power was growing. Of this, Adams
was also aware.

The increasing tension in Europe affected his outlook as, after 1786, he turned once more to America.
The principles of social and political development being
by definition everywhere the same, Adams took the opportunity to observe the European scene and glean from
it insights by which to make American society more
understandable. This was the whole point of his frequent warnings to America to avoid the errors of
Europe. His observations while abroad dramatized for
him what might be expected when any society matured.

At first, Adams had noticed mostly the beauties of
European civilization: the verdant, cultivated country-
side, the magnificent chateaus, the museums and shops,
the painting and architecture, the brilliance of social life
and the attention to intellect. Increasingly, however, he
became obsessed with other qualities: the wide disparities
of wealth, the rigid social distinctions, the looseness of
morals, the cynicism of politicians, and the startling
ignorance of the people. It all made a coherent picture
for him. "I cannot help Suspecting," he commented
from amidst the ostentation of the French court, "that
the more Elegance, the less Virtue in all Times and
Countries."[121] Especially was he impressed with the
antagonism between aristocratic and democratic interests
throughout European societies.

With the image of European society still freshly in
mind, then, Adams turned again to America—and
found many of the same disturbing signs. In his own

[120] Palmer, *Age of the Democratic Revolution: The Challenge*, pp.
29, 39-40, 40ff., 145-46.
[121] Adams to Abigail Adams, April 12, 1778: Adams Microfilm,
Reel 349.

thinking, the two societies became blurred. "It has been my fortune, good or bad," he later observed, "to live in Europe ten years, from 1778 to 1788, in a public character. This destiny, singular in America, forced upon my attention the course of events in France, Holland, Geneva, and Switzerland, among many other nations; and this has irresistibly attracted my thoughts more than has been for my interest."[122] Increasingly, Adams tended to link together European and American society and write similarly about both. Especially in his "Defense," is it difficult to determine at any given time which society he is considering, for he turns repeatedly from one to the other.

The confusion was compounded by his cyclical view of history. America had not matured as much as Europe, yet she ultimately would, for she was embarked upon the same course. Actually, Adams was warning in substantial measure against the future tendency of American development. In Europe, however, he saw what the end result would almost certainly be. Alarmed by the condition of European society and anxious to warn America about it, he confused warning with actuality, and described the American present in terms considerably darker even than he believed immediate conditions warranted.[123]

[122] Adams to John Taylor, 1814: *Works*, VI, 477.

[123] Edward Handler argues convincingly that Adams' confusion between American and European society worked both ways; that he tended to impose American values upon European situations which they did not fit, and conversely to read European conditions back into American society. Handler, *Europe and America*, Chapter 1. In accusing Adams of universalizing too freely, and of failing to consider the differences between European and American conditions, however, Handler fails to take account of the development in Adams' thought. As I have tried to show, before the 1780's Adams was struck most of all by America's uniqueness of moral character and social condition. Only after he came to believe that America had begun to develop along the European pattern, that is after about 1786, did he begin to write similarly of the two.

Chapter VII. "The Dangers of Party Faction"

In 1788, Adams had returned to America uncertain what his future would be. To his friends, he professed an interest only in retiring to his Quincy farm and leaving the controversy of public life behind. In fact, however, he was not yet ready to let ambition go. Though he turned aside suggestions that he serve as a delegate to the last session of the old Continental Congress, or as a Senator under the new constitution, or even as governor of Massachusetts, he clearly believed there were duties for him still to perform. There were only two offices, however, which he thought he could with honor accept—the Presidency or Vice-Presidency; but public sentiment, he grumbled, seemed to have decreed them for others.[1] As things turned out, of course, Adams had more than a decade of important public service still to complete—eight years as Vice-President and then a term as President. The experience of these twelve years was important for him, for it served to bear out in his own mind the warnings he had recently issued about the course of American political development, and thus to reinforce his whole changed conception of the American people.

The central problem confronting Adams during the 1790's was a familiar one—how best to promote the effective regulation of American society—yet it was newly complicated by the changes in circumstance that had occurred since twenty years before. The decline of American virtue and the division of society into opposing in-

[1] Adams to Miss Abigail Adams, August 16, 1788: Caroline De-Windt, ed., *The Journal and Correspondence of Miss Adams*, 2 vols. (Boston, 1876), II, 87-89.

terests threatened domestic stability, and the tendency of these interests to fall victim to foreign influence promised even greater danger. The ultimate consequence of this, he feared, would be civil discord and disunion, the break-up of the continent among separate warring parties. Internal order, Adams emphasized, depended upon continental union; and this, in turn, was the function of a firm and energetic national government supported by the majority of the people and capable of excluding foreign influence.

Union and harmony throughout the continent, however, Adams saw breaking down as a result of growing political division. One of the principles of republican political faith most widely held among Americans during the 1790's, stated that formal political parties were incompatible with popular republican government. Republican theory, whether derived from Locke, Montesquieu, or Rousseau, declared this to be so. In 1784, John Breckenridge, James Madison, John Taylor, and James Monroe had formed a group called "The Society for the Preservation of Liberty" whose principal object was to prevent the rise of faction in America.[2] Other men expressed similar sentiments. "In these United States," declared one individual in 1794, "where the people form one Republican society all constituted associations for promoting political views are useless, at least, if not dangerous, and should be discouraged."[3]

In this belief, Adams fully shared. The "spirit of faction" was the "Cankerworm" that had brought the downfall of every republic from Rome to Cromwell's Commonwealth. It threatened the new American republic as well. Parties accentuated the struggle for political spoils and made personal ambition rather than social virtue the touchstone of political success. Party con-

[2] "Documents": *American Historical Review*, XXXII (1926-27), 550-52.
[3] *Baltimore Daily Advertiser*, March 31, 1794.

flict, by exciting passions and clouding reason, corrupted elections more quickly than anything. In popular governments where there were no parties, the magistrates became at every election more beloved by the whole nation. Where parties intruded, however, and there were opposing candidates, each at the head of a faction, the people became divided and were set against each other. The clash of ambitions produced slanders first, mobs and seditions next, and civil turmoil at last.[4]

When stimulated by political factions, even "the most learned and virtuous men," made "wild work with the feelings and Interests and often with the rights of individuals."[5] How much greater the dangers among men of questionable virtue! All parties, Adams informed Benjamin Waterhouse in 1812, have been "violent Friends of Order, Law, Government, and Religion, when in Power" and "libellous, Seditious, and rebellious" when out.[6] France offered the grimmest evidence of the desolation which party faction could bring. Political faction, moreover, invited the encroachment of foreign influence. "The Resolution not to call in foreign Nations," Adams remarked in 1787, "will be kept untill a domestic difference of a serious nature shall break out."[7]

The ultimate danger was that the nation would finally divide into two powerful political parties locked in deadly struggle against each other. "There is nothing which I dread so much," Adams had exclaimed in 1780 concerning the first election to be held under the new Massachusetts Constitution, "as a division of the republic into two great parties, each arranged under its leader,

[4] "Davila": *Works*, VI, 254-55. Adams to Benjamin Waterhouse, April 2, 1806: Ford, ed., *Statesman and Friend*, pp. 35-36.

[5] *Ibid.*

[6] Adams to Benjamin Waterhouse, August 19, 1812: *Ibid.*, p. 86.

[7] Adams to Thomas Jefferson, October 9, 1787: Cappon, ed., *Adams-Jefferson Letters*, I, 202.

and concerting measures in opposition to each other. This, in my humble apprehension, is to be dreaded as the greatest political evil under our Constitution."[8] The danger was compounded in national elections where more powerful offices attracted ambitious men and greater impersonality rendered responsibility less certain. The greatest peril was that the election of the chief executive, the one official who should give focus to the whole nation's endeavors, would become the sport of party intrigue.[9]

Political division, however, is precisely what Adams saw developing during the 1790's. Two great factions were emerging, contesting elections, stirring up the people, attacking each other, allying themselves with foreign powers, appearing ready, as Adams believed, to compromise America's interests in any way necessary to increase their own power. In his Inaugural Address, Adams issued a stern warning against the dangers party division held for America. Americans would be unfaithful to themselves, he explained to the Congress assembled before him, if they failed to guard against political intrigue. If elections were to be determined by "artifice and corruption," the government would become "the choice of a party for its own ends, not of the nation for the national good." If the franchise was influenced by other nations through flattery or menace, the government would quickly fall under the control of foreign powers. Though Adams hoped that in the years ahead the name of Washington might help to allay such possibilities, he warned that the perils would increase.[10] And during his own term as President, of course, they did.

The story of party development during the 1790's, and more particularly of Adams' administration, has

[8] Adams to Jonathan Jackson, October 2, 1780: *Works*, IX, 511.
[9] "Davila": *Ibid.*, VI, 254.
[10] Richardson, ed., *Messages and Papers of the Presidents*, I, 218ff.

been frequently told. I propose only to sketch briefly
some of the episodes involved for the purpose of suggesting their relationship to the continuing development
of Adams' political thought. His disagreement with the
Jeffersonian Republican opposition was of long standing.
Its causes were many. As a high official in Washington's
two administrations, Adams was a prime target of Republican attacks, especially given his "anti-republican"
outbursts. He had, moreover, supported Hamilton's
funding and assumption schemes.[11] The area of foreign
policy, however, presented the issues most instrumental
in the development of opposing political alliances, and
here as well Adams found himself on the opposite side
from the Republicans. From the first, Adams stood in
fear of what the French Revolution might bring, not
only for France but for America as well. As we have
seen, he denied that France could ever successfully establish popular republican government. And he was
afraid that radical political ideas—of government in one
center, with no balance—would be transferred by Republican agents to America. Evidence of Republican perfidy was abundant: the welcome of Genêt, opposition
to the Jay Treaty in 1795, efforts to involve the United
States openly on France's side in the European war, appeals for the sequestration of British-held debts, and the
prohibition of all commercial intercourse with her.[12] The
Republicans, Adams complained, seemed ready to promote a needless war with Britain and a dangerous alliance with revolutionary France.[13]

[11] The national debt Adams described as "the instrument for
establishing a national government." The assumption of state debts
was "the pivot upon which the general government will turn."
Adams to Stephen Higginson, March 14, 1790: Adams Microfilm,
Reel 115.

[12] Adams to Abigail Adams, March 12, 1794: C. F. Adams, ed.,
Letters to his Wife, II, 146. Adams to Thomas Jefferson, May 11,
1794: Cappon, ed., *Adams-Jefferson Letters*, I, 255. Adams to Abigail
Adams, June 11, 1795: *Works*, I, 478.

[13] Adams to Abigail Adams, April 19 and May 10, 1794: C. F.

As the crisis with France deepened during Adams' own administration, so did his troubles with the growing Republican opposition. In spite of a brief flurry of congeniality between Jefferson and himself early in 1797, Adams and the Republicans very rapidly split further apart and went their opposite ways. Again, the source of disagreement was America's relations with France. The crisis arrived during 1798 and 1799, the period of the near war with France, the XYZ affair and the Alien and Sedition Acts, and the Virginia and Kentucky resolutions. From then on, Adams and the Republicans viewed each other with complete distrust. In reply to one of the hundreds of memorials that flooded in upon him during the summer of 1798, Adams expressed his fear that "in the last Extremity . . . We shall find Traitors who will unite with the invading Enemy and fly within their lines."[14] To another, he warned that the country had never appeared "in greater danger than at this moment, from within or without, never more urgently excited to assume the functions of soldiers."[15] Over the winter of 1798-1799, Adams became fully convinced that the "French, Jacobinical faction" was preparing to set up armed opposition to the national government. The Virginia and Kentucky resolutions had given warning, and the rumored arming of special troops to the south offered proof, he was sure, of imminent measures against the administration. In service to their French masters, the Republicans were ready to tear American society asunder.

Republican spokesmen, on the other hand, assailed Adams for his inflammatory speeches. The President's

---

Adams, ed., *Letters to his Wife*, II, 157, 159. Adams to Abigail Adams, April 19, 1796: *Ibid.*, pp. 223-24.

[14] "Reply to the Inhabitants of Kittery, Maine," August 17, 1798: Adams Microfilm, Reel 119.

[15] "Reply to the Young Men of Boston," May 22, 1798: *Works*, IX, 194.

public statements, Madison declared in disgust, were "abominable and degrading."[16] And Madison and others blamed him for passage of the whole body of Federalist security legislation: the Alien and Sedition Acts, the Army Bill, and the Excise.[17] Even Adams' final decision for peace in 1799, won scant praise from the Republicans. He could have done nothing else, Madison declared.[18]

By 1800, Adams had broken similarly with an important segment of his own party. He became convinced that there was an English as well as a French faction, devoted to just as dishonorable motives and equally threatening to American unity. These were the high Federalists, centering around Alexander Hamilton. Again, the sources of conflict between Adams and the Hamiltonians are well known. Stephen Kurtz and Manning Dauer, among others, have described them in considerable detail, and the story merits only brief recapitulation here.

There were, first of all, the conflicting ambitions of Adams and Hamilton, each contending for supremacy in the Federalist party after Washington's withdrawal. In 1796, Hamilton had schemed to reduce Adams' electoral vote and bring the second Federalist candidate, C. C. Pinckney in ahead of him. Adams was aware of this, as well as of the continuing influence Hamilton exerted on the administration through his friends in the Cabinet and Congress. Giving broader significance to this

[16] James Madison to Thomas Jefferson, April 2 and 15, 1798: Hunt, ed., *Writings of Madison*, VI, 312, 314-16.

[17] For Adams' role in the passage of this legislation, see Kurtz, *Presidency of John Adams*, pp. 322-31, and James M. Smith, *Freedom's Fetters, the Alien and Sedition Laws and American Civil Liberties* (Ithaca, New York, 1956), especially pages 20, 92-93, 152-63, 167-71. Also, Adams to Timothy Pickering, September 16 and October 16, 1798: *Works*, VIII, 596, 606-607 and Adams to Timothy Pickering, August 1 and August 13, 1799: Adams Microfilm, Reel 120.

[18] James Madison to Thomas Jefferson, February 8, 1799: Hunt, ed., *Writings of Madison*, VI, 330n.

contest was the difference between the two in social and political philosophy—Adams retaining something of a Jeffersonian faith in an essentially agrarian rather than commercial or manufacturing economy, an aversion to banks and speculation, a fear of extensive economic development, and a reluctance to cast America in an aggressive role internationally.[19] Adams, moreover, in spite of his growing disillusionment with American society, maintained a greater respect for republican forms of government.

As with the Republicans, the issue steadily driving Adams and the Hamiltonians apart after 1796 was how best to handle America's growing difficulties with France. They disagreed on whether to depend for defense upon a large standing army or an expanded naval force, whether Hamilton and other younger officers or Adams' old Revolutionary colleagues should be given command of the army, and most importantly whether or not the administration should seek a peaceful accommodation of the disputes with France. During the summer of 1798, when Adams became caught up in the anti-French uproar resulting from the XYZ affair, relations between him and the Hamiltonians seemed close. Hamilton's supporters applauded the vigor of Adams' public utterances. The President's conduct, noted Theodore Sedgwick approvingly, "has, indeed, increased the confidence of the friends of the government. . . ."[20] He had "elevated

[19] For Adams' criticism of banks and their tendency to promote speculation and accent social division, see Adams to Abigail Adams, January 9, 1793: C. F. Adams, ed., *Letters to his Wife*, II, 117 and Adams to Benjamin Rush, August 28, 1811: *Works*, IX, 638. Adams favored the national bank as an instrument of stability and national strength (though in later years he remembered that he had been against it), but believed it should be "Strictly limited in its operations. . . ." Adams to Abigail Adams, January 12, 1794: C. F. Adams, ed., *Letters to his Wife*, II, 138. See also, Dauer, *The Adams Federalists*, Chapters 3 and 4.

[20] Theodore Sedgwick to Rufus King, April 9, 1798: King, ed., *Life of Rufus King*, II, 311. Octavius Pickering, *The Life of Timothy Pickering*, 4 vols. (Boston, 1867-1873), III, 381-82.

the spirit, and cleared the filmy eyes, of the many," affirmed Fisher Ames. Every statement, declared Timothy Pickering, was "a step upstairs."[21]

During the winter of 1798-1799, however, Adams' emotions and his ardor for a war with France cooled dramatically. In February of 1799, to the utter dismay of the Hamiltonians, he made public his intentions of seeking a peaceful accommodation with France and appointed a new mission, instructing it to be ready to sail soon. The high Federalists were furious. "Yesterday we were all thunderstruck by the President's nominating Mr. Murray Plenipotentiary," muttered Secretary of State Pickering, Hamilton's chief confidant in the cabinet.[22] Other of the Hamiltonians were equally distraught. They had seen in the anti-French uproar an excellent opportunity, perhaps their last one, of doing away with the Republican opposition.[23] And now Adams was about to frustrate them. Much to Adams' annoyance, immediate pressure by some of the Federalists in the Senate forced him to add several other names to the peace commission. But he remained convinced by communications from the French government and from certain Americans then in Europe (among them his own son, John Quincy Adams) that an honorable accommodation was possible. Throughout the summer and early fall of 1799, Adams and the high Federalists in

[21] Fisher Ames to Timothy Pickering, July 10, 1798: Seth Ames, ed., The Works of Fisher Ames, 2 vols. (Boston, 1854), I, 232. Memorandum of Timothy Pickering, April 6, 1819: Pickering Papers, Massachusetts Historical Society.

[22] Timothy Pickering to Rufus King, February 19, 1799: Pickering Papers. King, ed., Life of Rufus King, II, 551. Ames, ed., The Works of Fisher Ames, I, 253.

[23] For a detailed treatment of high Federalist intentions, see James M. Smith, Freedom's Fetters, pp. 21, 113-22, 126-28. See also, George Cabot to Oliver Wolcott, Jr., October 25, 1798: George Gibbs, The Administrations of Washington and John Adams, 2 vols. (New York, 1846), II, 109. Stephen Higginson to Oliver Wolcott, Jr., July 11, 1798: Ibid., pp. 70-71.

his cabinet sparred to determine whether the mission should go or not. Finally, after repeated frustration (and a timely warning from Secretary of the Navy Stoddert), Adams rushed from Quincy to Trenton where the government was then resting and ordered the mission to depart. Once more, the Hamiltonians were left to gnash their teeth. Seeing their ambition finally frustrated, they gave themselves over to open and bitter condemnation of the President. Within a few months, when the Sixth Congress had met and begun to dismantle the security program, Adams was ready to push relations with the Hamiltonians to an open break.[24] On May 5, he confronted Secretary of War McHenry, accusing him, Secretary of State Pickering, and Secretary of the Treasury Wolcott of working against the administration. McHenry, Adams declared, must resign.[25] Adams agreed to allow McHenry to remain until June 1, so that he might prepare a defense of his official conduct. Five days later, the President demanded Pickering's resignation. When the Secretary refused, Adams on the 12th curtly dismissed him.[26] Again the Hamiltonians were outraged, but Adams was by this time persuaded that he could no longer afford to accommodate them, that they were both his and the nation's enemies.

By 1800, then, Adams believed a crisis had been reached. What he had most feared had come to pass; America stood divided between two warring factions, each prostituted to a foreign power and bent upon the gratification of its own political ambitions at whatever cost to the nation. Political discourse was characterized by an extraordinary violence of language, and the threat of actual physical conflict loomed over the land. The

[24] Stoddert recalled Adams' explanation of why he had waited. Benjamin Stoddert to Adams, October 27, 1811: Adams Microfilm, Reel 412.

[25] James McHenry to Adams, May 31, 1800: *Ibid.*, Reel 397.

[26] Adams to Timothy Pickering, May 10 and 12, 1800: *Ibid.*, Reel 120.

Republicans—or "Jacobins" as Adams called them—
were in active opposition to the government, rendering
homage to revolutionary France, and spouting radical
social and political doctrines at home. Convinced that
the administration was their mortal enemy, they appeared ready to risk disorder, even disunion, rather than
accept the Federalist program.

In the late fall of 1798, the Virginia and Kentucky
legislatures passed resolutions declaring that better the
union should be dissolved than a tyrannical government
allowed. Throughout the spring and summer following,
rumors grew of state militias arming to the south and
of groups forming in every major city from Baltimore to Boston preparing to resist forcibly the federal army when it moved against them. In Philadelphia, armed patrols had to walk the streets to
protect against mobs which gathered to threaten government officials.[27] Even the President thought it prudent to smuggle arms into his residence as a precaution.
In late February and early March of 1799, a group of
disgruntled farmers in the counties north of Philadelphia (significantly enough, a formerly Federalist area)
gathered at the urging of John Fries to protest the taxes
levied upon their land. Though the protest quickly collapsed when federal troops approached, it offered further evidence of the lengths to which opponents of the
administration were willing to go.[28]

On the other hand, the high Federalists, the "English
faction," seemed blind to the crisis facing the country.
Ready to return America to British control, they appeared bent upon pushing relations with France to an
open break and using this as an excuse for attacking the

[27] Adams to Thomas Jefferson, June 30, 1813: Cappon, ed.,
Adams-Jefferson Letters, ii, 346-48.
[28] Harry M. Tinkcom, *Republicans and Federalists in Pennsylvania, 1790-1801* (Harrisburg, 1950), pp. 215-19. Bernard Steiner,
The Life and Correspondence of James McHenry (Cleveland, 1907),
pp. 418, 431-37.

Republican opposition at home. Each side, Adams concluded, was willing to plunge the nation into civil strife in pursuit of its own political interest.

From 1789 on, Adams had believed that America should avoid foreign war if at all possible, especially for the immediate future. The new nation would require time to gather its strength and the government a chance to establish its authority. Thoughts such as these had led Adams to welcome the Jay Treaty in 1795. Similar considerations motivated him in 1799 and 1800. War, he feared, would necessitate a system of debts and taxes which America could hardly support. During the 1780's, he had witnessed in Massachusetts and elsewhere the resentment generated when Congress, and even local government, had attempted to place needed levies upon the people. More recently, the farmers of western Pennsylvania had risen to protest the tax placed by government upon their whiskey. In time of peace it was difficult enough to persuade the people to provide even the most essential financial support. War increased debts and made the load even heavier.

Adams' own advisors told how difficult it would be to raise revenue. The government, they warned, could borrow at no less than eight percent. Just a decade before, he exclaimed, he had borrowed money from the Dutch at half that rate![29] Another war, Adams had confided to Jefferson in 1794 during the war scare with England, would add "two or three hundred Millions of Dollars to our Debt, raise up a many headed and many bellied Monster of an Army to tyrannize over Us, totally disadjust [*sic*] our present Government, and accelerate the Advent of Monarchy and Aristocracy by at least fifty Years."[30]

[29] Adams to Oliver Wolcott, Jr., May 17, 1800: *Works*, IX, 57.
[30] Adams to Thomas Jefferson, May 11, 1794: Cappon, ed., *Adams-Jefferson Letters*, I, 255. While confessing the importance of Hamilton's tax system in giving strength to the national government, Adams had lamented the introduction of both taxes and expenses which would "accumulate a perpetual debt and lead to future

By 1799, Adams was alarmed at precisely this prospect. "This damned army," he broke out against Wolcott, "will be the ruin of this country. . . ." Debts and taxes, by arousing discontent and promoting political division, had levelled governments in Europe. America was in danger of suffering a similar fate.[31]

In the face of impending political crisis, Adams determined that peaceful accommodation with France was essential. To push ahead with the war program in the face of mounting Republican opposition would be folly. Two days before being sworn into office, he had told Jefferson that because of political factionalism a rupture with France "would convulse the attachments" of the country.[32] In the excitement of 1798, he had lost sight of his own warning; but by 1799 he had regained his earlier perspective. April 25, 1799 Adams proclaimed a fast day, imploring that God "would withhold us from unreasonable discontent, from disunion, faction, sedition, and insurrection. . . ."[33] Though the Hamiltonians appeared too blind to see it, the government simply could not command the support of the people for its war measures any longer.[34] Opposition, especially to the standing army and new taxes, was widespread and growing. To ignore the fact would be to risk serious disorder. It was essential for the well-being of the nation, he concluded, to restore the confidence of the people in the administration. The high Federalists, to protect their own political position, were ready to turn their backs on public senti-

---

revolutions." Adams to Abigail Adams, May 5, 1794: C. F. Adams, ed., *Letters to his Wife*, II, 158.

[31] Adams to James McHenry, July 27, 1799: Adams Microfilm, Reel 120.

[32] Samuel, ed., Jefferson's *Anas*, p. 184.

[33] "Proclamation for a National Fast," March 6, 1799: *Works*, IX, 172-74.

[34] Adams to James Lloyd, March 6 to 31 and April 24, 1815: *Ibid.*, X, 134-66. Adams made this point at length in this series of letters to Lloyd.

ment, to isolate the government from the people and impose their program by force if necessary. Adams recognized the dangers involved in this. He acknowledged the importance of leadership by an aristocracy, but an aristocracy of wisdom and virtue that remained ultimately responsible to the people. In opposition to Hamilton, Adams steadfastly denied that the distinctions among men were moral, or that the few could be trusted with political power any more than the many. If given the chance, all men would tyrannize over their fellows and had to be controlled equally. Adams thus differed from the Hamiltonians on the basic issue of who should govern in America. And so he moved to dampen political violence, to heal the divisions that plagued American society, and rebuild the broad consensus that had once supported the Federalist administration. As we have seen, he announced in February of 1799 the third mission to France, encouraged the dismantling of the security system, and ridded his cabinet of Hamilton's supporters.[35]

Adams was clearly wise in fearing the consequences of the high Federalist war policy. War with France in 1799, given the intensity of domestic opposition, would have put the nation to a desperate test. Serious internal turmoil would almost certainly have been the consequence. The Hamiltonians, if given the chance, were ready to push their advantage to the limit. Had this occurred, the Republicans would have had no alternative but to submit or mount an equally violent response. Adams was wise also in suspecting the military ambitions of Hamilton. This, in addition to Adams' long-

[35] In May of 1800, in a further effort to restore confidence in the government, he pardoned the Fries rebels who had already been convicted by two different state courts of treason and conspiracy. Adams had received petitions of clemency from the imprisoned men in August of 1799. Adams Microfilm, Reel 396. For Adams' exchange of communications with his cabinet on the matter during May of 1800, see *ibid.*, Reel 397.

standing aversion to a standing army, was the reason he was so recalcitrant in pressing the recruitment of officers (much to the Hamiltonians' annoyance), and tried to avoid the appointment of Hamilton as second in command of the new force under Washington. Not only did Adams dread the prospect of using troops against domestic opponents, he was alarmed at Hamilton's imperialistic ambitions. Mounting an overland campaign to the southwest, as Hamilton desired, Adams affirmed, would invite a Spanish war and add the problem of assimilating large new areas of alien territory. As the United States moved closer to reconciliation with France, moreover, there was less reason for maintaining a large armed force. If the nation saw an army to maintain without an enemy to fight, Adams warned McHenry, enthusiasms would arise not yet fully foreseen.[36]

Adams, of course, had his own political fate as well as the fortunes of the Federalist party very much in mind as he maneuvered for peace in 1800. Success in the coming election, he perceived, depended upon domestic tranquility. His only hope was to attract support from all moderate elements in the society, thus isolating the extremists on both sides. And this could be accomplished only by affirming a policy of honorable reconciliation with France. The "great Body of Federalists, as well as the whole of the other Party," he believed, were desirous of avoiding war if at all possible.[37] To proceed without negotiations would produce "a compleat revolution of sentiment" in favor of the Republicans (the thing to be avoided at all costs), the certain defeat of the Federal-

[36] Adams to James McHenry, October 22, 1798: *Works*, VIII, 613. Both at the time and later, Adams complained that the army had been forced upon him. Adams to Benjamin Rush, August 23, 1805: Biddle, ed., *Old Family Letters*, I, 76. Adams to H. G. Otis, May 9, 1823: Otis Papers, Massachusetts Historical Society.

[37] Adams' Notes for a Reply to Hamilton, 1800: Adams Microfilm, Reel 399.

ists, and ultimately another bitter war with Britain.[38]

By 1800, then, Adams was seriously alarmed by the dramatic changes that had taken place in American politics. To him they reflected a precipitate decline both in American moral character and the homogeneity of American society. Part of the problem, he identified with the appearance of a new generation of political leaders. The Old Patriots, men shaped by the experience of the Revolution, were passing from the scene. The initiative was passing to new men unfamiliar with the Revolution, unschooled in its principles. This was true, Adams observed, of both parties. Among the Federalists, Timothy Pickering, Fisher Ames, Robert Goodloe Harper—all had entered upon the political scene since 1783. Among the Republicans appeared another "set of young fellows" who had taken their college degrees "since the revolution in 1774" and were, consequently, unknowledgeable in its "great principles of civil and religious liberty."[39] Stability and dignity must be given to the laws, Adams had warned as far back as 1783, "and the old Hands must do this or it will not be done."[40] America, he had hoped, would look for leadership to "gentlemen who had some experience in life before the revolution. . . ."[41] During the first years of the national government, he had had reason to believe this would be the case. He was glad to see before him so many familiar faces, he had declared in his maiden speech to the Senate in 1789; men he had known ten and twenty years be-

---

[38] Adams to Thomas Boylston Adams, January 16, 1801: *Ibid.*, Reel 400. Adams to James Lloyd, February 15, 1815: *Ibid.*, Reel 122. Page Smith goes too far in denying to Adams any personal political motivations. Page Smith, *John Adams*, pp. 1,001-1,002, 1,029.

[39] Adams to John Trumbull, March 12, 1790: Adams Microfilm, Reel 115.

[40] Adams to Mercy Warren, January 29, 1783: "Warren-Adams Letters," Massachusetts Historical Society, *Collections*, LXXIII, 189.

[41] Adams to George Walton, September 25, 1789: *Works*, VIII, 495-96.

fore.[42] Much to his regret, however, the "Old Whigs" rapidly gave way to new men. "I am a solitary individual of 1774 men," he lamented in 1798. "All the rest have departed."[43] A change of generation, then, seemed to explain at least in part the political confusion into which the country had fallen. This was but another way of describing the decline in social virtue which the society had undergone.

Whatever Adams' reflections may explain about the political history of the 1790's, they shed important light upon his own situation.[44] By 1800, he felt a generation out of date; part of a glorious past during which the nation had come into being, but whose inspiration was rapidly fading. Many of the political leaders of the late 1790's were new to him (with a few exceptions such as Washington and Jefferson), and he did not really know or trust them. They had not shared with him the exhilaration of the Revolutionary struggle. They seemed more intent upon fashioning the nation along new lines, rather than looking back to the intent of the Revolutionary leaders.

Adams had formulated many of his ideas about the proper nature of America's social and political life during the early Revolutionary years. This had been a period of substantial agreement within American society on the dominant issues of the day: the injustice of British colonial measures, the danger of attacks upon American property and political liberties, and the need to defend them. Within this broad consensus, there had been disagreement as to tactics, some favoring vigorous resistance

[42] Adams to Abigail Adams, December 6, 1798: Adams Microfilm, Reel 124.

[43] Adams to Thomas Johnson, April 26, 1798: *Works*, VIII, 572.

[44] The problem of generation change between the Revolutionary leaders and the men coming into control of American politics during the 1790's merits much closer examination than anyone has yet given it. On both sides, the differences were frequently and somberly discussed.

and others more caution. But the only divergence on fundamentals had come from the Tories—always a minority voice and, after 1772-1774, an almost nonexistent one. Adams had come home from the first Continental Congress persuaded of the colonies' broad adherence to common principles. And in spite of his occasional frustrations, he continued, until his departure for France in 1778, to believe there existed a general consensus of opinion among Americans.[45]

Adams had been schooled in continental politics during this period. He had, furthermore, been eminently successful then as a political leader. He tended, as a consequence, to use his Revolutionary experience—at least his idealized recollection of it—as a touchstone by which to evaluate developments during the decades that followed. Whereas he remembered that there had once been a broad adherence to the public interest, he now confronted a society divided between groups seeking only their own satisfaction. Rather than closely knit and harmonious, the society of the 1790's proved factious and quarrelsome. Instead of being frugal and sparse, it appeared wealthy and rapidly growing in numbers. This constant comparison of present with past accentuated in Adams' mind the changes that American society had undergone, and made them seem particularly disheartening. Given his Revolutionary idealism, for example, Adams could make no peace with the notion of formal, national political parties. Their very existence seemed a sign of degeneration. Actually, they would in the future prove to be effective instruments of social control. Adams, however, never realized this.

Few politicians are able to make an effective transi-

---

[45] See the extended discussion by Irving Brant of strongly national sentiment during the 1770's in his *James Madison, Nationalist, 1780-1787*, pp. 409-20. John Marshall and others of the Revolutionary generation also reflected upon the spirit of unity they remembered as characteristic of the Revolutionary years, and the divisiveness of succeeding decades.

tion between significantly different historical epochs; that is, to retain the flexibility and freshness, the sense of anticipation necessary to consider problems constructively and on their own terms. Adams was no exception. When he returned home from Europe in 1788, he was already fifty-three years of age, for the eighteenth century a full lifetime in itself. The Revolution had constituted his great crusade. He had dedicated himself to it; and for it he retained an emotional attachment that dominated the rest of his life. Considering the Revolution's grandeur and his own successful role in it, this is understandable.

The hold that the Revolution had upon him, however, proved no blessing, for it stood in the way of his accommodation with the changing conditions of the 1790's. A greater tolerance of parties and willingness to use them as agencies of the general welfare, might have saved him considerable grief. He might then have been willing to challenge the Hamiltonians earlier for control of the Federalist party, and so have avoided much of the indecision that, by 1800, caused him such trouble. "It can never be the Duty of one Man to be concerned in more than one Revolution," he remarked in 1783, "and therefore I will never have any Thing to do with another."[46] With the peaceful "revolution" in American politics that took place during the 1790's, Adams had a great deal to do. Yet he never effectively understood it.

Beyond this, Adams' own predicament continued to dramatize America's condition for him, to add credibility to the belief that great changes had taken place among the American people. He found himself caught between Republicans and Hamiltonians, attacked from both sides, with few persons willing to speak up in his defense. He cast himself (with substantial reason) in the role of the disinterested Patriot, suffering abuse at the hands of his

[46] Adams to Mercy Warren, January 29, 1783: "Warren-Adams Letters," LXXIII, 188-89.

country's enemies. And he felt keenly the injustice of his condition. "How mighty a power is the spirit of party!" he cried. "How decisive and unanimous it is."[47] Men "merely national" were no longer heard; there were "no more Americans in America."[48] Patriotism had to be tinctured with English or French devotion, while "independent, unadulterated impartial Americanism," like "a decayed Tree in a vast desert plain of sand," was dead.[49]

As he looked back, his situation in 1800 seemed to him the logical culmination of a process begun in the mid-1780's; a process which had slowly eroded the close sense of identity he had once felt with the values and goals of American society. He recalled his embarrassments of the 1780's: the cancelled commissions, the altered instructions, the lack of diplomatic support by Congress and the states. His years as Vice-President under Washington had been little better. The office, he had quickly concluded, was less an honor than a burden, with its long hours of attendance upon (but not participation in!) tedious debate and its almost total lack of authority. ("It is, to be sure, a punishment to hear other men talk five hours every day," he complained to Abigail, "and not be at liberty to talk at all myself"—especially when so much of what he heard sounded "young, inconsiderate, and inexperienced.")[50] Both Washington's dominating figure and Adams' own stress upon the importance of a unitary executive combined to insure his clear subordination to the President.[51] (Adams acknowl-

[47] Adams to Elbridge Gerry, December 30, 1800: *Works*, IX, 577-78.

[48] Adams to Benjamin Stoddert, March 31, 1801: *Ibid.*, p. 582.

[49] Adams to Benjamin Rush, July 7, 1805: Biddle, ed., *Old Family Letters*, I, 71. Adams to Abigail Smith, September 26, 1802: Adams Microfilm, Reel 118.

[50] Adams to Abigail Adams, March 12, 1794: C. F. Adams, ed., *Letters to his Wife*, II, 146.

[51] Adams to John Lovell, September 14, 1789: Adams Microfilm,

edged the difficulty of refraining from "meddling improperly" with the executive power.) All patronage requests Adams directed to Washington.[52] "To be candid with you," he wrote in 1790 to John Trumbull, "the situation I am in is too inactive and insignificant for my disposition and I care not how soon I quit it."[53] His country had given him "the most insignificant office that ever the invention of man contrived or his imagination conceived."[54] And his experience in the Presidency after 1796, as we have seen, pushed disillusionment toward its limit. In spite of his dedicated service, the people had turned from him and embraced his tormentors. His defeat by Jefferson in 1800 was final confirmation of this.

Adams' attitude toward the election of 1800 was curiously ambivalent. He wanted the victory badly. A Federalist triumph, of course, he deemed essential to the country's well-being. The Jacobins must be kept from power. More than this, he longed for vindication in his own right; for evidence that the people appreciated the difficulty of his recent decisions and approved his conduct. He approached the contest, however, more in fear than confidence, suspecting that justice would not be done him. The Republicans continued their "disorganizing" activities in opposition, and the Hamiltonians, frustrated in their strongest desires, he believed, were equally bent upon insuring his defeat. Factionalism seemed to have gone too far to permit any moderate course success. At times, Adams seemed almost to court defeat; perhaps in the belief that it might prove his own continuing integrity. When defeat came, it provided the logical culmination of his experience over the last twenty years. "You

---

Reel 115. Adams to Stephen Higginson, March 14, 1790: *Ibid.* Adams to William Tudor, May 9, 1798: Tudor Papers.

[52] Adams to Mercy Warren, May 29, 1789: "Warren-Adams Letters," LXIII, 314.

[53] Adams to John Trumbull, March 7, 1790: Adams Microfilm, Reel 115. Adams to John Trumbull, January 23, 1791: *Ibid.*

[54] Adams to Abigail Adams, December 19, 1793: *Works,* I, 460.

may think me disappointed," he remarked to William Tudor in 1801; "I am not. All my life I have expected it."[55] The whole thing had for him an almost heroic aura. Yet in the end he was desperately disappointed. His conversation, reported one person, "was one continued theme of the most bitter complaint. . . ."[56]

Again his own defeat fitted neatly into the schema of American moral declension—indeed, witnessed clearly to it. The source of his troubles he found outside of himself, not within. He had remained constant while the society about him had changed. In times of "Simplicity and Innocence," he had observed back in the 1770's, "Ability and Integrity" were the principal recommendations for the public service, and the sole title to the honors that the public bestowed. When "Elegance, Luxury and Effeminacy" became established, however, he had warned that rewards would accrue to "Vanity and folly." When a people became totally corrupt, all the rules of good government would be reversed. "Virtue, Integrity and Ability" would become "the Objects of the Malice, Hatred and Revenge of the Men in Power, and folly, Vice, and Villany [sic]" would be cherished and supported.[57]

During the 1770's, Adams had believed that the virtuous man would find equitable reward. As long as one acted upon principles of truth, justice, and humanity, he had confided to Mercy Warren in 1774, one was certain of enjoying "the approbation of his Country," for this was "seldom refused to Integrity of Heart. . . ."[58] His own experience had borne witness to this. By 1800, the same logic had led him to a quite different conclusion. "I have been . . . strangely used in this country," he

[55] Adams to William Tudor, January 20, 1801: Tudor Papers.
[56] Benjamin Goodhue to Timothy Pickering, June 2, 1800: King, ed., *Life of Rufus King*, III, 263-64.
[57] Draft of a Newspaper Communication, August (?) 1770: *Diary and Autobiography*, I, 365.
[58] Adams to Mercy Warren, January 3, 1774: "Warren-Adams Letters," LXXII, 22-23.

remarked to Abigail, "so belied and undefended. . . ."[59]
The explanation was clear. The "virtue and good sense"
which he had once depended on, had proved ephemeral,
had "failed our expectation and disappointed all our
hopes."[60] Duty, patriotism, virtue seemed to have become "mere stalking Horses to Ambition and Avarice."[61]
The kingdom of virtue was not of this world, nor the
kingdom of merit. Convinced as he was of his own rectitude, Adams could find explanation for the attacks upon
him only in the iniquity of the American people.

Adams professed to scorn his critics, to rise above the
disappointment he felt. Yet he could not. He appreciated too keenly the applause of his fellow men not to
feel its absence. Whatever his vanity or ambition, he
had dedicated himself at considerable personal sacrifice—
forfeiture of a promising law practice, extended absence
from his family, the debilitation of his physical strength
—to America's well-being. And he felt bitter when the
people turned from him. As his son remarked, to be
shunted aside at the end of one's public career was
enough "to sink all generous Sentiments. . . ."[62] His
disappointment caused him to turn in upon himself,
until for a period even many of his virtues turned sour.
In the face of continuing criticism, Adams' pride in his
own integrity degenerated into self-righteousness. From
a belief that he knew better than most men where America's advantage lay, he came to affirm that he alone knew.
Where once he had assumed that virtue and popularity
could go hand in hand, he now questioned their relation-

[59] Adams to Abigail Adams, March 9, 1797: C. F. Adams, ed.,
Letters to his Wife, II, 247-48.
[60] Adams to Adrian Van der Kemp, July 24, 1802: Adams Microfilm, Reel 118. Adams to John Rogers, February 6, 1801: *Ibid.*,
Reel 120.
[61] Adams to Benjamin Waterhouse, June 29, 1806: Ford, ed.,
Statesman and Friend, p. 39.
[62] Thomas Boylston Adams to Abigail Adams, January 9, 1801:
Adams Microfilm, Reel 440.

ship increasingly until in his own mind the two became separated altogether. Experience had brought him to what Shaftesbury described as "that unfortunate Opinion of Virtue's being Naturally an Enemy to Happiness in Life."[63] He had once prided himself on speaking honestly to the people, however unpopular this might be. Now he seemed at times almost to flaunt his views intentionally. What had been a virtue thus became an obsession. His own righteousness and the depravity of his opponents; these came to be the terms in which he explained his relation to the society about him. In the end, the controversies in which he was engaged came to provide him the only means of affirming his own rectitude. Clinton Rossiter suggested this when he observed that Adams "wore the scratchiest hair shirt over the thinnest skin in American history."[64]

Early on the morning of Jefferson's inauguration, Adams left Washington and ended nearly forty years of public service. He returned to Quincy disillusioned by his own fate and anxious about his country's. America's prospects were not promising. "Clouds black and gloomy" hung over the nation, threatening "a fierce tempest arising . . . from party conflicts. . . ."[65] America, he feared, would be "tossed . . . in the tempestuous sea of liberty for years to come."[66] Where the bark could land but in political convulsion, he could not see.

[63] Anthony Ashley Cooper, the first Earl of Shaftesbury, *Characteristics* (London, 1711), II, 71.

[64] Clinton Rossiter, "The Legacy of John Adams": *Yale Review*, XLVI, No. 4 (January, 1957), 532.

[65] Adams to Joseph Ward, February 4, 1801: *Works*, IX, 97.

[66] Adams to Elbridge Gerry, February 7, 1801: Adams Microfilm, Reel 120. Adams to James McHenry, July 27, 1799: *Works*, IX, 4-5.

Chapter VIII. Retirement

For several years after returning to Quincy in 1801, Adams lived in almost complete isolation. He scarcely moved outside the limits of the village. His correspondence dropped off sharply with all but a few trusted individuals, and these he carefully instructed to conceal his views. "I want to pass off as little talk'd of and thought of as possible," he advised.[1] From the moment Adams left Washington on the morning of Jefferson's inauguration he turned his back completely on politics, occupying his time instead with administering his farm, enjoying his family, and visiting old friends—making up for all the years they had been denied him. Through the remainder of his life he held but one public office, Quincy representative to the Massachusetts Constitutional Convention of 1820; and this, falling in his eighty-fourth year, was purely an honorary appointment. Nor did he after 1801 have any further ambition for public life. "I have nothing to hope or wish but repose," he declared.[2] Over the last twenty years he had had his fill of politics and controversy. Now, weakened both physically and emotionally by the experience, he longed to be let alone; *"to remain in obscurity, and by no means to become the subject of conversation or speculation."*[3]

In retirement there was plenty of time to reflect upon his fate; and in spite of his denials, the thought of it

[1] Adams to Adrian Van der Kemp, March 3, 1804 and January 26, 1802: Van der Kemp Papers. See D. H. Stewart and G. P. Clark, "Misanthrope or Humanitarian? John Adams in Retirement," *New England Quarterly*, XXVIII (1955), 216-36.

[2] Adams to Benjamin Rush, January 18, 1808: Adams Microfilm, Reel 405. Adams to William Cunningham, September 27, 1808: E. M. Cunningham, ed., *Correspondence between the Hon. John Adams . . . and the late William Cunningham* (Boston, 1823), p. 28.

[3] Adams to William Cunningham, September 27, 1808: Cunningham, ed., *Correspondence between Adams and Cunningham*, p. 30.

still rankled. "The President, I am told," Timothy Pickering wrote to a friend in June of 1801, "is in a state of deep dejection. . . ."[4] Adams could not recall any part of his political life, he confessed to his son, John Quincy Adams, without pain. Every scene presented "Jealousy, Envy, treachery, Perfidy Malice without cause or provocation and revenge without Injury or Offence. . . ." He had served a master, he continued, who neither recognized his services nor cared for him.[5] Instead, his "generous fellow Citizens, the wisest and best People under heaven," had worn him out with hard service and then turned him adrift, "like an old Dray Horse."[6] The moral of his experience was clear: that "the Memory of Malice" was faithful, while that of kindness and friendship was "not only frail but treacherous."[7] This was the conclusion about his own life with which he had to live.

Adams carried with him into retirement the pessimistic view of American society that he had developed by 1801. The "cold blood" with which America had seen "faithfull officers cashiered, trusty servants discarded, and the best ships hove down in the Mud to rot," he affirmed, was "not much in favour" of American benevolence.[8] Intrigue decided everything. The vir-

---

[4] Timothy Pickering to Rufus King, January 5, 1801: King, ed., *Life of Rufus King*, III, 366.

[5] Adams to John Quincy Adams, November 30, 1804: Adams Microfilm, Reel 403.

[6] Adams to Benjamin Rush, February 2, 1807: Biddle, ed., *Old Family Letters*, I, 127.

[7] *Diary and Autobiography*, III, 294. Adams did not escape embarrassment even after 1800. Eighteen years later the General Court of Massachusetts refused to appropriate money for a bust of him. A number of private citizens then opened a subscription at two dollars apiece, but the money came in with painful slowness, amounting to less than one hundred dollars during the first week. Christopher Gore to Rufus King, February 24, 1818: King, ed., *Life of Rufus King*, VI, 119.

[8] Adams to Benjamin Waterhouse, April 2, 1806: Ford, ed., *Statesman and Friend*, pp. 36-37.

tue and good sense which he had once depended upon
had vanished. Adams was greeted upon his arrival in
Quincy in late March 1801, by a violent spring storm.
It seemed to him a token of the "moral and political
tempests and intellectual revolution" that had turned
the people from "wisdom and virtue to folly and vice."[9]

What the future held for America was uncertain.
Throughout all of Adams' comments after 1800 there
runs a vagueness that is in marked contrast to the certi-
tude of his earlier years. Adams admitted his own perplexity. He could not reason well upon public affairs,
he remarked. His sentiments had proven so different
from the people's that he could "lay down no principles,
nor conceive any system" in agreement with theirs.[10]
This feeling was in part a function of his political isolation. His "total retirement," he acknowledged to John
Quincy Adams, resulted in an almost complete want of
facts.[11] It derived also from his feeling of helplessness,
removed as he was from any effective influence. He
could no longer do anything, "even as an instrument."[12]
Yet his perplexity resulted most of all from his conviction that American society had changed, had set off on
a course of development he little understood.

Not only America, but the whole world seemed to
be "all afloat," struggling uncertainly with events whose
outcome Adams could not foresee. He could not believe that Providence had ceased to guide men's affairs.
Yet he confessed himself "wholly unable to comprehend
the vast System" of history. This was perhaps his

[9] Adams to Colonel Smith, March 24, 1801: Adams Microfilm,
Reel 118.
[10] Adams to William S. Smith, November 20, 1814: *Ibid.*, Reel
112.
[11] Adams to John Quincy Adams, January 8, 1808: *Ibid.*, Reel
405.
[12] Adams to John Jay, June 12, 1821: *Ibid.*, Reel 124.

greatest loss of all.[13] History seemed caught upon a balance, its course uncertain.

Ideology—fanatical commitment to absurd doctrines, religious and economic as well as political—held sway in Europe as in America. Adams could not escape the memory of the French Revolution, "the Pleasure which millions discovered in beholding the delicious Spectacle of the Guillotine in the Place de Louis quinze," the "spouting Trunks and gasping Heads" giving delight to "many People far above the . . . Paris mob."[14] Fanaticism had ended, as he had predicted, in tyranny. Napoleon now stood over France. And because of him, Europe wallowed in continuous war. Where was it to end?

Nor could Adams reach an accommodation with the emerging romantic temper of the nineteenth century. Obscurantism, emotionalism, it seemed to him; precisely the qualities of mind he most feared. "You know the Taste of this Age both in Europe and America," he remarked to Benjamin Waterhouse in 1807. "The nice palates of our modern men of Letters must have polished Periods and fashionable Words." Their aim was to run down and out of sight "all the old Writers."[15] The novels of Sir Walter Scott, already popular in America, Adams misconstrued completely. They appeared to him but gloomy tales of medieval tyranny. Edward Handler is quite right that Adams remained fixed in the perspectives of the eighteenth century, "an archaic survivor from a past age."[16]

Adams could not for any length of time remain disinterested in the world about him. The habits of a life-

[13] Adams to Elkanah Watson, August 11, 1812: Watson Papers, New York State Library.
[14] Adams to Benjamin Waterhouse, April 2, 1806: Ford, ed., *Statesman and Friend*, pp. 36-37.
[15] Adams to Benjamin Waterhouse, January 21, 1807: *Ibid.*, pp. 43-44.
[16] Handler, *America and Europe*, p. 197.

time could not so easily be broken. As the months passed and his spirits began to lift, his sense of involvement returned. "I cannot and will not be indifferent to the Condition and Prospects of my Country," he declared to Benjamin Rush.[17] Everything he read gradually turned his thoughts to the laws and government, the conditions and institutions of American society. Never did he recover the emotional engagement that had thrilled and exhausted him before 1800. Yet from about 1805 on, his interest in American affairs and his willingness to comment upon them returned.

Until about 1812, Adams' observations, though they gradually moderated, continued in much the same vein as during the 1790's. The dominant theme of his discourse remained the importance of maintaining the continental union. And the same tendencies, some enhanced, others relaxed, still threatened to destroy it: the growth of commerce and speculation, the increase of wealth and luxury, the increasing division of society into opposing economic and social interests, the continuation of party conflict, and the progressive decline of public virtue which all of these implied.

Commerce, luxury, and avarice, he warned again in 1808, had destroyed every republican government. Venice, Holland, Switzerland, all had fallen by the way. America seemed still in danger of following after them. Banks continued to proliferate, robbing people through interest and depreciated currency for the benefit of a few, promoting speculation, speeding the already "unnatural growth" of cities.[18] Adams found his views on banks and paper money stated perfectly by the French physiocrat, Destutt de Tracy; paper money was a fraud because it had "no real value"; specie alone

[17] Adams to Benjamin Rush, February 27, 1805: Biddle, ed., *Old Family Letters*, I, 64.

[18] Adams to John C. Gray, July 24, 1822: Adams Microfilm, Reel 124.

provided an honest medium of exchange (as long as it contained the actual face value of the metal).[19] In 1811, Adams opposed the recharter of the Bank of the United States.[20] He had always considered the Bank of the United States one of the "capital Errors" of the first administration, Adams wrote to William Branch Giles. By its practices of discounting and currency issue it had propagated "a system of Iniquity" never before equalled. Every paper dollar issued by the Bank, its branches, or the several state banks, beyond the amount of precious metals in their vaults, represented nothing and was a swindle of the people.[21] Banks of deposit alone he thought useful. The mania for banks of issue was a "national Injustice," a "Sacrifice of public and private Interest to a few Aristocratical Friends and Favourites."[22]

The growth of land speculation, fostered by the circulation of bank paper, Adams observed with equal alarm. It raged from New Hampshire to Georgia, creating immense fortunes and dividing the people into interests as hostile as opposing nations: debtors versus creditors, small farmers versus landed gentry, squatters versus absentee owners.[23] The "madness for land" threatened to keep growing until the continent was scattered over with manors larger than the Livingstons' and farms scarcely large enough to support a family.[24]

[19] Adams to John Taylor, March 12, 1819: *Ibid.*, Reel 123.

[20] Adams to John Quincy Adams, February 22, 1811: *Ibid.*, Reel 411. Adams gave no indication of understanding the moderating influence the Bank had upon local state banks.

[21] Adams to William Branch Giles, December 22, 1812: *Ibid.*, Reel 121.

[22] Adams to Thomas Jefferson, November 15, 1813: Cappon, ed., *Adams-Jefferson Letters*, II, 401-402. The growth of banks was rapid after 1800—from 29 in 1800 to 90 in 1811, to nearly 250 five years beyond this. By 1820, the total exceeded 300. Bray Hammond, *Banks and Politics in America before the Civil War* (Princeton, 1957), pp. 144-45.

[23] Adams to John Quincy Adams, February 12, 1808: Adams Microfilm, Reel 405.

[24] Adams to Thomas Jefferson, November 15, 1813: Cappon, ed.,

Sectional antagonism presented another source of internal discord. Since the first meeting of the Continental Congress in 1774, Adams had been conscious of a rivalry between New England and the southern states for influence in continental affairs. Both economic and social differences set the sections off from each other. Frequently he berated the "gentlemen" from Virginia for their "aristocratic" manners, at times going so far as to wonder whether they were capable of popular, republican government. During the 1790's, distinctions between North and South became more apparent. Under the new national government, disagreement over tariff and banking, commerce and land disposal, and treaty-making demonstrated that the dissimilarities ran deep.

After 1800, Adams believed that opposition between the sections raised serious obstacles to the maintenance of continental union. The "gentlemen" of the South, he observed to John Quincy Adams in 1805, had always been actuated by a hatred of New England. Heretofore they had been kept in check by fear of the North. Now, however, they had grown stronger. Indeed, they had gained control of the national administration. Were it not for the presence of the Negro, Adams warned, Southerners would eject New England from their union within the year.[25] The spirit of disunion was in the South. Always he remembered the Virginia and Kentucky resolutions of 1798.

As the new century wore on, Adams found to his dismay that even New England, in his own day the bulwark of continental loyalty, was not free from separatism. Faced with the prospect of permanent political subordination, some Federalists in the New England states became increasingly restive, especially as war

Adams-Jefferson Letters, II, 401. R. M. Robbins, *Our Landed Heritage: The Public Domain, 1776-1936* (Princeton, 1942), pp. 22-32.

[25] Adams to John Quincy Adams, January 8, 1805: Adams Microfilm, Reel 404.

with England again loomed close. In 1811, Josiah Quincy made a speech in Congress opposing the rapid admission of new states carved out of the Louisiana territory, and hinting at the dissolution of the union if necessary to prevent New England's being overrun in Congress. Quincy's speech, Adams believed unfortunate. There were "so many Seeds and Elements of division" already that it was dangerous to multiply them. Banks, non-intercourse, troubles with England and France were "setting us all on fire." Glances at dismemberment, however obscure, encouraged the idea and were therefore dangerous.[26] Madison's policies toward England, Adams lamented, were stimulating the spirit of factionalism in New England and giving encouragement to the high Federalists. Not just added taxes or the prospect of war, but the Embargo and inattention to the protection of American commerce had raised a storm of protest in Massachusetts, hurled Elbridge Gerry, a pillar of the national administration, out of the governorship, and "revolutionized all the subsequent Elections."[27]

Adams heard that Timothy Pickering, now representative from New York, carried to Congress in 1812 a project for dividing the continent at the Potomac, the Delaware, or even the Hudson. He represented the same faction that Adams had faced in 1799; men who wanted to plunge the nation into war with France, subdue or separate from the South, and set themselves up under English tutelage. A "blind, mad rivalry between the North and the South," Adams warned, "is destroying all morality and sound policy."[28] If things continued in their present course, there would be a

[26] Adams to John Quincy Adams, January 25, 1811: *Ibid.*, Reel 411.

[27] Adams to Thomas Jefferson, May 21, 1812: Cappon, ed., *Adams-Jefferson Letters*, II, 304-305.

[28] Adams' marginalia in his own copy of the 1806 edition of his "Davila" essays: Haraszti, *Adams and the Prophets of Progress*, pp. 173-74.

convulsion "as certainly as there is a Sky over our heads."[29] The people, he warned, should cling to the national government as their "only Rock of Safety against the Storm," and conform the state governments to it as much as possible. Only this could preserve America from fatal division.[30]

Had America been alone in the world, her internal divisions would have been serious enough. The fact that she was not compounded the danger. As during the 1790's, there were other nations ready to take advantage of her weakness for their own advantage. Adams watched the course of events in Europe following the French Revolution with a mixture of alarm and satisfaction. Alarm because it seemed to declare that the promise of civil liberty and rational enlightenment proffered by the American Revolution was ultimately to be denied; and satisfaction that his own warnings against French excesses were borne out. Not only France, but all of Europe and England appeared unsettled. France had found a modicum of stability only under the uncompromising rule of Bonaparte. In the midst of such disorder, neither civil nor religious liberty appeared to have much chance for survival. Adams hoped for tranquility; but he foresaw continuing turmoil. The nineteenth century, he remarked apprehensively, seemed likely to produce even greater changes than the eighteenth.[31]

The reassertion of legitimacy in Europe around 1815 offered the final grim contradiction to Adams' earlier hopes for the spread of liberty against "canon and feudal" tyranny. The process had not only been stalled, but reversed—even, perhaps, defeated. All over the

[29] Adams to Thomas Jefferson, May 3, 1812: Cappon, ed., *Adams-Jefferson Letters*, II, 303-304.
[30] Adams to Benjamin Waterhouse, March 11, 1812: Ford, ed., *Statesman and Friend*, pp. 76-78.
[31] Adams to John Adams Smith, October 10, 1819: Adams Microfilm, Reel 124.

world, Adams observed, the cause of liberty, justice, and humanity was in critical condition. The achievements of the eighteenth century had become odious and unpopular.[32] Where now, he asked Jefferson "very seriously," was the perfection of human nature, the progress of the human mind, the amelioration of society, or the diminution of human misery?[33] In every sphere—social, political, religious—reaction seemed ascendant.

Adams at first admitted to being a bit pleased at the restoration of the Bourbons—it offered final vindication of his prophecy. Yet his personal satisfaction was all but obscured by the alarming prospects which the restoration opened up. In France, Austria, Spain, even in England, sovereigns who called themselves legitimate were conspiring "in holy and unhallowed leagues, against the progress of human knowledge and human liberty." Conflict between rulers and people seemed everywhere imminent. The former, however, were strong and united; the latter divided among themselves.[34] Despotism and fanaticism were returning upon mankind like a flood; and men were disposed to submit.

Religious "Awakenings and Revivals"—Methodism, Swedenbourgism, Mesmerism—were running over the globe, erasing toleration, each declaring itself custodian of the true faith.[35] The Catholic Church, after facing a growing challenge for a century and more, appeared newly triumphant. Adams was "terrified with the prospect of an age of darkness."[36] Most ominous was the

[32] Adams to J. V. Yates, December 15, 1822: *Ibid.*

[33] Adams to Thomas Jefferson, July 15, 1813: Cappon, ed., *Adams-Jefferson Letters*, II, 357-58.

[34] Adams to James Madison, June 17, 1817: Hunt, ed., *Writings of Madison*, X, 267.

[35] Adams to Benjamin Waterhouse, December 19, 1815: Ford, ed., *Statesman and Friend*, pp. 118-21.

[36] Adams to Judge Sewall, November 4, 1815: Adams Microfilm, Reel 122. Though Adams espoused full toleration in matters of religious belief, he could not bring himself to endorse abolition of the religious establishment in Massachusetts. This, he feared, would have

for another.[44] Inevitably, the United States would become involved with the Latin American nations and with Europe—just the thing Adams sought to avoid. America, he acknowledged, could do nothing to prevent revolution to the south, but should do nothing to encourage it.[45]

In such a world setting, America's prospects were not encouraging. Europe afforded an "awefull subject of Consideration." Latin America appeared little better. Adams feared that America would surely suffer from both. "Who can look into futurity," he wondered, "without shuddering?" He gave thanks for all the blessings that America had enjoyed, "but not without trembling" at what was still to come.[46] Given America's internal divisions and the existence of a hostile world, there were ample reasons for concern about the years ahead.

ADAMS, however, did not despair. Indeed, as the years passed, he came more and more to believe not that America would succumb to internal division, but that the course of development was in just the opposite direction—toward greater domestic unity. And there was evidence, as well, to suggest that America would prove able to protect herself against enemies from abroad.

Domestically, the most notable development in Adams' thinking was the moderation of party animosity from about 1806 on. For the first few years after 1800, Adams' analysis of American politics was guided by the assumptions he had developed during the 1790's: with

[44] Adams to John Quincy Adams, June 8, 1818: Adams Microfilm, Reel 123.

[45] Adams to John Jay, March 18, 1822: *Ibid.*, Reel 124. Much to Adams' anger, his grandson, William Steuben Smith went off to Venezuela to enlist with Miranda against the Spanish. After Smith's capture, Adams refused to help him obtain pardon. Page Smith, *John Adams*, pp. 1,090-91.

[46] Adams to Richard Rush, March 17, 1815: Adams Microfilm, Reel 122.

all effective national sentiment gone, the country would continue divided between two factions. Control of the government would shift from party to party on a recurring twelve-year cycle (projected apparently from the span 1788-1800), raising a new crisis at each interval.

Gradually, however, Adams' fears began to temper. Rather than continuing on a course of party division, American politics seemed to have changed direction, to be moving into a period of stabilization. Two factors persuaded Adams of this: his unrelenting alienation from the remnant of high Federalists and his gradual accommodation with the Republicans.

Adams believed after 1800 that the revival of the Federalist party—a coalition of Hamiltonians, old Tories, the established clergy in New England, bankers, speculators, and commercial interests—was "totally impracticable."[47] He never again formally aligned himself with it. The Federalists, by their actions in openly discouraging the enlistment of volunteers and the floating of loans needed during the War of 1812, threatening to meet the Embargo with secession, and advocating radical changes in the constitution, continued to prove their irresponsibility. In 1808, James Hillhouse, Federalist senator from Connecticut, proposed several sweeping amendments to the federal constitution aimed chiefly at reconstituting the executive branch. According to them, the President would hold office for only one year, be chosen by lot from among the one-third of the senators to retire annually (senatorial terms were to be cut in half), receive a salary not to exceed $15,000 per year, and appoint and remove most important officials only with the advice and consent of both Senate and House.

[47] Adams' Notes for a Reply to Hamilton, 1809 (?): *Ibid.*, Reel 407. Adams to Thomas Boylston Adams, July 11, 1801: *Ibid.*, Reel 401.

In addition, the office of Vice-President was to be abolished with the Senate to choose its own speaker.[48]

Hillhouse's recommendation jarred Adams into a vigorous (though never published) reply. The purpose of weakening the Executive and strengthening the Senate seemed to him but an indication of further grasping for power by aristocratic, high-Federalist interests. In reaction, he launched again into a lengthy description of the American aristocracy and its dangers, its basis in wealth and family name, and the need to control it with a second legislative house and a strong executive. Hillhouse's recommendation to shorten the terms of President and Senators would exacerbate party conflict by increasing the number of contests for high national office. At the same time, the President would be weakened beyond any ability to make his influence felt in the political balance. In the past, Adams advised (thinking of his own experience), the President had become the victim of parties because he had not been independent enough. Rather than weakening him further, Adams would strengthen his powers by removing the Senate's role in appointments altogether. Hillhouse's proposals if effected, Adams concluded, would be fatal to the republican system, for the balance between executive and legislative branches would be destroyed.[49]

If aroused by Hillhouse's blatant efforts to expand aristocratical influence, however, Adams was gratified by the speed with which they were defeated. Neither in Congress nor in the country at large was there support for them. Adams found this encouraging because it added further evidence that the high Federalists were without influence. In 1808, he thought it not even worthwhile for the Federalists to present a Presidential candidate,

[48] James Hillhouse, *Proposals for Amending the Constitution of the United States* (New Haven, 1810).

[49] Notes for Adams' reply to Hillhouse's proposals: Adams Microfilm, Reel 406.

dwindled as they were to a handful of Hamiltonians. By their own "stiffrumped stupidity," they had destroyed themselves politically.[50]

As significant as Adams' continuing dissociation from the Federalists was his growing accommodation with the Republicans. If Jefferson could avoid falling under the control of the radicals around him, Adams held out hopes for the administration. As the years passed, Adams was pleased to find the forces of moderation gaining increasing strength. Through the terms of Jefferson and especially Madison and Monroe, the country gave evidence of moving toward the political unity Adams believed was so sorely needed.[51]

Adams was no Republican during the first years of the new century. He reported in disgust to John Quincy Adams in 1804 that for the first time the Massachusetts electors would not be Federalists. The governorship, he hoped, would not go the same way.[52] Nor did he approve of Jefferson's extensive removals of Federalist appointees from office, or the efforts to impeach Federalist judges. Both, he thought, set precedents inimical to political stability.[53] Adams, moreover, was fearful that the new administration would inevitably fall under French domination. For the past eight years, he warned in 1804, there had been "strange, unknown, mysterious

[50] Adams to John Quincy Adams, January 8, 1808: *Ibid.*, Reel 405; Adams to John Quincy Adams, December 14, 1804: *Ibid.*, Reel 403.

[51] I am, of course, describing Adams' evaluation of political developments rather than the developments themselves. Among historians, the question of how calm the American political climate was after 1815 remains moot.

[52] Adams to John Quincy Adams, November 16 and December 14, 1804: Adams Microfilm, Reel 403.

[53] Adams to John Quincy Adams, December 6, 1804: *Ibid.* For a discussion of Adams' and Jefferson's appointment policies and procedures, see Sidney Aronson, *Status and Kinship in the Higher Civil Service* (Cambridge, Massachusetts, 1964), Chapter 1; Leonard White, *The Federalists* (New York, 1948), Chapters 21 and 22; and Leonard White, *The Jeffersonians* (New York, 1951), Chapter 24.

Persons" running all over New England offering themselves as schoolmasters and even laborers, praising
France, preaching Republicanism, and clamoring down
the Federalist administrations. Foreign agents, all of
them, he suspected. Could one believe that French policy
was not at work, he further wondered not quite rele-
vantly, when the Spanish minister Yrujo was married
to the governor of Pennsylvania's daughter, when the
infamous Genêt was the spouse of the New York governor's daughter, and when the brother of Emperor
Napoleon was wed to an eminent lady of Baltimore?[54]
Let Jefferson say what he would, he could continue in
office no other way than by satisfying the French in all
essential measures.

As Adams watched Jefferson operate, however, his
fear that the President would not be truly national or
independently American faded. In domestic affairs
Adams detected no insidious influences, "no very great
or lasting evil" in the policy Jefferson pursued. Adams
did not lament Jefferson's repeal of the Alien laws—
they "were never favorites with me," he explained—
though he thought that as a consequence, naturalization
became too easy. Nor did he protest when Jefferson allowed the Sedition law to expire. Adams, moreover,
rejoiced that the 8 percent loan, unpopular as it had
been, was ended.[55]

In the area of foreign affairs, Adams believed the
Republican administrations would meet their severest
test; and here he watched them achieve their greatest
success. Jefferson's early foreign policy bothered Adams.
He resented, for example, reductions in the naval force
that he had worked so hard to build up. Adams always
thought the navy America's most important line of defense; by reducing it, Jefferson seemed to be compro-

[54] Adams to John Quincy Adams, December 2, 1804: Adams
Microfilm, Reel 403.
[55] Adams to John Quincy Adams, December 6, 1804: *Ibid.*

mising America's security. Adams took exception, as
well, to the Embargo and non-importation policies—
not because they were directed chiefly at England and
might provoke retaliation, but because Adams thought
they would prove futile and only serve to increase internal division.[56] Adams agreed that the disrespect
shown American commerce by both France and England
was intolerable. But voluntarily withdrawing American
ships from the seas and closing American ports seemed
hardly the way to achieve redress. Adams had learned
his lesson well during the 1780's. England would not
halt her depredations until openly challenged and forced
to do so by American privateers, armed merchantmen,
and naval forces. The futile embargoes of 1775 and
1794, Adams recalled, had demonstrated this. The only
tangible result of Jefferson's timid policy would be to
ruin American trade and create economic hardship in
New England, something that section would not long
tolerate.[57] In Jefferson's action, Adams detected a lingering sectional bias. Persistence in an embargo, he warned,
would certainly convince many people in the eastern
states that southern leaders were still insensitive to New
England's commercial interests. In January of 1808,
he reported to John Quincy Adams that a hundred
sailors had recently marched in the streets of Boston in
protest. Humiliation of the northern states could not
long endure without producing passions very difficult to
control.[58]

The greatest single event in effecting Adams' accommodation with the Republicans was the War of 1812.
During this episode, while the New England Federalists
threatened disunion, the Republicans demonstrated im-

[56] John Quincy Adams endorsed both policies; his father made
no attempt to dissuade him.

[57] Adams to Joseph Varnum, December 7, 1812: Adams Microfilm,
Reel 121.

[58] Adams to John Quincy Adams, January 29, 1806: *Ibid.*, Reel
404. Adams to John Quincy Adams, April 12, 1808: *Ibid.*, Reel 406.

pressively that they harbored national, not just sectional or party sentiments. This, more than anything else, moved Adams into support of the Republican administration and persuaded him that under its direction America faced a promising future.

By about 1808, Adams was convinced that America would soon have to fight another war to defend her rights against foreign interference. He had no difficulty in anticipating that the contest would be against England rather than France.[59] With France troubled internally and preoccupied with affairs on the continent, the English navy offered the gravest threat to American commercial interests. Moreover, Adams had repeatedly cautioned since his stay in England that hatred for her former colonies continued to fester there, that she would never behave honorably toward them unless forced to it. Events since 1783 had borne him out: the refusal of England during the 1790's to abide by the articles of peace concerning evacuation of the western posts and indemnification for American property; her Orders in Council restricting neutral trade with Europe. Most annoying of all, English impressment of American sailors continued. George III's proclamation of October 16, 1807, laying claim to the right of impressment of suspected English nationals found on all foreign ships convinced Adams that a clash was imminent.

In a long and indignant letter, written just after the proclamation became known (though not published until January of 1809), Adams made his reply. The proclamation, he declared, had no basis either in English law or the law of nations, and was, in fact, in direct contradiction to the principles of English liberty. It was, moreover, directed specifically at American ships and seamen. No other insults America had ever received from any foreign nation, Adams continued excitedly, held such

[59] Adams to John Quincy Adams, January 8, 1808: *Ibid.*, Reel 405.

dangerous consequences as this. If allowed, it would mean the humiliation of the country, the demoralization of American seamen, the existence of a state of constant warfare on the high seas, and continuous turmoil domestically. Americans, Adams emphasized, would even rather be "embargoed" than impressed. The proclamation, itself, was "dictated by a spirit as hostile and malicious as it was insidious. . . ."[60] England seemed determined to press America as far as she would permit. Though Adams had thought peace might have been possible before the King's action, he saw "no possibility of it" afterward.[61] By itself, the proclamation provided adequate grounds for an immediate declaration of war.

Adams' attitude toward the War of 1812 was curiously different from the near-war with France in 1798-1799. He had always harbored a somewhat bellicose spirit. And from his early years, he had admired the military virtues of discipline and courage. In the Continental Congress, he had enjoyed nothing more than his work on the Continental Board of War and Ordnance. During the first two decades after the peace of 1783, however, he had urged America to avoid hostilities if at all possible in order to give herself time to gather her strength. Always, of course, he had accepted the possible necessity of fighting when national honor was involved; but as his actions in support of Jay's Treaty and in seeking accommodation with France demonstrated, he had been willing to interpret "national honor" rather flexibly. A war so soon after independence, he had argued, would raise taxes and dissensions at home before the nation was strong enough to support them, while almost surely throwing her into the arms of some European "ally" abroad.

After 1800, Adams retained some apprehension of

---

[60] Letter, January 9, 1809: *Boston Patriot.*

[61] Adams to John Quincy Adams, January 8, 1808: Adams Microfilm, Reel 405.

what war would bring. A contest with England, he acknowledged, might create too great a dependence on France.[62] Yet by 1812, the arguments for war and even the advantages to be gained by it seemed to him preponderant. War had become necessary to sustain American independence, to reawaken America to the dangers surrounding her, to preserve her from the fanaticism spreading around "like a Fire of Clapboards and Shingles."[63] The greatest fear Adams had of the Republican administration was not that it might precipitate a break with England, but that it might not be aggressive enough. He was apprehensive that things would go along indecisively, with New England growing increasingly restive under commercial restrictions and Congress unwilling to effect a solution.[64] Not only did Adams refuse to join Worcester's peace society, he handed down stern lectures on the follies of pacifism itself. War, Adams replied, "in many cases" was fully consistent with Christianity. The military education of youth, furthermore, was in no way at odds with the principles of "philanthropy, humanity, or religion."[65]

More surprisingly, Adams now offered the disturbing notion, somewhat akin to Jefferson's endorsement of periodic revolutions, that occasional wars were necessary for the health of society. Harkening up the old "furnace of affliction" idea from his Revolutionary days, Adams argued that human nature could not long bear prosperity. Long periods of peace allowed the people to become soft and corrupt, to lose touch with their former virtues. There was never a republic nor any people under any government, he insisted, that could maintain their in-

[62] Adams to Benjamin Rush, January 18, 1808: *Ibid.* Adams to Adrian Van der Kemp, April 30, 1806: Van der Kemp Papers.

[63] Adams to John Quincy Adams, April 7, 1812: Adams Microfilm, Reel 413. Adams to John Adams Smith, December 14, 1808: *Ibid.*, Reel 406.

[64] Adams to John Quincy Adams, April 12, 1808: *Ibid.*

[65] Adams to Judge Sewall, November 23, 1819: *Ibid.*, Reel 124.

dependence, much less grow and improve, without the stimulation effected by war.[66] Adversity was the great reformer. A contest every twenty-five years or so would call the people to attention, marshall them beneath a common patriotism, and rid them of their divisions.[67] True, war raised the danger of encouraging too much veneration for military figures; France offered melancholy evidence of this. And for this reason, Adams claimed to rejoice in American military victories with "trembling."[68] Yet he did not hesitate to rejoice.

As things turned out, Adams believed the war experience created among the American people just the sense of unity and purposefulness he had anticipated. Military successes, particularly the dramatic victories of the small American fleet, Adams found especially gratifying. After the long trial of British impressment and seizures, the retribution exacted by McDonough and Perry and Hull was sweet. More than any other event since the Revolution, meeting and repulsing the mightiest naval power in the world reawakened America's sense of greatness. Past troubles with both England and France, Adams declared, had arisen because America had had "no feeling of its Strength nor any Sense of its Glory."[69] These naval victories, he expected, would ferment in the minds of the people until they generated "a national self respect a spirit of Independence and a national pride . . . never before felt. . . ."[70]

The glow, Adams hoped, would obscure the divisions that had plagued American society. Whatever result the war in fact had upon American society, it had this effect

[66] Adams to John Quincy Adams, September 2, 1815: *Ibid.*, Reel 122.

[67] Adams to Richard Rush, March 23, 1809: *Ibid.*, Reel 407.

[68] Adams to Benjamin Waterhouse, September 17, 1813: Ford, ed., *Statesman and Friend*, p. 109.

[69] Adams to Richard Rush, December 8, 1812: Adams Microfilm, Reel 121.

[70] Adams to Benjamin Waterhouse, March 23, 1813: *Ibid.*

upon him. After 1812, he believed the American people were joined in common enterprise as at no time since the days of the Revolution. He was aware, of course, that in areas of New England opposition to the war ran high. Among some Americans, he complained, there was "little sense of national honour, and little real knowledge of national duty and interests."[71] Motivated by considerations of their own financial interest, they wished for war against France and peace with England at any price.[72] Adams seemed more disgusted with New England's eccentricity, however, than alarmed by it. The "Tory Project" of Hillhouse, Pickering, and the others, he thought, was not likely to make much headway. The gathering at Hartford he termed "ineffably ridiculous," little more than an electioneering device arranged with "the cunning of an Ostrich."[73]

Most of all, Adams was impressed by the fortitude of the rest of the nation. His prediction that "calamity alone and extreme distress" would again bring forth the real character of the nation seemed borne out. Especially was he gratified by the national fervor displayed in the South and West. He had always been skeptical about the national loyalties of the Southern states. And with countless other New Englanders, he was apprehensive about the rapid growth of the trans-Appalachian area. Yet these sections proved to be the most vigilant defenders of American rights. Even though their own interests had not been directly involved—Adams believed maritime rights, not the acquisition of new lands or defense against Indian raids had been the immediate cause of the war —they had supported the contest with unequalled vigor.

[71] Adams to Thomas McKean, October 30, 1814: *Ibid.*, Reel 122.

[72] Adams to James B. Hammond, February 9, 1813: *Ibid.*, Reel 121.

[73] Adams to Governor Plummer, December 4, 1814: *Ibid.*, Reel 122; Adams to John Quincy Adams, February 19, 1812: *Ibid.*, Reel 413.

The war demonstrated clearly that they were the equals of any Americans in bravery and patriotism.

The war clarified, as well, another once-disputed point: whether under the existing constitution and with Republican leadership, the country could make war and contract a peace acceptable to all the sections without serious internal dislocations.[74] Adams worried about the outcome of the peace negotiations at Ghent. He still did not fully trust Gallatin, the reputed leader of the Whiskey rebels of 1794; and Clay, being from the West, remained an unknown. Throughout 1814, Adams sent off repeated missives to John Quincy Adams, another of the peace commissioners, exhorting him to look after the New England fisheries and northern boundaries in the negotiations, as well as the western territories and use of the Mississippi. Adams found the treaty as finally agreed upon, however, fully satisfactory.[75]

The war, then, was important in shaping Adams' final evaluation of American society. Americans seemed to have recovered somewhat from the low point of the 1790's, to have retrieved a sense of national honor and independence. Adams acknowledged that he was "astonished" at the "rapid growth of a national character." It had been a plant "feeble in its origins" and "for a long course of years . . . slow in its growth, and . . . little cultivated."[76] After 1815, he was able to look with greater equanimity upon the nation's future.

During the postwar years, Adams entered upon a period of political euphoria. America seemed embarked upon a sea of extraordinary calm. Political factions would not disappear; Adams was now reconciled to this. There were still sources of friction: personal ambition, family jealousy, wealth, commerce, sectional differences, reli-

[74] Adams to Thomas McKean, July 6, 1815: *Ibid.*, Reel 122.

[75] Adams to John Quincy Adams, April 1, 1815: *Ibid.* Adams to William S. Smith, February 22, 1815: *Ibid.*

[76] Adams to Rufus King, July 29, 1818: *Ibid.*, Reel 123.

gion. Many "seed Plotts of Division" remained.[77] Elections to powerful national offices were still to be held. And each state contained "virtually a White Rose and a Red Rose a Caesar and a Pompey. . . ."[78] Yet party animosity had unquestionably moderated, especially on the national scene. The violent factions present in 1800, tearing at government, law, and social order, had disappeared. After the fiasco at Hartford, the "British faction" was wholly discredited. A "forlorn minority," Adams described them, "incarcerated in a Kind of St. Helena in Massachusetts."[79] The Republican administration, on the other hand, had become truly national in appeal, gathering in support the vast majority of the population, "honest Federalists" as well as moderate Republicans.

Following the war, Adams' identification with the administration became even more pronounced. In 1812, through the good offices of Benjamin Rush, he was reconciled with Jefferson, beginning the long, second friendship with him that proved so fruitful. Throughout the postwar years, Adams was active in introducing young men of New England to the political leaders of the South, writing letter after letter of introduction to Jefferson, Madison, and Monroe.[80] This seemed one way of "softening asperities and promoting Union. . . ."[81]

Important to Adams' reconciliation with the Republicans was his son's more complete alliance with them. It was easier, of course, for John Quincy Adams to dissociate himself from the Federalists. He was, furthermore, convinced with his father of the folly of the Ham-

[77] Adams to Thomas Jefferson, March 3, 1814: Cappon, ed., *Adams-Jefferson Letters*, II, 427.

[78] Adams to Thomas Jefferson, November 15, 1813: *Ibid.*, 401.

[79] Adams to John Quincy Adams, April 11, 1817: Adams Microfilm, Reel 123.

[80] Adams to James Monroe, December 6, 1816: *Ibid.*

[81] Adams to Thomas Jefferson, February 2, 1817: Cappon, ed., *Adams-Jefferson Letters*, II, 507.

Retirement

policies after 1800: financial policies, the Louisiana Pur-
chase, and the Embargo. Finally, John Quincy Adams
was regarded with special favor by Jefferson, both because of Jefferson's earlier relationship with the Adamses in Europe, and because John Quincy represented the
kind of capable person Jefferson wanted to attract to the
administration. So the Republicans continued the younger Adams in public service after 1800, Jefferson appoint-
ing him ambassador to Russia, and Madison naming
him American minister to the peace conference at Ghent.
Finally, of course, he became Secretary of State under
Monroe.[82] John Adams was understandably ambitious
for his gifted son, and was gratified at the responsibilities given him. That the Republicans were interested in
using John Quincy and that he, in turn, willingly allied
himself with them, made it easier for John Adams to
become convinced of their worth.

All signs by 1815, then, indicated that the nation
faced a period of political calm. We are now in the midst
of a "profound tranquility," Adams observed to Richard
Sharp, "more united and unanimous than ever."[83] How
long it would last was uncertain. But for the moment,
all seemed serene. Madison's administrations, in spite of
some blundering, constituted "a glorious epoch" in American history; the President, by his effective prosecution
of the war, had "acquired more glory and established
more Union" than all his predecessors.[84] Monroe's terms
were still more placid. In Monroe's wide margin of victory over Rufus King in 1816, Adams found further

[82] The best examination of John Quincy Adams' early career is
Samuel Flagg Bemis, *John Quincy Adams and the Foundations of
American Foreign Policy* (New York, 1949).

[83] Adams to Richard Sharp, April 27, 1817: Adams Microfilm,
Reel 123.

[84] Adams to Richard Rush, August 26, 1815: *Ibid.*, Reel 122.
Adams to Thomas Jefferson, February 2, 1817: Cappon, ed., *Adams-
Jefferson Letters*, II, 508.

evidence that serious political conflict had come, at least momentarily, to an end.[85] His own son's election in 1824, bitter as its circumstances were, offered final hope for America's future.

The effectiveness with which the states set about re-doing their constitutions around 1820, suggested further that this hope was not an illusion. By 1820, Adams was eighty-five years of age and clearly unable to follow with any attention the movement toward constitutional re-form. He did serve for a few days, however, in the Mas-sachusetts convention. Initially, two things about the con-ventions disturbed him: whether they would continue the constitutional balance in the state governments, and whether, as some people were advising, they would do away with property qualifications and institute universal manhood suffrage. Adams heard arguments in the Mas-sachusetts convention for ending property requirements and read of its consideration in New York and else-where.[86]

Adams opposed the move. He still thought a moder-ate property requirement necessary to insure the voter's economic independence and freedom of judgment, and he argued the point as forcefully as strength would per-mit in the Massachusetts convention. The great object of government, he warned in one of the few speeches he was able to make, was to render property secure. This was the foundation upon which civilization rested; and it would be dangerously weakened if the franchise were indiscriminately handled by men with no property at all. Wise men all over the world had agreed on the neces-sity of pecuniary qualifications for officers and electors. And Massachusetts, he hoped, would heed their coun-sel.[87]

[85] Adams to John Quincy Adams, November 21, 1817: Adams Microfilm, Reel 123.
[86] Adams to Judge Peters, March 31, 1822: *Ibid.*, Reel 124.
[87] *Journal of the Massachusetts Constitutional Convention* (Boston,

In the end, Adams found nothing alarming about the new constitutions. The balance seemed adequately guaranteed and suffrage requirements were not significantly changed. Massachusetts, he noted approvingly, confirmed her existing system of government with near unanimity.[88] New York expanded its franchise, and Adams had some reservations about that; yet there too, things had generally gone well. Improvements, in fact, had been made with the abolition of the Councils of Revision and Appointment (thus clarifying the separation between legislature and executive).[89]

Adams did not live long enough to become involved in the slavery question. Missouri's application for admission to the union brought the problem to his attention, and he was vaguely aware of its importance. Slavery, he remarked, "hangs like a Cloud over my imagination."[90] Like most men of his age, he felt little sympathy for the Negro. Yet he was convinced that slavery as an institution, unless eradicated, would bring calamities upon the nation. There would be "Insurrection" of blacks against whites, he warned, encouraged by America's enemies.[91]

1823), p. 134. Adams to Adrian Van der Kemp, December 13, 1821: Adams Microfilm, Reel 124.

[88] Adams to John Jay, May 13, 1821: *Ibid.*

[89] Adams to Adrian Van der Kemp, December 13, 1821: *Ibid.* Adams' brief observations on the franchise encourage speculation on what his reaction would have been to the political temper of the Jacksonian period. He, of course, did not live long enough to confront it. Adams knew of Andrew Jackson only as the military hero of Florida and New Orleans. On this basis, he believed Jackson "one of the most exalted of the choice spirits, both as a Statesman and a warrior." Adams to Louisa Catherine Adams, March 1, 1819: *Ibid.*, Reel 123.

[90] Adams to Louisa Catherine Adams, December 23, 1819: *Ibid.*, Reel 124.

[91] Adams to Louisa Catherine Adams, January 30, 1820: *Ibid.*, Reel 124. England, he advised, had already several times attempted to arouse the slaves to revolt. And in Nova Scotia, she was planning to train Negroes already stolen from America to infiltrate the South

On principle, Adams' position was clear. "Every measure of prudence" ought to be taken for the "eventual total extirpation" of the evil from the United States. "Humanity" demanded it.[92] Adams recalled with considerable pride that he had never employed slaves on his farm, even when this had been acceptable among the best circles of New England society and in spite of the fact that it had cost him both convenience and money.[93] His words, however, betrayed reservations about the difficulty of the issue. He favored no precipitate action; always he counselled restraint. Doing away with slavery would leave the problem, especially for the South, of dealing with the Negro. "All possible humanity" should be shown the Negro, he explained more precisely, "consistent with public safety."[94] No unwelcome measures should be forced upon the South. The nation should not by any "rash and violent measures" expose the lives and property of citizens who were "so unfortunate as to be surrounded with these fellow Creatures."[95] Sudden abolition would be calamitous. What should be done with the free Negroes, he did not know. He considered the feasibility of colonization, but concluded reluctantly that it would not work.[96]

Adams resolved the problem simply by setting it aside; by leaving it to future generations to handle as best they could. He had constantly declared to the gentlemen of the South, Adams remarked in 1821, that he could not adequately comprehend the issue and

---

and incite the slaves to rebellion. Adams to Rev. Henry Colman, January 13, 1817: *Ibid.*, Reel 123.

[92] Adams to Robert J. Evans, June 8, 1819: *Ibid.*
[93] Adams to Robert J. Evans, June 8, 1819: *Ibid.*
[94] Adams to Peter Ludlow, Jr., February 20, 1819: *Ibid.*
[95] Adams to Robert J. Evans, June 8, 1819: *Ibid.*
[96] Rev. Henry Colman to Adams, January 1, 1817: *Ibid.* Adams to Rev. Henry Colman, January 13, 1817: *Ibid.*

would leave it to them. He would support no measures against their judgment.[97]

As encouraging as Adams found America's prospects to be after 1812, however, he did not end his life on a note of complete optimism. Not so easily could he escape the lessons history had taught. The logic of his historical thought maintained too strong a hold to permit him the delusion that all America's problems had been resolved. The day of reckoning had been postponed; he could not bring himself to believe it had been erased. Every example from history told him it could not be. There remained potential sources of conflict at home, and a hostile world abroad always ready to do America in.

Adams, furthermore, was unable to shake off fully the continuing disappointment of his personal experience and the lessons about American society which this had taught him. His own past, in fact, dominated his years of retirement. Though he lived for twenty-six years after 1800, time passed always in the shadow of what had gone before. This latter period of his life had meaning for him not as the beginning of experiences fresh and new, but as a further working out of processes earlier begun. His observations on American society after 1800 were considerably more fragmentary and less perceptive than before. He made no serious effort to reexamine the assumptions of his political thought developed during the 1790's. Nor did he add anything substantially new to them, other than to suggest that the process of social maturity might for the moment have slackened its pace. Though his interest in American society returned, it remained detached and perfunctory; understandably enough, given his age and condition.

Only in consideration of his own past, only when engaged in defense of his administration, or his activities abroad, or his role in the Continental Congress did some-

[97] Adams to Thomas Jefferson, February 3, 1821: Cappon, ed., *Adams-Jefferson Letters*, II, 571.

thing like the old enthusiasm return. In reliving the years before 1800 and defending himself against his detractors, lay his real interest. He spent more energy on this than anything else over the whole period of his retirement. Denied at the end of his career the acclaim he so ardently desired, he turned for vindication to the future, to the writings of historians who might finally do him justice. Even in this, however, he feared his enemies would triumph.

America's history for the past fifty years, he replied in 1815 to Dr. Jedediah Morse's request for materials on the Revolution, was already as much corrupted as any half-century of ecclesiastical darkness. And Adams expressed little faith that things would in the future be much different.[98] In plain English, he concluded, the true history of the Revolution and the establishment of the new constitution had been lost forever; nothing but misrepresentations remained.[99] The account would be "one continued Lye from one end to the other."[100] This meant, of course, that his own reputation would be abused, left as it had been in the hands of scribblers hired by the "English faction" or the "Jacobins." The "few traces" of him that remained would go down to posterity in confusion and distraction, as his life had been passed.[101]

During the years of his retirement, Adams did what he could to set the record straight. He spent months poring over his letter files and notebooks, formulating his defense, reworking his arguments. With Mercy Warren, who in her *History of the Revolution* had played down Adams' importance, he carried on a heated exchange. Day after day during 1804 and 1805, he inun-

[98] Adams to Jedediah Morse, March 4, 1815: Adams Microfilm, Reel 122.
[99] Adams to Hezekiah Niles, January 3, 1817: *Ibid.*, Reel 123.
[100] Adams to Benjamin Rush, April 9, 1790: Biddle, ed., *Old Family Letters*, I, 55-56.
[101] Adams to Benjamin Rush, July 23, 1806: *Ibid.*, p. 107.

dated her with letters of prodigious length, detailing his
activities in Massachusetts and the Congress until she,
in sheer exhaustion, ceased to reply.[102] Between 1803 and
1813, he exchanged a long series of letters with a distant
relative, William Cunningham, who had written initially
to request information that might be used against Jefferson. Rapidly, Adams guided the discussion around to
his own administration, and launched forth upon the
wickedness of Hamilton's and Pickering's opposition to
him.[103] In the interval between 1808 and 1813, Adams
sent off an extended series of letters to the *Boston Patriot*, intended in part as a defense of his son against
attacks by the Essex Junto, but also as an exercise in public self-justification. He devoted a substantial number of
the letters to an examination of the British doctrine of
impressment and its illegality. These, however, remained
stale and uninspired. More animated was his discussion
of his relationship with the "English faction."[104] The
publication in 1814 of John Taylor's *Inquiry into the
Principles and Policy of the Government of the United
States* with its heavy attack upon Adams' "Defense,"
roused Adams to a vigorous reply. In thirty-two letters,
most of them running to several pages, he defended
himself against Taylor's accusations of anti-republicanism, again detailing what he meant by "aristocracy" and
arguing the importance of the political balance.[105]

All of these exchanges represented a prodigious out-
put for a man of Adams' years, especially when set along-
side the less dramatic but equally heavy correspondence

[102] Adams' "Correspondence with Mercy Warren," 1807: Massachusetts Historical Society, *Collections*, Series 5, IV, 321-491.
[103] Cunningham, ed., *Correspondence Between Adams and Cunningham*. The letters were published against Adams' explicit wishes
in 1823, and some of their contents were used against his son in the
election of 1824.
[104] *Boston Patriot*, 1808-1813. Only a portion of these letters is
in Adams' *Works*, IX, 241-331.
[105] Adams' side of the full exchange can be found in Adams
Microfilm, Reels 112, 417-21; Taylor's side in Reels 417-21.

he maintained with others. Adams, however, could not let the past alone, not when it had stung him so. He could not allow his enemies to have the last word, to defeat him in the eyes of posterity as they had among his contemporaries. He had to carry the burden himself. The great body of "honest federalists," he complained, remained silent; not one stepped forward to vindicate him. (Curiously enough, he wished on numerous occasions that a Tory history of the Revolution would be written; in the belief, one suspects, that it would give him his due as a Revolutionary leader.) Yet his own efforts, he feared, would not be acknowledged; his protests would be pushed aside as the effusions of self-love. It was vain, he concluded, to expect justice from future generations any more than his own. Too many falsehoods had already been transmitted. The truth was irrecoverable.[106] This was the burden Adams carried with him to the grave. This, probably more than his ideological convictions about American growth and moral decay, was the reason Adams could not fully shake off his earlier disenchantment with American society or his forebodings about its fate.

It is difficult to reconstruct Adams' exact mood at the close of his life. There was an ambivalence to his remarks, a tension between hope and pessimism that at times stretched one way and at times another. On balance, however, he inclined to be hopeful, though cautiously so. As he cast his glance backwards, he could see that there had in fact been "splendid improvements in human society" and "vast ameliorations" in the condition of mankind.[107] As he looked about him, he found it "delightful" to contemplate the "glory and prosperity"

[106] Adams to William Cunningham, April 24, 1809: Cunningham, ed., *Correspondence Between Adams and Cunningham*, pp. 114-15.

[107] Adams to John Jay, September 24, 1821: Adams Microfilm, Reel 124.

of his country.[108] Among the American people, there was "a confused [though] general sense of a common Interest or Public Good." And to this, all intrigues were compelled to pay regard.[109]

When he looked ahead, he became more circumspect. Trying to anticipate the future was like looking through a kaleidoscope; every turn brought a new, unexpected configuration.[110] "The vast, the incomprehensible futurity," precluded confident anticipation.[111] Yet in the end, Adams continued to hope for improvement, though he recognized that progress would be "awfully slow." History had proven again and again that men could turn even the noblest dreams into nightmares. Still, he thought America's prospects "cheering."[112] He would leave the world better than he found it—superstition, persecution, bigotry somewhat abated; governments a little ameliorated; science and literature generally improved. His enthusiasm was considerably more temperate than Jefferson's. Years would be required, he kept reminding Jefferson, to determine what effects "the Wonders of the Times" would ultimately have.[113] Yet, with Jefferson, he affirmed his belief in the gradual amelioration of human affairs.

Perhaps the most remarkable thing of all is that Adams remained as confident as he did. The elements of a much greater pessimism were present. His own bitter disappointment had never been rectified. Throughout the last quarter century of his life, he remained in virtually complete political isolation. The physical debilities of old age crept constantly in upon him: palsy,

[108] Adams to Charles Carroll, August 2, 1820: *Ibid.*

[109] Adams to George Washington Adams, June 11, 1821: *Ibid.*

[110] Adams to Dummer Sewall, May 12, 1819: *Ibid.*, Reel 123.

[111] Adams to Adrian Van der Kemp, October 4, 1813: Van der Kemp Papers.

[112] Adams to Thomas Jefferson, September 18, 1823: Cappon, ed., *Adams-Jefferson Letters*, II, 598.

[113] Adams to Thomas Jefferson, July 16, 1814: *Ibid.*, pp. 435-36.

blindness, rheumatism, a congenital anemia. His extraordinarily long period of retirement, "a second lifetime" one biographer has described it, offered ample opportunity to reflect upon his own misfortunes. One by one, his friends dropped away, until toward the end only Governor Thomas McKean and Jefferson remained. In October of 1818, the severest blow of all fell; Abigail died of typhoid fever after a protracted illness. On July 4, 1826, Adams' own death finally came—just a few hours, as his astonished countrymen observed, after Jefferson's. He died without regret; longing for release from the trials of this world that had weighed so heavily upon him; not fully reconciled to the society that had wronged him; yet, in spite of everything, wishing it well.

Bibliographical Essay

As the reader can easily surmise, this book depends for its effectiveness not upon an exhaustive search of all materials relating to John Adams and the historical period in which he lived, but upon what is intended to be a fresh and imaginative reading of materials for the most part already familiar. Most of my time was thus spent in the vast body of the Adams Family Papers, reading and rereading—often as many as ten or a dozen times. The Adams Family Papers (referred to in the text as Adams Microfilm) are housed in the Massachusetts Historical Society, but are available on microfilm in major research libraries elsewhere. I worked for the most part from the microfilm copy, using first the one in Yale's Sterling Memorial Library and then in the Princeton Firestone Library.

The Adams Family Papers include far and away the majority of Adams' extant writings: letterbooks, diary, account books, literary notebooks, manuscript autobiography. This collection, however, is not exhaustive; and so I turned to certain other manuscript collections to complete my research. Mr. L. H. Butterfield and his staff, in the process of editing John Adams' papers, have scoured repositories the world over for materials not included in the Family Papers, and they have been kind enough to let me read some of this material. In addition, I read personally certain other items written by or to Adams, or relating to him, located in other collections. Among the most important of these were materials in the Adams, Warren, Tudor, and Pickering papers in the Massachusetts Historical Society; Adams' personal library in the Rare Book Room of the Boston Public Library; Adams' letters to Francis Adrian Van der Kemp in the Historical Society of Pennsylvania; and the John Adams papers in the Manuscript Division of the Library of Congress. Other small holdings of Adams papers, varying from five to seventy items, are lodged in various archives from Massachusetts to North Carolina.

Beyond this, I used the standard printed sources containing Adams' writings and the writings of his contemporaries. Full citation of a particular work may be found at its first occurrence in the footnotes. For a more complete listing of printed materials, both primary and secondary, relating to Adams and his times, I refer the reader to the bibliographies listed in such books as Catherine Drinker Bowen's *John Adams and the American Revolution* (Boston, 1951), Manning J. Dauer's *The Adams Federalists* (Baltimore, 1953), Stephen G. Kurtz's *The Presidency of John Adams* (Philadelphia, 1957), and more general studies such as John C. Miller's *The Federalist Era, 1789-1801* (New York, 1960).

Index

Index